Lecture Notes in Artificial Intelligence   10003

Subseries of Lecture Notes in Computer Science

LNAI Series Editors

Randy Goebel
University of Alberta, Edmonton, Canada
Yuzuru Tanaka
Hokkaido University, Sapporo, Japan
Wolfgang Wahlster
DFKI and Saarland University, Saarbrücken, Germany

LNAI Founding Series Editor

Joerg Siekmann
DFKI and Saarland University, Saarbrücken, Germany

More information about this series at http://www.springer.com/series/1244

Nardine Osman · Carles Sierra (Eds.)

Autonomous Agents and Multiagent Systems

AAMAS 2016 Workshops, *Visionary Papers*
Singapore, Singapore, May 9–10, 2016
Revised Selected Papers

 Springer

Editors
Nardine Osman
Campus de la UAB
IIIA-CSIC
Bellaterra
Spain

Carles Sierra
Campus de la UAB
IIIA-CSIC
Bellaterra
Spain

ISSN 0302-9743 ISSN 1611-3349 (electronic)
Lecture Notes in Artificial Intelligence
ISBN 978-3-319-46839-6 ISBN 978-3-319-46840-2 (eBook)
DOI 10.1007/978-3-319-46840-2

Library of Congress Control Number: 2016952511

LNCS Sublibrary: SL7 – Artificial Intelligence

Printed on acid-free paper

This Springer imprint is published by Springer Nature
The registered company is Springer International Publishing AG
The registered company address is: Gewerbestrasse 11, 6330 Cham, Switzerland

Preface

AAMAS is the leading scientific conference for research in autonomous agents and multiagent systems, which is annually organized by the non-profit organization the International Foundation for Autonomous Agents and Multiagent Systems (IFAAMAS). The AAMAS conference series was initiated in 2002 by merging three highly respected meetings: the International Conference on Multi-Agent Systems (ICMAS); the International Workshop on Agent Theories, Architectures, and Languages (ATAL); and the International Conference on Autonomous Agents (AA).

Besides the main program, AAMAS hosts a number of workshops, which aim at stimulating and facilitating discussion, interaction, and comparison of approaches, methods, and ideas related to specific topics, both theoretical and applied, in the general area of autonomous agents and multiagent systems. The AAMAS workshops provide an informal setting where participants have the opportunity to discuss specific technical topics in an atmosphere that fosters the active exchange of ideas.

This book compiles the most visionary papers of the AAMAS 2016 workshops. In total, AAMAS 2016 ran 16 workshops. To select the most visionary papers, the organizers of each workshop were asked to nominate two papers from their workshop and send those papers, along with the reviews they received during their workshop's review process, to the AAMAS 2016 workshop co-chairs. The AAMAS 2016 workshop co-chairs then studied each paper carefully, in order to assess its quality and whether it was suitable to be selected for this book. One paper was selected from each workshop, although not all workshops were able to contribute. The result is a compilation of 12 papers selected from 12 workshops, which we list below.

- The 18th International Workshop on Trust in Agent Societies (Trust 2016)
- The First International Workshop on Security and Multiagent Systems (SecMAS 2016)
- The 6th International Workshop on Autonomous Robots and Multirobot Systems (ARMS 2016)
- The 7th International Workshop on Optimization in Multiagent Systems (OptMAS 2016)
- The Second International Workshop on Issues with Deployment of Emerging Agent-Based Systems (IDEAS 2016)
- The 17th International Workshop on Multi-Agent-Based Simulation (MABS 2016)
- The 4th International Workshop on Engineering Multiagent Systems (EMAS 2016)
- The 14th International Workshop on Adaptive Learning Agents (ALA 2016)
- The 9th International International Workshop on Agent-Based Complex Automated Negotiations (ACAN 2016)
- The First International Workshop on Agent-Based Modelling of Urban Systems (ABMUS 2016)

- The 21st International Workshop on Coordination, Organization, Institutions and Norms in Agent Systems (COIN 2016), with a special joint session with the 7th International Workshop on Collaborative Agents Research and Development: CARE for Digital Education (CARE 2016)
- The 15th International Workshop on Emergent Intelligence on Networked Agents (WEIN 2016)

We note that a similar process was carried out to select the best papers of the AAMAS 2016 workshops. While visionary papers are papers with novel ideas that propose a change in the way research is currently carried out, best papers follow the style of more traditional papers. The selected best papers may be found in the Springer LNAI 10002 book.

Revised and selected papers of the AAMAS workshops have been published in the past (see Springer's LNAI Vol. 7068 of the AAMAS 2011 workshops). Despite not publishing such books regularly for the AAMAS workshops, there has been a clear and strong interest on other occasions. For instance, publishing the "best of the rest" AAMAS workshops volume has been discussed with Prof. Michael Luck, who was enthusiastic concerning AAMAS 2014 in Paris. This book, along with Springer's LNAI 10002 volume, aim at presenting the most visionary papers and the best papers of the AAMAS 2016 workshops. The aim of publishing these books is essentially to better disseminate the most notable results of the AAMAS workshops and encourage authors to submit top-quality research work to the AAMAS workshops.

July 2016   Nardine Osman
                                                                             Carles Sierra

Organization

AAMAS 2016 Workshop Co-chairs

Nardine Osman	Artificial Intelligence Research Institute, Spain
Carles Sierra	Artificial Intelligence Research Institute, Spain

AAMAS 2016 Workshop Organizers

Trust 2016

Jie Zhang	Nanyang Technological University, Singapore
Robin Cohen	University of Waterloo, Canada
Murat Sensoy	Ozyegin University, Turkey

SecMAS 2016

Debarun Kar	University of Southern California, CA, USA
Yevgeniy Vorobeychik	Vanderbilt University, TN, USA
Long Tran-Thanh	University of Southampton, Southampton, UK

ARMS 2016

Noa Agmon	Bar-Ilan University, Israel
Alessandro Farinelli	University of Verona, Italy
Manuela Veloso	Carnegie Mellon University, USA
Francesco Amigoni	Politecnico di Milano, Italy
Gal Kaminka	Bar Ilan University, Israel
Maria Gini	University of Minneapolis, USA
Daniele Nardi	Sapienza – Università di Roma, Italy
Pedro Lima	Institute for Systems and Robotics, Portugal
Erol Sahin	Middle East Technical University, Turkey

OptMAS 2016

Archie Chapman	University of Sydney, Australia
Pradeep Varakantham	Singapore Management University, Singapore
William Yeoh	New Mexico State University, USA
Roie Zivan	Ben-Gurion University of the Negev, Israel

IDEAS 2016

Adam Eck	University of Nebraska-Lincoln, USA
Leen-Kiat Soh	University of Nebraska-Lincoln, USA
Bo An	Nanyang Technological University, Singapore

Paul Scerri   Platypus LLC, USA
Adrian Agogino   NASA, USA

MABS 2016

Luis Antunes   University of Lisbon, Portugal
Luis Gustavo Nardin   Center for Modeling Complex Interactions, USA

EMAS 2016

Matteo Baldoni   University of Turin, Italy
Jörg P. Müller   Technische Universität Clausthal, Germany
Ingrid Nunes   Universidade Federal do Rio Grande do Sul, Brazil
Rym Zalila-Wenkstern   University of Texas at Dallas, TX, USA

ALA 2016

Daan Bloembergen   University of Liverpool, UK
Tim Brys   Vrije Universiteit Brussels, Belgium
Logan Yliniemi   University of Nevada, Reno, USA

ACAN 2016

Katsuhide Fujita   Tokyo University of Agriculture and Technology, Japan
Naoki Fukuta   Shizuoka University, Japan
Takayuki Ito   Nagoya Institute of Technology, Japan
Minjie Zhang   University of Wollongong, Australia
Quan Bai   Auckland University of Technology, New Zealand
Fenghui Ren   University of Wollongong, Australia
Chao Yu   Dalian University of Technology, China
Reyhan Aydogan   Ozyegin University, Turkey

ABMUS 2016

Pascal Perez   University of Wollongong, Australia
Lin Padgham   RMIT, Australia
Kai Nagel   Technische Universität Berlin, Germany
Ana L.C. Bazzan   Universidade Federal do Rio Grande do Sul, Brazil
Mohammad-Reza   University of Wollongong, Australia
  Namazi-Rad

COIN 2016, with a special joint session with CARE 2016

Samhar Mahmoud (COIN)   King's College London, UK
Stephen Cranefield   University of Otago, New Zealand
  (COIN)
Fernando Koch (CARE)   Samsung Research Institute, Brazil
Tiago Primo (CARE)   Samsung Research Institute, Brazil

Andrew Koster (CARE)   Samsung Research Institute, Brazil
Christian Guttmann   UNSW, Australia, IVBAR, and Karolinska Institute,
  (CARE)   Sweden

WEIN 2016

Satoshi Kurihara   University of Electro-Communications, Japan
Hideyuki Nakashima   Future University-Hakodate, Japan
Akira Namatame   National Defense Academy, Japan

Contents

A Language for Trust Modelling

Tim Muller[⊠], Jie Zhang, and Yang Liu

Nanyang Technological University, Singapore, Singapore
{tmuller,zhangj,yangliu}@ntu.edu.sg

Abstract. The computational trust paradigm supposes that it is possible to quantify trust relations that occur within some software systems. The paradigm covers a variety of trust systems, such as trust management systems, reputation systems and trust-based security systems. Different trust systems have different assumptions, and various trust models have been developed on top of these assumptions Typically, trust models are incomparable, or even mutually unintelligible; as a result their evaluation may be circular or biased. We propose a unified language to express the trust models and trust systems. Within the language, all trust models are comparable, and the problem of circularity or bias is mitigated. Moreover, given a complete set of assumptions in the language, a unique trust model is defined.

1 Introduction

People interact over the internet. Opportunities may arise for people to betray others. Hence, people need to trust over the internet. Computational trust is a paradigm that deals with quantifying trust, mitigating risks and selecting trustworthy agents [9].

Within the computational trust paradigm, there are different *trust systems.* A trust system, here, refers to online systems involving trust values. A typical centralised trust system, for example, collects ratings, aggregates these into a single score, and distributes these scores. The effectiveness of a trust system is not straightforward to ascertain. What is, e.g., the correct way to aggregate the ratings into a single score, and what does it mean? In order to interpret the trust values and determine their validity, a trust model is required.

Within the computational trust paradigm, there are also different *trust models.* A trust model dictates the meaning of trust values, and what appropriate trust values are. A trust model can be used to evaluate trust systems, for example for simulations to measure the effectiveness of a trust system. Different trust systems can be compared using a sufficiently general trust model. However, there is no fully general trust model that everyone agrees on.

In fact, there probably cannot such a fully general trust model, since different trust systems require different assumptions. For example, some trust models assume trust is transitive (A trusts B and B trusts C implies A trusts C) to some extent, and others do not [1]. The variety of assumptions that underlie different trust models (which underlie different trust systems) leads to confusion:

© Springer International Publishing AG 2016
N. Osman and C. Sierra (Eds.): AAMAS 2016 WS, Visionary Papers, LNAI 10003, pp. 1–12, 2016.
DOI: 10.1007/978-3-319-46840-2_1

Implicit assumptions may cause misinterpretation. Overly strong assumptions may yield meaningless results. Assumptions may be shared between the system and its (experimental) analysis, making its analysis pointless. Two systems may have similar assumptions, which unexpectedly lead to fundamentally different conclusions.

We propose a shared language for these assumptions. The computational trust paradigm is captured in three core *principles* (see Sect. 3). We assert that every trust model should adhere to these principles. Moreover, if indeed a trust models adheres to the principles, then it can be described in our language. In this paper, we demonstrate the generality and validity of the principles within the computational trust paradigm. Moreover, we reformulate existing trust models into the universal language, both to show feasibility and to exemplify the approach.

The language to express the assumptions is a distribution over strategies for each class of users. An assumption about honest users must define exactly what the behaviour of an honest user can be, and the prior probability that a user is honest. (The different strategies need not be finite, or even countable.) The major benefit of the proposed format for assumptions, is that if the assumptions are sufficiently strong, they define a trust model. We refer to the process of obtaining a trust model by merely formulating the assumptions as *trust model synthesis*. There are yet many hurdles to take before trust model synthesis leads to automated trust modelling in practice. We demonstrate, in this paper, both the potential of trust model synthesis (see Sect. 2) and the feasibility of trust model synthesis in practice (see Sect. 5).

The document is organised as follows: First we look at the concrete consequences of our proposal in Sect. 2. There, we also address the shortcomings of the traditional approaches, and motivate our alternative. Then we formally introduce the principles that the framework is built on, in Sect. 3. Finally, we discuss the feasibility of automated trust modelling in Sect. 5, and look ahead for possible future challenges and improvements in Sect. 6.

2   Modelling Trust

Existing trust models and trust systems are being improved by ongoing research and by superior implementations. We refer to the general notion of continuous improvement as the life cycle. The skeleton of the life cycle, is that first a problem or shortcoming is identified, then a solution or idea is proposed, implemented, verified, and possibly accepted. There are some problems with the life cycle, that we address in this section. Throughout this section, we suppose that our three core principles (discussed in Sect. 3) are sufficient to perform trust model synthesis (discussed in Sect. 5).

Figure 1 depicts the typical life cycle of trust models and trust systems. The two life cycles are tightly coupled.

The trust system life cycle starts with a set of requirements on a system. The requirements are implemented into a trust system. The implementation of the

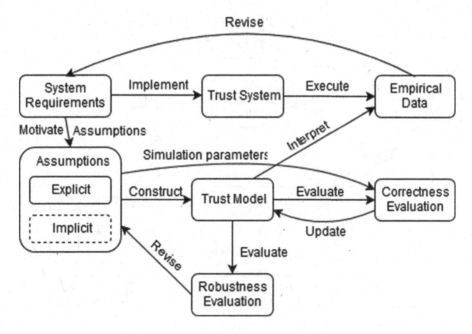

Fig. 1. The typical life cycle of trust models.

trust system asserts a certain trust model. Then, the trust system is executed. (Partial) runs of the system are analysed using a trust model (same or other). The empirical analysis may lead to updating the requirements (e.g. if a new attack is found) or to updating the trust model (e.g. if the trust model incorrectly models real users).

The trust model life cycle starts with a set of explicit assumptions, partially based on the requirements of the system. Based on the assumptions, a trust system can be formulated. Typically, the trust system introduces a set of implicit assumptions. The trust model can be theoretically analysed using simulation or verification. Its results may lead to identifying a correctness problem. Typically, correctness problems are addressed by updating the trust model, not the assumptions. Occasionally, the correctness problems leads to the identification of an implicit assumption. Another theoretical analysis is robustness evaluation, where at least one user may violate any assumptions made about him. Its results may lead to identifying a robustness problem. A robustness problem typically induces updating the assumptions.

Not all modellers follow the life cycle to the letter, but it is a reasonable description of how different factors influence or determine others. Some research focusses only on particular phases. Ideally, their solutions can be reused across different settings. Unfortunately, the classic life cycle hinders this to some extent. For example, it may be difficult to publish a paper that merely identifies some problem, as the audience may expect a solution. Similarly, a solution may require an implementation, and an implementation may require an empirical evaluation, etc (Fig. 2).

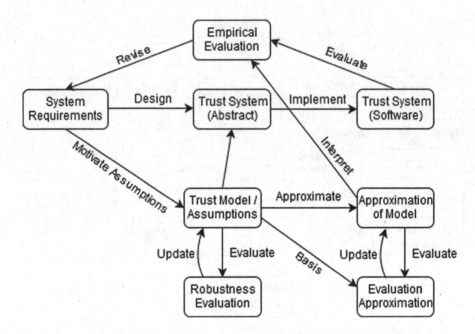

Fig. 2. The proposed life cycle of trust models.

The life cycle of the trust system remain largely unchanged, except that it now includes an abstraction of the trust system. Note that the abstraction could be made after or before implementation. The trust model life cycle lacks implicit assumptions. The explicit assumptions and the trust model are one and the same. Unfortunately, there is no guarantee that the trust model is computationally feasible. We may be satisfied with trust values that are approximations of the true values predicted by the model. However, these approximations would need additional analysis. Correctness evaluation is no longer a necessity (unless we need approximations, in which case their analysis suffices), and robustness evaluation is streamlined.

Empirical, correctness and robustness evaluation. When it comes to theoretical evaluation, in the classic life cycle of trust systems, correctness evaluation of trust models is emphasised heavily as a motivation to use the trust model. Correctness evaluation allows one to ascertain that the model satisfies the assumptions. It is performed under the assumptions made in the trust model, and the assumptions themselves are not scrutinised. This problem is known, and efforts to mitigate this problem are not novel. The ART testbed [2], for example, is a well-known example of a testbed designed to validate different trust models with a unified procedure.

However, fully general correctness evaluation methods cannot exist [8]. Even the ART testbed can only evaluate those trust models that relate to e-commerce, and then over a limited amount of aspects. More importantly, the ART testbed can only evaluate complete trust systems with trust models, that cover all aspects of e-commerce. It is not a tool that can validate partial models intended to solve specific problems.

An alternative evaluation is empirical evaluation. Empirical evaluation suffers less from circularity issues. However, empirical data still requires interpretation, and is not immune to biased assumptions. Any healthy life cycle of trust systems must incorporate empirical data at some point. However, as our life cycle does not suffer from the issue of circularity of correctness evaluation, empirical data is not necessary to show internal consistency. As a result, the empirical evaluation is much more loosely coupled to the theoretical evaluation. This allows researchers to specialise on specific subproblems, rather than to force all research to directly translate to a complete trust system.

In our proposed life cycle, it is the assumptions themselves that are evaluated. Since, with trust model synthesis, the model is merely the assumptions, evaluating the trust model equates to evaluating the model assumptions. Note that with the classical approach, there may be implicit or ambiguous assumptions, meaning that evaluating the stated assumptions is insufficient. In our approach, the model assumptions must be assumptions about the behaviour of the agents – concrete and explicit. Our argument is that by forcing the model assumptions to be concrete and explicit, evaluation and comparison of the trust models is more transparent.

3   The Principles of Computational Trust

The three principles that we introduce to capture the paradigm of computational trust are: (1) a trust system is a (timed) process with partially observable states, (2) users' behaviour is dictated by a (probabilistic) strategy and (3) trust values reflect the user's possible behaviour based on evidence. Multi-agent systems, including trust systems, typically satisfy (1) and (2). Furthermore, principle (3) has also been asserted in the computational trust paradigm [10]. Principles (1), (2) and (3) are not novel. The notion that, together, the three principles are sufficiently strong to define a trust model, is novel.

A variation of each of the principles is present in many trust systems. Trust models typically treat trust systems as a process with some properties – specifically what actions are possible at which time. When reasoning about a trust model, one must reason about what certain past actions of an agent say about future actions, and to do this, one must categorise users. The last principle is typically seen as a requirement, e.g. a "good" trust model provides trust values that reflect the user's behaviour. We are going to sever the ties with existing methods, and rigourously define the three principles, even if that excludes some existing models.

Principle 1: Trust System. Principle one is based on processes that can be expressed as deterministic labelled transition systems:

Definition 1. *A deterministic labelled transition system is a tuple* (S, A, s_0, t), *where S is a set of states, A is a set of actions, $s_0 \in S$ is the initial state and $t : S \times A \to S$ is the transition function.*

A trace τ is a list of actions $a_0, \ldots, a_n$, and T the set of all traces.

Users $u \in U$ are agents that use the system. Users may fully, partially, or not observe particular actions.

Definition 2. *A blinding is a partial function* $\delta : A \times U \nrightarrow A$.

When u cannot observe a, then $\delta(a, u)$ is undefined. When u can only partially observe a, then $\delta(a, u) = a'$, where a' is the partial observation. We also allow blinding of traces, denoted with Δ. In $\Delta(\tau, u)$, the elements a in τ are replaced by $\delta(a, u)$, if defined, and omitted otherwise. Thus, $\Delta(\tau, u)$ provides the perspective of agent u, when the system trace is τ.

Based on the notion of deterministic labelled transition systems, blinding and users, we can formally define trust systems:

Definition 3. *A trust system is a tuple* $(S, U, A, s_0, t, \delta)$, *where S is a set of states, U is a set of users, A is a set of actions, s_0 is the initial state, $t : S \times U \times A \to S$ is the transition function and δ a blinding.*

Principle 1 supposes that a real trust system can be represented as our abstract notion of trust system.

Principle 2: Strategies. The trust system is simply an automata with branching. We need to grant the users agency, which we provide in the form of a strategy. Strategy may refer to a rational strategy, as often assumed in game theory [6]. But a strategy may also refer to, e.g., a taste profile – what are the odds that a user enjoys something.

In most trust systems, several agents may be allowed to perform an action at a given time. Quicker agents may have an advantage, so timing must play a role in the agents' strategies. We suppose that the time before an action happens is exponentially distributed – for its convenient properties. The exponential distribution has one parameter, which is the expected time until the action, called the *rate* – not to be confused with a (trust) rating.

Traces, users and actions are as defined in the trust system. A (rated) *move* is an assignment of rates to actions, denoted $A \to \mathbb{R}^{\geq 0}$. Every user u has a strategy, which dictates the moves of the user, given the circumstances. We use the notion of (blinded) traces to model the circumstances.

Definition 4. *A strategy of a user is a function* $f : T \times A \to \mathbb{R}^{\geq 0}$. *A behaviour of a user is a distribution over strategies, $b : (T \times A \to \mathbb{R}^{\geq 0}) \to [0, 1]$. W.l.o.g. $f \in F = \{f | b(f) > 0\}$.*

The strategy of a user is in the extensive form. That definition has been chosen for maximal generality. In practice, models of users are often far simpler.

Remark 1. Definition 4 asserts that all users operate independently. To model Sybil attacks (or forms of collusion), the designer needs to allow a single user to operate multiple accounts. Any cooperative strategy of a set of users that all own a single account can be mimicked by a strategy of single user creating/owning multiple accounts.

Principle 2 supposes that every user initially has a behaviour.

Principle 3: Trust Values. The trust values should reflect the probabilities of the possible actions that a user may perform. In a simple trust model, for example, actions may be classified as "good" or "bad", and a trust value denotes the probability of "good". In more sophisticated models, more actions are available, and cannot generally be classified as just good or bad. We want our trust values to reflect the likelihood of all possibilities.

We propose to use behaviour (i.e. a distribution over strategies) as a trust value. Suppose that the user is aware of the unblinded trace τ. Assuming discrete probability distributions, users can compute the rate of an action a by u, as $\sum_{f \in F} b(f) \cdot f(\tau, a)$, and the probability as $\sum_{f \in F} b(f) \cdot \frac{f(\tau,a)}{\sum_{a' \in A} f(\tau,a')}$. (1) The generalisation to blinded traces is not much more complicated, and presented in Sect. 5.

The trust value can typically not be displayed as a single value. In special cases, a compact representation exists (e.g. in Subjective Logic [3], with three values). Usually, however, there is no human-friendly representation.

4   Assumptions

The format of assumptions that exist to support trust models is currently heterogeneous. There have been statistical assumptions, axiomatic assumptions, logical assumptions and informal assumptions. The assumptions are made about trust itself, the trust system, honesty and malice, and about behaviour. The principles cover assumptions about the trust system (1), and about trust itself (3). We further argue that (2) implies that it suffices to formulate the remaining assumptions about behaviour.

In [11], the authors propose a way of dividing model assumptions into two groups. They introduce *fundamental assumptions* and *simplifying assumptions*. Fundamental assumptions are assumptions intended to reflect the nature of the object of study (in [11], "trustee and truster agents are self-interested" is an example). Simplifying assumptions are assumptions necessitated by practical limitations of the model (in [11], "the majority of third-parties testimonies are reliable" is an example). Trust models cannot be formulated without a good deal of fundamental and simplifying assumptions on top of the three principles and a trust system.

Both fundamental assumptions and simplifying assumptions can be encoded into a selection of behaviours. The example simplifying assumption can be

encoded by letting the behaviour of those agents that sometimes provide testimonies assign a probability of over 0.5, to those strategies that are reliable[1].
The example fundamental assumption – that users are self-interested – can be
encoded by assigning no probability to dominated strategies. User will not have
strategies where users can unilaterally increase their own profit.

Without loss of generality, let $C = \{c_0, c_1, \dots\}$ be a partition over U (thus
every u_i occurs in exactly one c_j). We call c_i a class of users. For example, we
may have a class of buyers and a class of sellers. For each class c, we must assume:

– A set F_c of strategies that users in class c may have.
– A distribution b_c over these strategies.

Our *language* is a partition of users into classes, with a prior behaviour for each
class of users. The language covers all the assumptions that a trust model needs
to make (at least in combination with the three principles), and it fulfills the
role of a trust model.

The important question is whether it is always possible to translate the
assumptions from arbitrary format, to our language. Note that in the classic life
cycle (Fig. 1), a correctness evaluation is performed, typically using a simulation.
All users in that model are simulated using agents with a defined behaviour –
the simulation code defines the behaviour of the agents. That code must define,
in all possible traces, what the behaviour of the agent is. Therefore, there exists
a behaviour for a user, such that it acts exactly like the simulation. Thus, if there
exists a trust model with a positive correctness evaluation, then there exists a
set of assumptions in our language for the same trust model.

5   Trust Model Synthesis

In order to do trust model synthesis, the modeller must supply a trust system and
behaviour, according to principles 1 and 2. Typically, the trust system is a given.
The synthesised trust model can provide trust values, according to principle 3.
To illustrate the approach with an example:

Example 1. Take a simple system called MARKET(4,3) with seven users, divid-
able into two classes: four buyers b_1, b_2, b_3, b_4 and three sellers s_1, s_2, s_3. Buyers
b may $initiate(b, s)$ a purchase with any seller s, whenever they do not have
an outstanding purchase, after a purchase, they can score it $score(b, s, r)$ where
$r \in \{1, 2, 3, 4, 5\}$. The seller can either $deliver(s, b)$ or $betray(s, b)$, which finalises
b's purchase. Only the b and s can see $initiate(b, s)$, $deliver(s, b)$ or $betray(s, b)$,
meaning that $\delta(initiate(b, s), u) = initiate(b, s)$, if $u = b$ or $u = s$, and undefined
otherwise; and similarly for $deliver$ and $betray$.

---

[1] By making encoding assumption into behaviour, we realise that we have an implicit
assumption about what it means to be reliable. Forcing such implicit assumptions to
be made explicit is an important benefit of our proposed approach. Here, an educated
guess would be that reliable recommenders always provide truthful testimonies about
objective events.

There is only one buyer strategy. The rate for $iniate(b, s)$ is 1, if the seller(s) has the highest probability of $deliver(s, b)$ according to the buyer's trust value, and 0 otherwise. Letting the unit of time, e.g., be a week, then the buyer buys from a maximally reliable seller on average once per week. There are two seller strategies, *honest* and *cheater*, where, after $initiate(s, b)$, the honest seller performs $deliver(s, b)$ with rate 0.9 and $betray(s, b)$ with rate 0.1, and the cheater vice versa. Both honest sellers and cheaters take, on average, a week to act, but the honest seller delivers with high probability, whereas the cheater betrays with high probability. After receiving $deliver(s, b)$, b performs $score(b, s, r)$ with rate r. and after $betray(s, b)$, b performs $score(b, s, r)$ with rate $6 - r$.

The two buyers are users of the trust system. The trust system facilitates interactions between buyers and sellers, by allowing buyers to initiate interactions and sellers to finalise them. Furthermore, the system allows buyers to send ratings, which the other buyers can use. The question is, what will happen in the system? What should a buyer do when given a set of ratings? What will a buyer do? The (synthesised) trust model can answer these questions.

Given the three principles, we can make exact predictions. Given a blinded trace τ, let $\nabla(\tau, u)$ be the set of traces τ', such that $\Delta(\tau', u) = \tau$. Assuming the set of actions A is finite (countable), $\nabla(\tau, u)$ is finite (countable), and can be computed in at most finitely[2] (countably) many steps. Using equation (1), we can compute the probability of performing action a_{i+1}, given $a_0, \ldots, a_i$, and the behaviours of the agents. Since the trust system is deterministic, that implies that for each $\tau' = a_0, \ldots, a_n \in \nabla(\tau, u)$, we can compute the probability of τ' in n steps. Given a distribution over traces, a user can perform a Bayesian update of the behaviours, using equation (1), when he observes an action a. The complexity of the Bayesian update is linear in the number of traces and the number of agents (and constant in the length of the traces). The approach is highly similar to POMDPs, except for the existence of invisible actions and the lack of reward.

Remark 2. So far, we have not discussed the notions of rewards or goals. The reason is that goals are orthogonal to our approach. A modeller is simply asked how he expects the users to behave, and to write this down mathematically, and he can synthesise a trust model. However, in reality users do have goals, and their goals are relevant to other aspects than the synthesis. First, the modeller may expect the behaviour because of the goals. In Example 1, the fact that buyers select the most trustworthy seller reflects their goal of not being betrayed. The split between the two classes of sellers as honest and cheater also reflects that sellers may have two goals (to make money honestly, or to cheat). Second, the goals pop up in robustness analysis. If a strategy is found that achieves the goals far better than other strategy and/or harms other users in achieving their goals, then it may be prudent to add that strategy into the behaviour of users of that class. (Example 1 is not robust against a reputation lag attack. A seller becomes the most trustworthy one, lets others buy from him, but wait with betraying

---

[2] As long as the probability of extremely large invisible subtraces is negligible.

until all four have made a purchase. Such a strategy can then be added to the behaviour of sellers.)

Although the problem is theoretically computable, the approach is nevertheless intractable in full generality. Observe the following challenges: behaviours with incomputable probability density, strategies encoding NP-hard problems, and statespace explosion (number of traces). These practical issues are, of course, to be expected. However, practical models typically have simple probabilities, strategies are not based on hard problems, and agents do not exploit the entire statespace.

To illustrate the practical computability, consider Example 1: In the system MARKET(4,3), for all τ, $\nabla(\tau, b_1)$ is infinite. However, all $\tau' \in \nabla(\tau, b_1)$ are *probabilisticly bisimilar* [5], when we restrict to blinding all actions with b_1. When two states are probabilisticly bisimilar, it means that the two states are completely identical, and we can collapse the two states.

6   Research Problems

Implementation. The first step towards real automated trust modelling, is a prototype tool. The simplest approach to such a tool is to transform the assumptions into a probabilistic automaton, and use probabilistic verification tools, such as PRISM [4], to automate the synthesis. Likely, general purpose tools are not sufficiently powerful, and specialised tools need to be developed for simple, realistic models (e.g. Beta-type models [3]).

The problems that the special purpose tool would have to overcome, are similar to those of probabilistic verification tools. We cannot yet envision the precise challenges, but statespace reduction will be a necessity. We saw that for MARKET, probabilistic bisimulation [5] reduces the statespace from countably infinite to 1. More importantly, possible forms of statespace reduction exist for our purpose, such as: Letting the system signal partial information about an action (e.g. an e-market place could signal that a transaction occurred, even if it is unaware of the outcome), and generating equivalence classes over blinded traces.

The user of the synthesised trust model may not be interested in the exact probability values. If the user allows an absolute error ϵ, and there is an upper bound m to the rate of the outgoing actions, then the statespace can be trivially bounded to a finite size. Assuming all states have an outgoing rate of m, the probability that the length of the trace exceeds n, at time x, is exponentially distributed as $e^{-\frac{m}{n} \cdot x}$. Given m, x, ϵ, it is always possible to pick n, such that $e^{-\frac{m}{n} \cdot x} < \epsilon$. Thus, by introducing a small error ϵ, we can restrict the traces to the traces of length at most n.

The authors are currently working on a tool that can do robustness verification for generic trust models. Robustness verification is an excellent way to find new possible attacks, which, in turn, can help us construct behaviours that take into account future attacks and responses to defences.

Application. The theoretical concepts of trust model synthesis are surprisingly powerful. In order to judge the practical power of trust model synthesis, a real model should be encoded, synthesised and compared with the original. The second core principle forces the modeller to be explicit and concrete with model assumptions. This means that, e.g., "trust is transitive" is not a valid assumption, and should be replaced by assumptions about the behaviour of users. Finding a general, but concrete, translation of that assumption is an interesting challenge. A multitude of similar assumptions exist, which pose equally interesting challenges for the modeller.

Evalutation and Analysis. We have shortly addressed the notions of evaluation and analysis. Our approach to validation is complementary to the orthodox approach to validation (e.g. ART testbed [2]). Due to the concrete nature of the assumptions, they can directly be contrasted with reality. There is, however, always a degree of interpretation. How to minimise the effect of interpretation is currently an open question.

The approach opens new doors for robustness analysis. In security analysis, it is common to reason about users that violate the assumptions of a security protocol, and to automatically verify the security of the protocol. The question is to what extend these methods can apply to our domain. Recent research indicates that such methods are feasible for the domain [7]. Attempting to automatically verify the impact of breaking the assumptions is a difficult challenge.

7 Conclusion

We have presented a novel approach to constructing trust models. The main advantage is the lack of hidden assumptions that may introduce unseen problems. The key contribution is a generic language to formulate assumptions about trust models. The language consists of describing the behaviour of (classes of) users. We have formulated 3 major principles that we argue apply to all trust systems. The validity of the language hinges on these principles. We have formulated how the design and construction of trust systems and models can be streamlined by our proposal. Finally, parts of the tasks of the trust system can be generated automatically, using trust model synthesis.

There are several ways in which the language can help in future research: One way is by providing a link towards automation helps researchers tackle problems that are more suitable to be address by computers. Furthermore, two mutually intelligible trust models can now be provided a common foundation for comparison. Finally, we hope that vague or hidden assumptions are eventually considered unacceptable, and our language is one of several approaches to bring rigour.

References

1. Falcone, R., Castelfranchi, C., Transitivity in trust: a discussed property. In: Proceedings of the 10th Workshop on Objects and Agents (WOA) (2010)
2. Fullam, K.K., Klos, T.B., Muller, G., Sabater, J., Schlosser, A., Topol, Z., Suzanne Barber, K., Rosenschein,J.S., Vercouter, L., Voss, M.: A specification of the agent reputation, trust (art) testbed: experimentation and competition for trust in agent societies. In: Proceedings of the Fourth International Joint Conference on Autonomous Agents and Multiagent Systems, pp. 512–518. ACM (2005)
3. Jøsang, A.: A logic for uncertain probabilities. Int. J. Uncertainty Fuzziness Knowl. Based Syst. **9**(03), 279–311 (2001)
4. Kwiatkowska, M., Norman, G., Parker, D.: PRISM: probabilistic symbolic model checker. In: Field, T., Harrison, P.G., Bradley, J., Harder, U. (eds.) TOOLS 2002. LNCS, vol. 2324, pp. 200–204. Springer, Heidelberg (2002). doi:10.1007/3-540-46029-2_13
5. Larsen, K.G., Skou, A.: Bisimulation through probabilistic testing (preliminary report). In: Proceedings of the 16th ACM SIGPLAN-SIGACT Symposium on Principles of Programming Languages, pp. 344–352. ACM (1989)
6. Leyton-Brown, K., Shoham, Y.: Essentials of game theory: a concise multidisciplinary introduction. Synth. Lect. Artif. Intell. Mach. Learn. **2**(1), 1–88 (2008)
7. Muller, T., Liu, Y., Mauw, S., Zhang, J.: On robustness of trust systems. In: Zhou, J., Gal-Oz, N., Zhang, J., Gudes, E. (eds.) IFIPTM 2014. IAICT, vol. 430, pp. 44–60. Springer, Heidelberg (2014). doi:10.1007/978-3-662-43813-8_4
8. Robinson, S.: Simulation model verification and validation: increasing the users' confidence. In: Proceedings of the 29th Conference on Winter Simulation, WSC 1997, pp. 53–59 (1997)
9. Sabater, J., Sierra, C.: Review on computational trust and reputation models. Artif. Intell. Rev. **24**(1), 33–60 (2005)
10. Wang, Y., Singh, M.P.: Formal trust model for multiagent systems. In: IJCAI, vol. 7, pp. 1551–1556 (2007)
11. Han, Y., Zhiqi Shen, C., Leung, C.M., Lesser, V.: A survey of multi-agent trust management systems. IEEE Access **1**, 35–50 (2013)

Abstraction Methods for Solving Graph-Based Security Games

Anjon Basak[1]([⊠]), Fei Fang[2], Thanh Hong Nguyen[2],
and Christopher Kiekintveld[1]

[1] University of Texas at El Paso,
500 W University Ave, El Paso, TX 79902, USA
abasak@miners.utep.edu, cdkiekintveld@utep.edu
[2] University of Southern California,
941 Bloom Walk, SAL 300, Los Angeles, CA 90089, USA
{feifang,thanhhng}@usc.edu

Abstract. Many real-world security problems can be modeled using Stackelberg security games (SSG), which model the interactions between defender and attacker. *Green security games* focus on environmental crime, such as preventing poaching, illegal logging, or detecting pollution. A common problem in green security games is to optimize patrolling strategies for a large physical area such as a national park or other protected area. Patrolling strategies can be modeled as paths in a graph that represents the physical terrain. However, having a detailed graph to represent possible movements in a very large area typically results in an intractable computational problem due to the extremely large number of potential paths. While a variety of algorithmic approaches have been explored in the literature to solve security games based on large graphs, the size of games that can be solved is still quite limited. Here, we introduce abstraction methods for solving large graph-based security games. We demonstrate empirically that these abstraction methods can result in dramatic improvements in solution time with modest impact on solution quality.

Keywords: Security · Green security · Abstraction · Contraction · Game theory

1 Introduction

As a society, we face a wide variety of security challenges in protecting people, infrastructure, computer systems, and natural resources from criminal activity. A common challenge across all of these different security domains is making the best use of limited resources to improve security, even in the face of intelligent, highly motivated attackers. Green security domains focus particularly on the problem of protecting wildlife and natural resources against illegal exploitation, such as poaching and illegal logging. Resource limitations are particularly acute in fighting many types of environmental crime, due to a combination of limited

N. Osman and C. Sierra (Eds.): AAMAS 2016 WS, Visionary Papers, LNAI 10003, pp. 13–33, 2016.
DOI: 10.1007/978-3-319-46840-2_2

budgets and massive physical areas that need to be protected. For example, it is common for small numbers of rangers, local police, and volunteers to patrol protected national parks that may cover thousands of square miles.

Recent work on *green security games* [8,11] has proposed formulating the problem of finding optimal patrols to prevent environmental crime as a Stackelberg security game [23]. In these games, the defender (e.g., park ranger service) must decide on a randomized strategy for patrolling the protected area, limited by the geographic constraints and the number of available resources. The attacker (e.g., poacher) selects an area of the park to attack based on the intended target and the patrolling strategy. For example, a poacher will try to target areas of high animal density where patrols are the least likely to occur. The goal in solving the green security game is to find the patrolling strategy for the defender that maximizes the environmental protection.

Green security games typically model the movement constraints for the defender patrols using a graph to capture the physical terrain. Unfortunately, this leads to a major computational challenge because the number of possible paths grows exponentially with the size of the graph, and enumerating all possible combinations of paths that could be followed by the available resources makes the problem even more intractable [27,33]. Several algorithms have been proposed in the literature to solve these games more efficiently [22,26]. Most of these rely on incremental strategy generation (known as double oracle algorithms, or column/constraint generation) to solve an integer programming formulation of the problem without enumerating the full strategy space. The most recent application called PAWS [10] approaches the scalability issue by incorporating cutting plane and column generation techniques. While these methods have improved scalability dramatically, it is still not possible to solve real-world problems covering large areas with a fine-grained resolution on the terrain.

In this paper we introduce a new direction for solving large security games based on graphs by using abstraction to reduce the size of the problem before applying an equilibrium solver. This direction is motivated by the success of automated abstraction methods in solving other very large games, most notably computer poker [16,17,19,20,38]. In addition, there has been work on using abstraction methods for graphs in the literature on pathfinding algorithms (e.g., [4,14,15,32]). We introduce a new solution technique for green security games that first applies a graph abstraction method to simplify the graph used to define the strategy space, and then apply an equilibrium solver to the reduced game. Once the simplified game has been solved, we map the solution back into the original game. We note that this overall approach can be used in combination with previous work on incremental strategy generation to further improve scalability, since the faster incremental algorithms can be used as equilibrium solvers in our method.

We empirically evaluate our abstraction techniques on graph-based security games motivated by the problems encountered in green security domains. Our experiments demonstrate that abstraction has great potential to scale up algorithms for green security games to much larger problem sizes. In particular, we show that applying our graph abstraction methods dramatically improves computation time, while introducing relatively modest reductions in the solution quality. Future work to improve the abstraction methods should yield even greater advantages.

2   Related Work

The first approach to compute strategic resource allocations for security was to find a randomized strategy after enumerating all possible resource allocations [27], which is used by the Los Angeles Airport Police as an application called ARMOR [28]. After that a more compact form security game representation was used [23] to achieve a faster algorithm (IRIS [33]), which is used by Federal Marshal Service (FAMS). Another algorithm, ASPEN [22], was introduced to prevent the exponential explosion of the variables since all the possible resource allocation were used to get the strategy for the defender. ASPEN uses branch-and-price approach to alleviate problems of previous algorithms. In this algorithm, joint scheduling was used to get a probability distribution over the pure strategy space. Most recently, to tackle more massive games an approach based on cutting planes was introduced [36] to make the solution space more manageable. Game theoretic algorithms are also used to secure ports [30] and trains [37].

Recently, successful deployment of game theoretic applications motivated researchers to use game theory in green security domains [8,21,35]. The transition to green security domain provided new challenges and research questions. For example rather than using the SSG game model a new game model called GSG [11] has been introduced. Assumptions about attacker being able to fully observe the defenders strategy was also not suitable with the real world scenario, where the poacher doesn't have the capability to observe the complete patrolling strategy. So, partial observability and bounded rationality have been introduced to make the attacker model more realistic. The defenders also have the issue of limited observability which results in payoff uncertainty. To address this issues an algorithm called ARROW [26] was introduced.

Many abstraction techniques have also been developed for extensive form games with uncertainty including both lossy [29] and lossless [18] abstraction. There also has been some work which gives bounds on the error introduced by abstraction [24]. There is also imperfect recall abstraction which considers hierarchical abstraction [9] and earth mover's distance [13].

Contraction technique [14] has been used to achieve fast routing in road networks, where contraction acts as a pre-processing step. One issue with the contraction algorithm was finding the shortest path. To alleviate the issue a bidirectional Dijkstra [15,31] algorithm is used which is fast. A time dependent contraction algorithm also has been introduced for time dependent road network [4].

Another area where game abstraction is used extensively is in making computer poker agents. A simple version of full scale Texas hold'em poker, 2 player limit Texas hold'em poker, has $O(10^{18})$ nodes [5]. Without any kind of abstraction solving poker is extremely hard. Even though recently heads-up limit hold'em poker is solved [6] without any abstraction, it required giganic amount of data processing.

3 Domain Motivation

Wildlife plays a major role in our ecosystem by thriving and balancing every aspect of the environment. Illegal activities such as poaching pose a major threat to biodiversity in wildlife and marine areas, and many endangered species such as rhinos and tigers are under extreme threat of extinction due to human activity. A report [1] from the Wildlife Conservation Society (WCS) on May 2015 stated that the elephant population in Mozambique has shrunk from $20,000$ to $10,300$ in last five years. Recently, elephants have been added to the IUCN Red List [2].

Marine species are also facing danger because of overfishing and illegal fishing. This is not only hampering the biodiversity of our ecosystem but also causing harm to the people of coastal areas where people depend on fishing for both

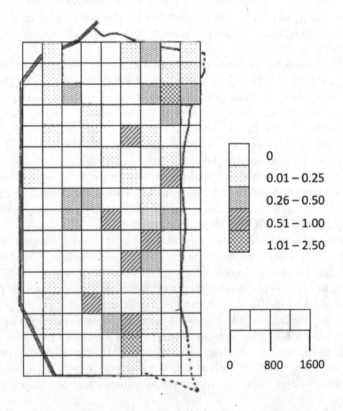

Fig. 1. Mean numbers of elephants/$0.16\,km^2$ in Queen Elizabeth National Park, Uganda

sustenance and livelihood. According to World Wide Fund for Nature (WWF), the global estimated financial loss due to illegal fishing is $23.5 billion [3]. Different organizations like WCS are providing strategies which involve patrolling of forest areas to prevent poaching and protect wildlife habitats.

PAWS [10] is a new application based on solving green security games which helps to design patrolling strategies to protect wildlife in threatened areas. It is based on a kind of virtual street map to define the area the needs to be patrolled. In the application, the area of interest is divided into grid cells that capture information about the terrain, as well as other important information such as the animal density. For example, Fig. 1 shows the mean number of elephants in each area of the grid representing the Queen Elizabeth National Park in Uganda [12].

Each cell is $400\,m$ by $400\,m$. The first thing we notice is there are many cells which have no animal count at all, and if there is minimal activity it is very inefficient to consider these areas as targets to patrol. Even if we give less priority to the cells with low animal activity, it is still very difficult for the patroller to patrol even a single target without any path strategy inside those cells, because each cell is $0.16\,km^2$. PAWS solve this problem by having a finer grained structure. For example each grid cell in Fig. 1 can be divided into $50m$ by $50m$ cells. However, this results in large number of targets, so the existing algorithms are not able to compute a strategy directly on the full problem with the large number of small cells. Our goal in considering abstraction methods is to make it computationally feasible to directly analyze games with this fine-grained structure.

4 Game Model

A typical green security game (GSG) model is specified by dividing a protected wildlife area into grid based cells, as shown in the example in Fig. 1. Each cell is considered a potential target t_i where an attacker could attempt a poaching action. We transform this grid-based representation into a graph representation as shown in Fig. 2. Each node represents a target t_i. There are utilities on both the nodes and edges in our graphs. $U_d^c(i,j)$ represents the utility on the edge between target i and j.

To patrol a cell t_i the patroller needs to cover a certain distance s_{t_i}. We use $d(i,j)$ to represent the distance from target i to j, as shown in Fig. 2, where $s_{t_1} = 100\,m$ and $d(2,3) = 1\,km$. A patrolling path is a sequence of consecutive targets covered by the defender. Inside a target (i.e., grid region) the defender covers some distance then he moves to the next target. The defender has a constraint on the maximum length of a patrol, so each path must be shorter than a given maximum value d_{max}. Typically the patrol starts in a base station and ends in the same base station. For example, a patrolling path is shown in Fig. 3 where the patrol starts at t_0 and traverses through targets $t_1 \rightarrow t_6 \rightarrow t_9 \rightarrow t_4$ and ends back in target t_0.

In a GSG the defender's pure strategies are the set of joint patrolling paths $J_m \in J$. The defender has a limited number of resources R, each of which can be

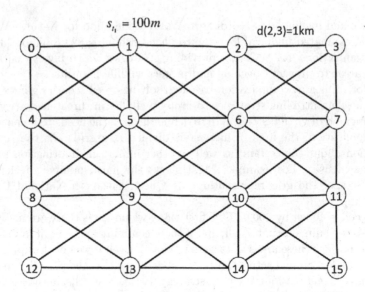

Fig. 2. A graph representation of a grid based GSG

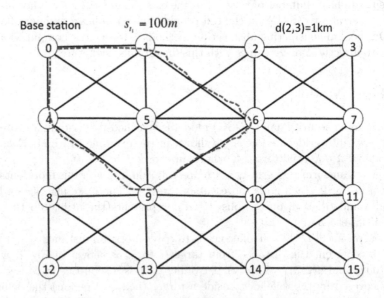

Fig. 3. A patrolling path

assigned to at most one patrolling path. Each joint patrolling path J_m assigns each resource to a specific path. Each path $p_k \in J_m$ in a joint patrolling path covers a set of targets $t \in T$. Every path p_k is unique and is generated using breadth first search where we have a base target t_b. The length of each patrolling path must be less than the distance constraint d_{max}.

We use a matrix $P = P_{J_m t} = (0,1)^n$ to represent the mapping between joint patrolling paths and the targets covered by these paths, where $P_{J_m t}$ represents whether target t is covered by the joint patrolling path J_m. We define the defender's mixed strategy x as a probability distribution over the joint patrolling paths J where x_m is the probability of patrolling a joint patrolling path J_m. The coverage probability for each target $c_t = \sum_{J_m} P_{J_m t} x_m$. Table 1 shows an example of matrix P. This matrix P grows exponentially with the number of targets and resources, which makes performing computations on this representation intractable as the size of the game gets very large.

Table 1. Matrix P for joint patrolling paths

	J_1	J_2	...	J_n
t_1	1	1	...	1
t_2	1	1	...	0
t_3	1	0	...	1
.	.	.		.
.	.	.	...	.
.	.	.		.
t_n	0	1	...	1

If target t is protected then the defender receives reward $U_d^c(t)$ when attacker attacks target t, otherwise a penalty $U_d^u(t)$ is given. In the domain, these values are based on the density of the animals in the area attacked, as a proxy for the expected losses due to poaching activities. We assume that the number of losses decreases when the defender is patrolling the area. The attacker receives reward $U_a^u(t)$ if the attack is on an uncovered area, where the defender is not patrolling, or penalty $U_a^c(t)$ if the attack is executed in a patrolled area. We also assume $U_d^c(t) > U_d^u(t)$ and $U_a^u(t) > U_a^c(t)$. The expected payoffs for defender and attacker are given by:

$$U_d(c,t) = \sum_{t \in T} a_t (c_t U_d^c(t) + (1 - c_t)(U_d^u(t))) \tag{1}$$

$$U_a(c,t) = \sum_{t \in T} a_t (c_t U_a^c(t) + (1 - c_t)(U_a^u(t))) \tag{2}$$

We use the Stackelberg model for the GSG, as in previous work on GSG. In this model the patroller, who acts as defender, moves first and the adversary observes the defender's mixed strategy and chooses a strategy afterwards. The defender tries to protect targets $T = t_1, t_2, ..., t_n$ from the attackers by allocating R resources. The attacker attacks one of the T targets. a_i is the binary attack vector for attacking target t_i. The solution concept used to find equilibrium in this game model is called Strong Stackelberg Equilibrium(SSE) [7,25,34]. In this equilibrium the defender selects a mixed strategy (in this case a probability distribution x over joint patrolling paths J_m), assuming that the adversary will be able to observe his strategy and will choose a best response and break ties in favor of the defender.

5   Solution Approach

We first present a basic method for solving our games using a mixed-integer programming formulation identical to baselines presented in previous work [22]. Solving this mixed integer linear program (MILP) will determine the optimal patrolling strategy for the given game as a probability distribution over the joint patrolling paths. This formulation is somewhat naïve, and it does not scale well to large games due to the exponential number of possible joint paths as the graph grows larger (result in a very large P matrix). We could improve this formulation with any of the more advanced methods based on incremental strategy generation to solve larger problem instances. However, our focus here is on investigating the benefits of abstraction, rather than improving the base algorithm for equilibrium computation, so this basic formulation is sufficient for our purposes. The MIP is represented by the following equations:

$$max \quad \mathbf{d} \tag{3}$$

$$\mathbf{d} - DPx - U_d^u \leq (1 - a)M \tag{4}$$

$$k - APx - U_a^u \leq (1 - a)M \tag{5}$$

$$APx + U_a^u \leq k \tag{6}$$

$$\sum_{x_i} = 1 \tag{7}$$

$$\sum_{a_i} = 1 \tag{8}$$

$$x, a \geq 0 \tag{9}$$

Equation 3 represents the objective function, which maximizes the expected payoff for the defender. Equations 4–6 enforce the players to choose mutual best responses. Equation 7 makes sure that the probability distribution over the joint patrolling paths sums to one. Equation 8 enforces the attacker to attack only one target.

This MIP solves for the probability distribution x over the joint patrolling paths J. This is the strategy defender commits to. In an SSG, attacker observes the defender strategy then attacks a target. We find this attacked target by taking the target with the maximum expected payoff for the attacker using Eq. 2. The attacker breaks tie in favor of defender, as specified in the Strong Stackelberg Equilibrium solution concept. That means if there are multiple targets with same expected payoff for the attacker, the attacker chooses the target with the maximum expected payoff for the defender. Then we can easily calculate the defender expected payoff using Eq. 1.

6   Abstraction for Graph-Based Security Games

Abstraction techniques play a vital role in solving large game models in game theory. Typically, abstraction techniques exploit action space similarity to shrink the game model before applying a solver (such as an equilibrium finding algorithm) to the simpler game. We have already seen successful computer poker agents which uses abstraction techniques where an original game tree can have approximately 10^{71} nodes.

Our approach here applies this idea of game abstraction to green security games. The main idea we exploit in our abstraction is that there are often relatively few important targets in a GSG. The key regions of high animal density are relatively few, and may areas have low density, as shown in Fig. 1. Based on this observation, we believe that many targets in the game can be effectively removed from the analysis to reduce the complexity of large GSG while retaining the important features of the game.

The main idea of our abstraction methods is based on the idea of graph contraction, a version of which has been developed for pathfinding in road networks [14,15]. The idea in contraction is to systematically remove unnecessary nodes from a graph by introducing edges and maintaining the shortest path structure from the complete graph. However, we must also consider the utilities of the nodes when performing contraction in a GSG, since we are interested not only in the shortest path but also the value of the targets on the path. We contract nodes depending on their utility to the defender, relying on the observation that there may be many targets with very low utilities.

The first step in our contraction process is selecting the targets we want to contract. The selection process works according to Pareto optimality. This Pareto optimality will give us a notion about which targets give the defender less utility even after traveling a long distance compared with other targets. Each target in the graph has reward $U_d^c(t), t \in T$ if the total distance s_t of the target is covered. A target t_i is not Pareto optimal if $\exists j \in N, i \neq j, U_d^c(t_i) < U_d^c(t_j)$ and $s_i \geq s_j$. Since we are contracting the graph to get a patrolling strategy for the defender, we only use the utility for the defender to find targets which are not Pareto optimal. Pareto optimality is one of the possible ways of selecting targets to be contracted. Contracting a dominated target may lead to a loss in the solution quality. We defer a further investigation of the the the selection criteria to future work.

Contraction of a node t is done by replacing edge (v, t, v') with a shortcut (v, v'), where $v \neq v'$ and v, v' are neighbors of t. Next we evaluate the edges to determine whether to keep them or not. We do not need direct edge (v, v'), if $d(v, t) + d(t, v') \geq d(p)$, where p is another shortcut. To find the shortest path we use a brute force approach. We check if there exists another path (v, t', v') where $d(v, t') + d(t', v') \leq d(v, t) + d(t, v')$. We keep expanding node t' if $d(v, t') < d(v, t) + d(t, v')$. If $t' = v'$ and $d(v, t') < d(v, t) + d(t, v')$ then we do not need edge (v, v'). If the shortcut (v, v') is necessary then we assign the node's utility on that new edge. Since shortest path computation can become expensive we can limit our search for shortest path where can consider only the neighbors of the contracted node. This search space limit does not affect the correctness of the graph since we are introducing the shortcut (v, v') if we do not find another shortcut path.

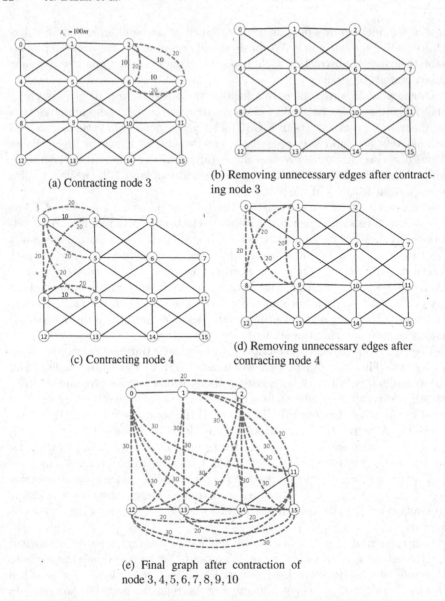

(a) Contracting node 3

(b) Removing unnecessary edges after contracting node 3

(c) Contracting node 4

(d) Removing unnecessary edges after contracting node 4

(e) Final graph after contraction of node $3, 4, 5, 6, 7, 8, 9, 10$

Fig. 4. Contraction procedure for different nodes

In this problem, adding shortcut for neighbors of node t is sufficient to make sure the shortest paths in the original graph are preserved. If there exist two nodes v_1, v_2 between which the shortest path must include node t, then in this shortest path, the node prior to t (denoted as v_3) and the node right after t (denoted as v_4) are neighbors of t and a shortcut (v_3, v_4) will be added for sure according to our approach. Otherwise the optimality of the shortest path between v_1 and v_2 is violated. Therefore, after contraction, the shortest path between v_1 and v_2 can be replaced by one containing the shortcut (v_3, v_4) and the distance is unchanged.

Figure 4 shows how the contraction procedure works on the example graph shown in Fig. 2. The number on the edge represents the distance of the two nodes which are connected by that edge. Figure 4a shows the new edges introduced as red dotted curve after removing target 3. After that we compute the shortest path for each of the new edge. Figure 4b shows that there were already existing shortest paths. So all of the new edges were pruned because they are unnecessary. Similarly, Fig. 4c shows the new edges introduced as red dotted lines after contracting target 4. Then Fig. 4d shows what happened to the graph as we compute shortest path calculation. As we notice that some new edges remained (e.g. $t_0 \rightarrow t_8$) because those nodes are in the shortest path. Figure 4e shows the final graph after contracting nodes $(3, 4, 5, 6, 7, 8, 9, 10)$.

Algorithm 1. Contraction Procedure

```
 1: procedure CONTRACTGRAPH                                          ▷
 2:     G ← Graph()                                ▷ Initiate the graph to contract
 3:     n_d ← ContractedNodes()                       ▷ Get the nodes to contract
 4:     for t ← n_d.pop() do                            ▷ for every node t in n_d
 5:         for v ← n_c.neighbors() do
 6:             for v' ← n_c.neighbors() do
 7:                 if v ≠ v'j then
 8:                     d_mid ← Dist(v, t, v')
 9:                     d_s ← ShortestDist(v, v')
10:                     if d_mid ≤ d_s then                    ▷ t in shortest path
11:                         AdjustNeighbors(v, t, v')
12:                     end if
13:                 end if
14:             end for
15:         end for
16:     end for
17: end procedure
```

Algorithm 1 shows how the contraction procedure works. Lines $2-3$ initialize the variables. Lines $4-16$ check whether a contracted node t falls into the shortest path between node v and v'. In line 8 $Dist(v, t, v')$ returns the distance of edge $v \rightarrow t \rightarrow v'$. In line 9 $ShortestDist(v, v')$ finds the shortest path between v and v'. If t is in the shortest path (line 10), we add a direct edge between v and v' using method $AdjustNeighbors()$ shown in Algorithm 2. Algorithm 2 also makes sure that there is a path between v and v' which consists of node t. Lines $2-4$ in Algorithm 2 builds an edge that consists of node t. $Path(v, t)$ returns the intermediate nodes to reach t from v including v. We do this because there might be previously contracted nodes in the edge from v or v' to t. Suppose $Path(v, t_5)$ returned $p_v^{t_5} = (v \rightarrow t_1 \rightarrow t_2)$. $Path(v', t_5)$ returned $p_{v'}^{t_5} = v' \rightarrow t_6 \rightarrow t_7$. After

---

Algorithm 2. Adjust Neighbor Procedure

1: **procedure** ADJUSTNEIGHBORS(v, t, v')   ▷
2:     $p_v^t \leftarrow Path(v, t)$
3:     $p_{v'}^t \leftarrow Path(v', t)$
4:     $p \leftarrow Merge(p_v^t, t, p_{v'}^t)$
5:     $v.AddNeighbor(v', p)$
6:     $v'.AddNeighbor(v, p)$
7:     $v.RemoveNeighbor(t)$
8:     $v'.RemoveNeighbor(t)$
9: **end procedure**

---

that $Merge(p_v^{t_5}, t_5, p_{v'}^{t_5})$ will merge these two paths and return $v \rightarrow t_1 \rightarrow t_2 \rightarrow$ $t_5 \rightarrow t_7 \rightarrow t_6 \rightarrow v'$. Next in line $5 - 6$ v and v' adds each other as neighbor inside method $AddNeighbor(v, p)$.

Once we have the contracted graph we can follow the same procedure described in Sect. 5 to solve the game based on the smaller. The only difference is that we have fewer nodes and the edges can represent paths that c over multiple underlying nodes. Solving for the optimal solution of this contracted game will not necessarily result in finding the optimal solution to the original game, but we will show in our experimental results that it is a good approximation.

6.1 Reverse Mapping

The MIP returns a probability distribution over the joint patrolling paths J. But the P' matrix used by the MIP was constructed from the contracted graph, where patrolling paths do not reflect the original graph: each edge in the contracted graph can represent multiple nodes and edges in the original graph. We need to find the P matrix which will consider those contracted nodes. Given the defender's strategy, found from the MIP, using a P matrix which considers all the targets including the contracted node, we can find the target with the maximum expected payoff for the attacker. What we present now is a reverse mapping function which transform the P' matrix into P. For each of the joint patrolling paths this function $ReverseMap(P') \rightarrow P$ checks if two consecutive nodes have edges with contracted nodes. If so, the node is marked as covered in the P matrix. There is an alternative of first mapping the routes in the contracted graph to routes in the original graph, and then solve a MIP. Either way is correct as the reversemapping does not depend on solving the MIP.

The reverse mapping function $ReverseMap(P') \rightarrow P$ gives us joint patrolling paths for the original graph. Algorithm 3 shows how the $ReverseMap$ method works. For every joint patrolling path J_m (line 4) and for every path p_m in J_m (line 5) we mark two consecutive nodes as covered (line 9–10). Then we check if two consecutive nodes have any edge consists of contracted nodes. If so, we mark those targets covered (line 11–14). Once we have the joint patrolling paths P for the original graph, we can compute the attack vector and also defender's expected payoff.

Algorithm 3. Reverse Mapping Procedure

```
 1: procedure REVERSEMAP
 2:     J ← JointPaths()
 3:     index ← 0
 4:     for Jₘ ← J.pop() do
 5:         for pₖ ← Jₘ.pop do
 6:             for i ← pₖ.len − 1 do
 7:                 t ← pₖ(i)
 8:                 tₙₑₓₜ ← pₖ(i + 1)
 9:                 P[t][index] ← 1
10:                 P[tₙₑₓₜ][index] ← 1
11:                 eₙₒₐₑₛ ← EdgeNodes(t, tₙₑₓₜ)
12:                 for tₑ ← eₙₒₐₑₛ.pop() do
13:                     P[tₑ][index] ← 1
14:                 end for
15:             end for
16:         end for
17:         index ← index + 1
18:     end for
19: end procedure
```

7   Experiments

We begin by showing what the solution of the example game shown in Fig. 4e looks like. We computed this solution based on Fig. 2 after contracting targets $(3, 4, 5, 6, 7, 8, 9, 10)$. We show the reduced P' matrix for the contracted graph is formed, and then we show how we find the P matrix after reverse mapping. For simplicity we use only two joint patrolling paths which have a positive probability distribution. We used the maximum distance 6 to generate 9 patrolling paths without any duplicates for the contracted graph. The joint patrolling paths are $J_0 = (p_6, p_8)$ and $J_1 = (p_6, p_7)$ where $p_6 = (t_0 \rightarrow t_{15} \rightarrow t_0), p_7 = (t_0 \rightarrow t_2 \rightarrow t_1 \rightarrow t_0), p_7 = (t_0 \rightarrow t_{11} \rightarrow t_1 \rightarrow t_0)$. The MIP returns a probability distribution x where $x_0 = 0.076$ and $x_1 = 0.250$. There are other joint patrolling paths for which x_i has a positive probability, but we are only showing part of the solution. A part of P' matrix is given in Table 2 for the contracted graph shown in Fig. 4e.

Next we use the reverse mapping function $ReverseMap(P') \rightarrow P$ to obtain the P matrix (Table 3) for the graph shown in Fig. 2. The $ReverseMap(P') \rightarrow P$ checks whether a target t_i is in an edge between two consecutive target in a patrolling path which belongs to a joint patrolling path. If so, t_i is marked as covered. For example, t_5, t_{10} are marked as covered because they are part of an edge from t_0 to t_{15} for joint schedule J_0 and J_1.

Now we present the results of our initial experimental evaluation of the the the effectiveness of abstraction based on graph contraction on security games. The baseline solution provides us with a defender strategy on joint patrolling paths for any given graph (contracted or not). We did our analysis by comparing the baseline case with different levels of contraction. The comparisons are done

Table 2. A part of the P' matrix for example game in Fig. 4e,

	$x_0 = 0.0769$	$x_1 = 0.2507$	...
	J_0	J_1	...
t_0	1	1	...
t_1	1	1	...
t_2	0	1	...
t_{11}	1	0	...
t_{12}	0	0	...
t_{13}	0	0	...
t_{14}	0	0	..
t_{15}	1	1	...

Table 3. A part of P matrix for example game in Fig. 2

	$x_0 = 0.0769$	$x_1 = 0.2507$	...
	J_0	J_1	...
t_0	1	1	...
t_1	1	1	...
t_2	0	1	...
t_3	0	0	...
t_4	0	0	...
t_5	1	1	...
t_6	1	0	...
t_7	0	0	...
t_8	0	0	...
t_9	0	0	...
t_{10}	1	1	...
t_{11}	1	0	...
t_{12}	0	0	...
t_{13}	0	0	...
t_{14}	0	0	..
t_{15}	1	1	...

for two metrics: solution quality and runtime. For each level of contraction we measured the level of error introduced and how much time we could save by introducing that error. We denote the error by epsilon(ϵ),which can be defined as follows, where $U'_d(c, a)$ is the expected payoff for defender when using contraction where $U_d(c, a) \geq U'_d(c, a)$:

$$\epsilon = \frac{[U_d(c, a) - U'_d(c, a)]}{U_d(c, a) * 100} \tag{10}$$

For our experimental setup we used 100 randomly generated, 2-player security games intended to capture the important features of typical green security games. Each game has 25 targets (nodes in the graph). Payoffs for the targets are chosen randomly from the range -10 to 10. The rewards for defender or attacker are positive and the penalties are negative. We set the distance constraint to 6. In the baseline solution we have no contraction. For different level of abstraction the number of contracted nodes (#CN) varies between the values: $(0, 2, 5, 8, 10)$. Figure 5 shows us how contraction affects contraction time (CT), solution time (ST) and reverse mapping time (RMT). CT only consider the contraction procedure, ST considers the construction of the P matrix and the solution time for the MIP, and RMT considers time to generate the P matrix for the original graph from the solution to the abstracted game.

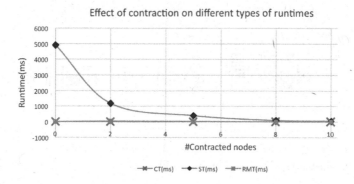

Fig. 5. Effect of contraction on contraction time(CT), solving time(ST) and reverse mapping time(RMT)

We first note that as the graph becomes more contracted ST takes much less time, as shown in Fig. 5. The next experimental result presented in Fig. 6 shows how much error is introduced as we increase the amount of contraction and the amount of time we can save by using contraction. The amount of time saved is very significant compared with the amount of error introduced.

In the next experiment we tried to see how the density of high-valued targets in the graph affects the expected utility of defender if we use contraction. If a

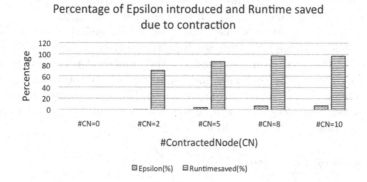

Fig. 6. Effect of contraction on Epsilon and runtime saved

graph has $y\%$ density, we set the same utility for the defender and attacker for 10 % of targets in a graph. The rest of the targets have 0 utility, meaning that those targets are insignificant. Figure 7 shows that when we have a small number of significant targets contraction results in better solution quality. This indicates that contraction will be a particularly effective method for games with relatively few important areas to protect relative to the size of the geographic area, which is often the case for GSG. The reason why the expected utility decreased as we increased density is we kept the distace limit for the patrolling fixed.

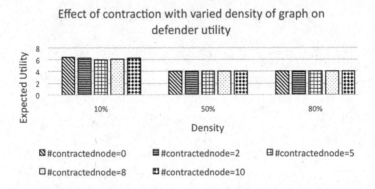

Fig. 7. Effect of contraction for different graph densities

In the next experiment result shown in Figs. 8 and 9 we consider how increasing patrolling distance can affect the solution quality with different levels of contractions and how much time was saved by using contraction. For different level of abstraction the number of contracted nodes used were : $(0, 2, 5, 8, 10)$. The number of resources was fixed at 3. For the baseline algorithm, there was no epsilon because it provides the optimal solution and is what we compare the solution quality of the graph contraction approach to. One key observation is as the distance increases, the percentage of epsilon increased. This is because our resource was fixed but when maximum distance increased we had more joint patrolling paths to consider. This had the effect of introducing more error, but we were able to save a huge amount of time as shown in Fig. 9.

For our final experiment we kept the same experimental setup as the previous experiment except this time we kept the maximum distance fixed at 6 and we varied the number of resources. For the number of resources we considered $(1, 2, 3)$. The results are shown in Figs. 10 and 11. We notice in Fig. 8 that epsilon decreased as we increased our resources. This is expected behavior: as we increase our resources there will be less error introduced, and we were able to save more time(Fig. 9) when resources were increased.

7.1   Discussion and Future Work

Our experimental results demonstrate that using graph contraction as a method for abstraction in green security games has significant potential to increase the

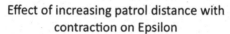

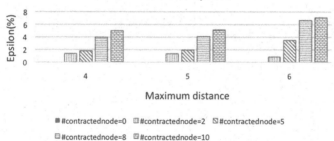

Fig. 8. Effect of contraction on Epsilon with increasing distance

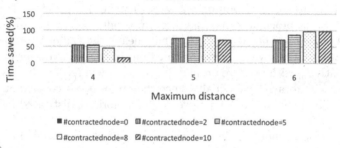

Fig. 9. Effect of contraction on runtime saved with increasing distance

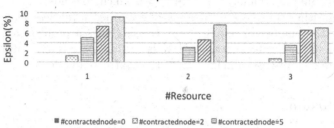

Fig. 10. Effect of increasing patrolling resource with contraction in epsilon

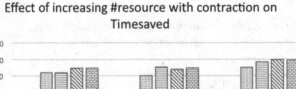

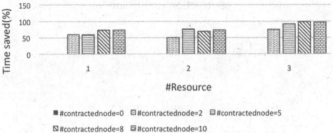

Fig. 11. Effect of increasing patrolling resource on runtime

scalability of solution methods for this class of games. However, we also note several issues with the current methods, and opportunities for improvement in future work.

One of the important issues in the contraction procedure is the selection of targets we want to contract. Suppose a target has been contracted. It can happen in the current procedure that the target was not used in any edge between two targets, which are not contracted. That means the target will not be covered when we use the reverse mapping function. In this scenario for every joint patrolling path J_m with positive probability attacker will receive the reward, and the defender will always have penalty since the target is not covered at all. This kind of situation may be avoidable if we design a more sophisticated method for determining which targets to contract.

Another issue is there might be contraction which can result in very long edges. The difficulty arises if all the edges from base target are further away than the distance constraint. We will not be able to generate any legal path in this case. This kind of scenario can be avoided by not doing contraction if the edge results an edge longer than a threshold.

A final part of our contraction method that could be improved is when we need to find out whether (v, t, v') is the shortest path. We use a shortest path finding algorithm to find another shortest path which does not use t. This shortest path algorithm continues until v' can be reached using less distance than (v, t, v'). As the number of nodes grows, this becomes a problem for runtime. One solution of this problem is to reduce the search space. For example we can only compare edges between neighbors of the contracted node.

8   Conclusion

Stackelberg security games are currently being used in real-world green security domains. In this domain the defenders try to find out an efficient patrolling strategy to prevent illegal wildlife poaching. One of the big issues of this approach, modeling the scenario with GSG, is scalability. In reality, wild animals spread over very large area. As a result, the problem space becomes huge to solve within feasible time. In this paper we focused on improving the scalability of methods for solving a general class of graph-based security games that includes green security games in particular. We showed that using graph contraction as a method of abstraction can speed up the solution process by a huge amount. With further work to refine the abstraction method, we believe that we can achieve a very large improvement in the scalability for green security games.

References

1. Govt of Mozambique announces major decline in national elephant population (May 2015). http://press.wcs.org/News-Releases/articleType/ArticleView/article Id/6760/Government-of-Mozambique-Releases-Elephant-Population-Numbers. aspx
2. The IUCN Red List of threatened species, April 2015. http://www.iucnredlist.org/
3. Estimate of global financial losses due to illegal fishing, February 2016. http://www.worldwildlife.org/threats/illegal-fishing
4. Batz, G.V., Geisberger, R., Neubauer, S., Sanders, P.: Time-dependent contraction hierarchies and approximation. In: Festa, P. (ed.) SEA 2010. LNCS, vol. 6049, pp. 166–177. Springer, Heidelberg (2010). doi:10.1007/978-3-642-13193-6_15
5. Billings, D., Burch, N., Davidson, A., Holte, R., Schaeffer, J., Schauenberg, T., Szafron, D.: Approximating game-theoretic optimal strategies for full-scale poker. In: The International Joint Conference on Artificial Intelligence (IJCAI), pp. 661–668 (2003)
6. Bowling, M., Burch, N., Johanson, M., Tammelin, O.: Heads-up limit hold'em poker is solved. Science **347**(6218), 145–149 (2015)
7. Breton, M., Alj, A., Haurie, A.: Sequential Stackelberg equilibria in two-person games. J. Optim. Theory Appl. **59**(1), 71–97 (1988)
8. Brown, M., Haskell, W.B., Tambe, M.: Addressing scalability and robustness in security games with multiple boundedly rational adversaries. In: Poovendran, R., Saad, W. (eds.) GameSec 2014. LNCS, vol. 8840, pp. 23–42. Springer, Heidelberg (2014). doi:10.1007/978-3-319-12601-2_2
9. Brown, N., Ganzfried, S., Sandholm, T.: Hierarchical abstraction, distributed equilibrium computation, and post-processing, with application to a champion no-limit Texas hold'em agent. Technical report (2014)
10. Fang, F., Nguyen, T.H., Pickles, R., Lam, W.Y., Clements, G.R., An, B., Singh, A., Tambe, M., Lemieux, A.: Deploying paws: field optimization of the protection assistant for wildlife security. In: Proceedings of the Innovative Applications of Artificial Intelligence (IAAI) (2016)
11. Fang, F., Stone, P., Tambe, M.: When security games go green: designing defender strategies to prevent poaching and illegal fishing. In: International Joint Conference on Artificial Intelligence (IJCAI) (2015)
12. Field, C., Laws, R.: The distribution of the larger herbivores in the Queen Elizabeth National Park, Uganda. J. Appl. Ecol. 273–294 (1970)
13. Ganzfried, S., Sandholm, T.: Potential-aware imperfect-recall abstraction with earth mover's distance in imperfect-information games. In: Conference on Artificial Intelligence (AAAI) (2014)

14. Geisberger, R., Sanders, P., Schultes, D., Delling, D.: Contraction hierarchies: faster and simpler hierarchical routing in road networks. In: McGeoch, C.C. (ed.) WEA 2008. LNCS, vol. 5038, pp. 319–333. Springer, Heidelberg (2008). doi:10.1007/978-3-540-68552-4_24

15. Geisberger, R., Sanders, P., Schultes, D., Vetter, C.: Exact routing in large road networks using contraction hierarchies. Transp. Sci. **46**, 388–404 (2012)

16. Gilpin, A., Sandholm, T.: A competitive texas hold'em poker player via automated abstraction and real-time equilibrium computation. In: Proceedings of the National Conference on Artificial Intelligence (AAAI), vol. 21, p. 1007 (2006)

17. Gilpin, A., Sandholm, T.: Better automated abstraction techniques for imperfect information games, with application to texas hold'em poker. In: International Foundation for Autonomous Agents and Multiagent Systems (AAMAS), p. 192 (2007)

18. Gilpin, A., Sandholm, T.: Lossless abstraction of imperfect information games. J. ACM (JACM) **54**(5), 25 (2007)

19. Gilpin, A., Sandholm, T., Sørensen, T.B.: Potential-aware automated abstraction of sequential games, and holistic equilibrium analysis of texas hold'em poker. In: Proceedings of the Conference on Artificial Intelligence (AAAI), vol. 22, p. 50 (2007)

20. Gilpin, A., Sandholm, T., Sørensen, T.B.: A heads-up no-limit texas hold'em poker player: discretized betting models and automatically generated equilibrium-finding programs. In: International Conference on Autonomous Agents and Multiagent Systems (AAMAS), pp. 911–918 (2008)

21. Haskell, W.B., Kar, D., Fang, F., Tambe, M., Cheung, S., Denicola, E.: Robust protection of fisheries with compass. In: Association for the Advancement of Artificial Intelligence (AAAI), pp. 2978–2983 (2014)

22. Jain, M., Kardes, E., Kiekintveld, C., Ordónez, F., Tambe, M.: Security games with arbitrary schedules: a branch and price approach. In: Association for the Advancement of Artificial Intelligence (AAAI) (2010)

23. Kiekintveld, C., Jain, M., Tsai, J., Pita, J., Ordóñez, F., Tambe, M.: Computing optimal randomized resource allocations for massive security games. In: Proceedings of The 8th International Conference on Autonomous Agents and Multiagent Systems-, vol. 1, pp. 689–696. International Foundation for Autonomous Agents and Multiagent Systems (AAMAS) (2009)

24. Kroer, C., Sandholm, T.: Extensive-form game abstraction with bounds. In: Proceedings of the Fifteenth ACM Conference on Economics and Computation, pp. 621–638 (2014)

25. Leitmann, G.: On generalized stackelberg strategies. J. Optim. Theory Appl. **26**(4), 637–643 (1978)

26. Nguyen, T.H., Fave, F.M.D., Kar, D., Lakshminarayanan, A.S., Yadav, A., Tambe, M., Agmon, N., Plumptre, A.J., Driciru, M., Wanyama, F., Rwetsiba, A.: Making the most of our regrets: regret-based solutions to handle payoff uncertainty and elicitation in green security games. In: Khouzani, M.H.R., Panaousis, E., Theodorakopoulos, G. (eds.) GameSec 2015. LNCS, vol. 9406, pp. 170–191. Springer, Heidelberg (2015). doi:10.1007/978-3-319-25594-1_10

27. Paruchuri, P., Pearce, J.P., Marecki, J., Tambe, M., Ordonez, F., Kraus, S.: Playing games for security: an efficient exact algorithm for solving bayesian stackelberg games. In: Proceedings of the 7th International Joint Conference on Autonomous Agents and Multiagent Systems, vol. 2, pp. 895–902. International Foundation for Autonomous Agents and Multiagent Systems (AAMAS) (2008)

28. Pita, J., Bellamane, H., Jain, M., Kiekintveld, C., Tsai, J., Ordóñez, F., Tambe, M.: Security applications: lessons of real-world deployment. ACM SIGecom Exchanges 8(2), 5 (2009)
29. Sandholm, T., Singh, S.: Lossy stochastic game abstraction with bounds. In: Proceedings of the 13th ACM Conference on Electronic Commerce, pp. 880–897 (2012)
30. Shieh, E., An, B., Yang, R., Tambe, M., Baldwin, C., DiRenzo, J., Maule, B., Meyer, G.: Protect: a deployed game theoretic system to protect the ports of the united states. In: Proceedings of the 11th International Conference on Autonomous Agents and Multiagent Systems, vol. 1, pp. 13–20. International Foundation for Autonomous Agents and Multiagent Systems (AAMAS) (2012)
31. Skiena, S.: Dijkstra's Algorithm. Implementing Discrete Mathematics: Combinatorics and Graph Theory with Mathematica, pp. 225–227. Addison-Wesley, Reading (1990)
32. Storandt, S.: Route planning for bicycles-exact constrained shortest paths made practical via contraction hierarchy. In: International Conference on Automated Planning and Scheduling (ICAPS), vol. 4, p. 46 (2012)
33. Tsai, J., Kiekintveld, C., Ordonez, F., Tambe, M., Rathi, S.: Iris-a tool for strategic security allocation in transportation networks (2009)
34. Von Stengel, B., Zamir, S.: Leadership with commitment to mixed strategies (2004)
35. Yang, R., Ford, B., Tambe, M., Lemieux, A.: Adaptive resource allocation for wildlife protection against illegal poachers. In: Proceedings of the 2014 International Conference on Autonomous Agents and Multi-agent Systems, pp. 453–460. International Foundation for Autonomous Agents and Multiagent Systems (AAMAS) (2014)
36. Yang, R., Jiang, A.X., Tambe, M., Ordonez, F.: Scaling-up security games with boundedly rational adversaries: a cutting-plane approach. In: The International Joint Conference on Artificial Intelligence (IJCAI) (2013)
37. Yin, Z., Jiang, A.X., Tambe, M., Kiekintveld, C., Leyton-Brown, K., Sandholm, T., Sullivan, J.P.: Trusts: scheduling randomized patrols for fare inspection in transit systems using game theory. AI Mag. 33(4), 59 (2012)
38. Zinkevich, M., Johanson, M., Bowling, M., Piccione, C.: Regret minimization in games with incomplete information. In: Advances in Neural Information Processing Systems (NIPS), pp. 1729–1736 (2007)

Can I Do That? Discovering Domain Axioms Using Declarative Programming and Relational Reinforcement Learning

Mohan Sridharan[(✉)], Prashanth Devarakonda, and Rashmica Gupta

Department of Electrical and Computer Engineering,
The University of Auckland, Auckland, New Zealand
{m.sridharan,vdev818}@auckland.ac.nz, rashmicy@gmail.com

Abstract. Robots deployed to assist humans in complex, dynamic domains need the ability to represent, reason with, and learn from, different descriptions of incomplete domain knowledge and uncertainty. This paper presents an architecture that integrates declarative programming and relational reinforcement learning to support cumulative and interactive discovery of previously unknown axioms governing domain dynamics. Specifically, Answer Set Prolog (ASP), a declarative programming paradigm, is used to represent and reason with incomplete commonsense domain knowledge. For any given goal, unexplained failure of plans created by inference in the ASP program is taken to indicate the existence of unknown domain axioms. The task of learning these axioms is formulated as a Reinforcement Learning problem, and decision-tree regression with a relational representation is used to generalize from specific axioms identified over time. The new axioms are added to the ASP-based representation for subsequent inference. We demonstrate and evaluate the capabilities of our architecture in two simulated domains: *Blocks World* and *Simple Mario*.

1 Introduction

Robots[1] are increasingly being used to assist humans in complex domains such as disaster rescue and health care. While it is difficult for robots to operate in such domains without considerable domain knowledge, human participants may not have the time and expertise to equip robots with comprehensive and accurate domain knowledge. Robots receive incomplete but useful commonsense knowledge about the domain, including *default* knowledge that holds in all but a few exceptional circumstances, e.g., "books are typically in the library, but cookbooks may be in the kitchen". Robots also receive unreliable information by processing inputs from sensors such as cameras and microphones. Furthermore, the axioms governing the dynamics of the domain may be known partially and may change over time. To truly assist humans in such domains, robots need the ability to represent, reason with, and learn from, such different descriptions of knowledge and uncertainty at both the cognitive level and the sensorimotor level.

---

[1] We use the terms "robot", "agent" and "learner" interchangeably in this paper.

N. Osman and C. Sierra (Eds.): AAMAS 2016 WS, Visionary Papers, LNAI 10003, pp. 34–49, 2016.
DOI: 10.1007/978-3-319-46840-2_3

Towards addressing the challenges described above, we have developed architectures that have combined the non-monotonic logical reasoning capabilities of declarative programming with the uncertainty modeling capabilities of probabilistic graphical models. These architectures allow robots to represent and reason with logic-based and probabilistic representations of knowledge and uncertainty, for planning and diagnosis [1–4]. The architecture describe in this paper builds on our prior work [5,6] to support incremental and interactive discovery of previously unknown domain axioms. The key features of the architecture are:

- An action language is used to describe the dynamics of the domain. This description and histories with initial state defaults are translated to an Answer Set Prolog (ASP) program that is solved for inference, planning and diagnostics.
- For any given goal, unexplained failures during plan execution are taken to indicate the existence of previously unknown domain axioms. The task of interactively discovering such unknown axioms is formulated as a reinforcement learning problem.
- Decision-tree regression and a relational representation are used to improve computational efficiency, and to generalize from specific axioms identified through reinforcement learning. These newly discovered axioms are added to the ASP program and used for subsequent reasoning.

These features are demonstrated in two simulated domains: *Blocks World* and the *Simple Mario* game. We show experimentally that the proposed architecture and the relational representation allow the robot to reliably discover previously unknown domain axioms more efficiently than traditional reinforcement learning.

The remainder of this paper is organized as follows. First, Sect. 2 summarizes prior work and describes some background material. Next, Sect. 3 describes the problem formulation and the proposed architecture. The experimental results are discussed in Sect. 4, followed by conclusions in Sect. 5.

2   Related Work

We motivate the proposed approach by reviewing some related work. We also provide some background information about ASP, reinforcement learning and relational representations, and their use on robots.

Probabilistic graphical models are used widely to formulate planning, sensing, navigation, and interaction, on robots [7,8], but these formulations, by themselves, make it difficult to reason with commonsense knowledge. Research in planning has provided many algorithms for knowledge representation and reasoning on robots [9,10], but these algorithms require considerable prior knowledge about the domain. Many of these algorithms are based on first-order logic, and do not support non-monotonic logical reasoning, default reasoning, and the ability to merge new, unreliable information with the current beliefs. Other logic-based formalisms address some of these limitations, e.g., Answer Set Prolog (ASP), a declarative language designed for representing and reasoning with common-sense knowledge [11], has been used by an international research community for cognitive robotics applications [12–14]. However, ASP does not support proba-bilistic models of uncertainty, and does not inherently support incremental and interactive learning from experience.

Combining logical and probabilistic reasoning is a fundamental research prob-lem in robotics and AI. Architectures have been developed to support hierarchi-cal representation of knowledge in first-order logic, and probabilistic processing of perceptual information [15,16]. Existing approaches have combined determin-istic and probabilistic algorithms for task and motion planning [17,18], switched between probabilistic reasoning and first-order logic based to use semantic maps and commonsense knowledge in a probabilistic relational representation [19], and used a three-layered organization of knowledge to combine first-order logic and probabilistic reasoning for open world planning [20]. Other approaches for com-bining logical and probabilistic reasoning include Markov logic networks [21], Bayesian Logic [22], probabilistic first-order logic [23], first-order relational POMDPs [24], and probabilistic extensions to ASP [25,26]. Many of these algo-rithms are based on first-order logic, and have the corresponding limitations, e.g., non-monotonic logical reasoning and reasoning with default knowledge are chal-lenging. Other algorithms based on logic programming do not support all desired capabilities such as reasoning with large probabilistic components, reasoning with open worlds, and incremental and interactive learning of domain knowledge.

Many tasks that require the agent to learn from repeated interactions with their environment have been posed as Reinforcement Learning (RL) prob-lems [27] and modeled as Markov Decision Processes (MDPs). It is challenging to design RL algorithms that scale to complex domains, and allow the transfer of knowledge between related tasks or domains. Relational reinforcement Learning (RRL) combines relational representations of states and actions with regression for Q-function generalization [28]. An RRL formulation enables the use of struc-tural similarities, and the reuse of relevant experience in related regions of the state-action space [29]. Existing approaches, however, use RRL for planning, and generalization, e.g., with a decision tree [30], is limited to a single MDP corre-sponding to a specific planning task. Furthermore, these approaches do not fully support the ability to reason with commonsense knowledge.

We have designed architectures that combine the complementary strengths of declarative programming and probabilistic graphical models for planning and diagnostics in robotics [1–3]. In this paper, we abstract away the unreliability of perception, and combine declarative programming with RRL for incrementally and interactively discovering axioms, and generalizing across individual axiom instances. Unlike prior work that used inductive logic and ASP to monotoni-cally learn causal rules [31], or integrated ASP with RL for discovering domain axioms [5], we use relational representation for generalization. Unlike existing work in RRL that primarily focuses on planning, our approach uses relational representations for discovering domain axioms, and generalizes across different MDPs, i.e., different decision making tasks in the domain.

3   Proposed Architecture

This section describes the proposed approach for incrementally and interactively discovering previously unknown axioms governing domain dynamics. The overall architecture is shown in Fig. 1. For any given goal, ASP-based non-monotonic reasoning with a coarse-resolution domain description provides a sequence of abstract actions. Each such action is implemented as a sequence of concrete actions, using a partially observable Markov decision process (POMDP) to probabilistically model the relevant part of the fine-resolution description obtained by refining the coarse-resolution description. In this paper, we abstract away the uncertainty in perception for simplicity, and thus do not discuss probabilistic planning. Instead, we represent the domain at a single resolution, use ASP-based reasoning with commonsense knowledge for planning and diagnosis, and focus on RRL-based interactive discovery of domain axioms. We illustrate the capabilities of this architecture using two simulated domains.

1. **Blocks World (BW):** A tabletop domain where the agent's objective is to stack blocks characterized by different colors, shapes, and sizes, in specific configurations on a table. Figure 2 illustrates a scenario with four blocks, which corresponds to ≈70 states under a standard RL/MDP formulation [28]. In this domain, the agent may not know, for instance, that a block should not be placed on a prism-shaped block, and any corresponding action should not be attempted.

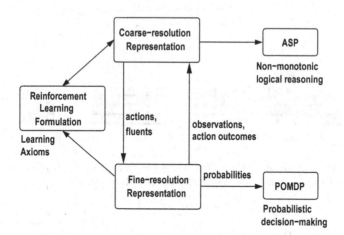

Fig. 1. The overall architecture integrates the complementary strengths of declarative programming, probabilistic graphical models, and reinforcement learning.

Fig. 2. Blocks world scenario with four blocks.

2. **Simple Mario (SM):** A simplified version of the popular Mario game, where
   the agent (*mario*) has to navigate between specific locations while avoiding
   obstacles and hazards. The domain has ≈80 states and 4 parametrized actions
   in a standard MDP formulation. Figure 3(a) shows the safe actions (moving
   or jumping left or right), while the unsafe actions are shown in Fig. 3(b)
   (colliding with a monster), Fig. 4(a) (landing on spikes), and Fig. 4(b) (landing
   on an empty space).

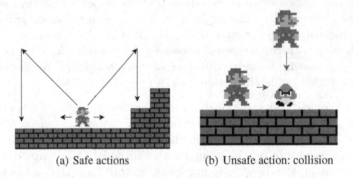

(a) Safe actions   (b) Unsafe action: collision

Fig. 3. Examples of safe actions (e.g., moving, jumping to unoccupied locations) and
unsafe actions (e.g., collision with a monster) in the Simple Mario domain.

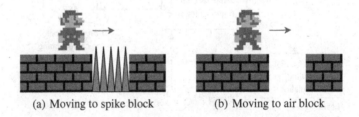

(a) Moving to spike block   (b) Moving to air block

Fig. 4. Examples of unsafe actions that cause episode termination (e.g., moving to a
block made of *spike* or *air* material) in the Simple Mario domain.

3.1   Knowledge Representation

The transition diagram of our illustrative domain is described in an *action language AL_d* [11]. Action languages are formal models of parts of natural language
used for describing transition diagrams. AL_d has a sorted signature containing
three *sorts*: *statics*, *fluents* and *actions*. Statics are domain properties whose
truth values cannot be changed by actions, while fluents are properties whose
truth values can be changed by actions—actions refer to a set of elementary
actions. Fluents are of two types: *inertial fluents* obey the laws of inertia and

are changed directly by actions, whereas *defined fluents* do not obey the laws of inertia and cannot be changed directly by actions—they are changed based on other fluents. A domain property p or its negation $\neg p$ is a domain literal. AL_d allows three types of statements:

a **causes** l_{in} **if** $p_0, \ldots, p_m$	(Causal law)
l **if** $p_0, \ldots, p_m$	(State constraint)
impossible $a_0, \ldots, a_k$ **if** $p_0, \ldots, p_m$	(Executability condition)

where a is an action, l is a literal, l_{in} is an inertial fluent literal, and $p_0, \ldots, p_m$ are domain literals. The causal law states that action a causes inertial fluent literal l_{in} if the literals $p_0, \ldots, p_m$ hold true. A collection of statements of AL_d forms a system description.

The domain representation consists of a system description $\mathscr{D}$ and history $\mathscr{H}$. $\mathscr{D}$ consists of a sorted signature Σ and axioms used to describe the transition diagram τ. The sorted signature Σ is a tuple that defines the names of objects, functions, and predicates available for use in the domain. For instance, the sorts of the BW domain include elements such as *block*, *place*, *color*, *shape*, *size*, and *robot*, whereas the sorts of the SM domain include elements such as *location*, *block*, *material*, *size*, *direction* and *thing*. When some sorts are subsorts of other sorts, e.g., *agent* (i.e., *mario*) and *monster* may be subsorts of *thing*, they can be arranged hierarchically.

We describe the fluents and actions of the domain in terms of the sorts of their arguments. The BW domain's fluent *on(block, place)*, defined in terms of the sorts of the arguments, states that a specific block is at a specific place. This is an inertial fluent that obeys the laws of inertia. There are some statics for block attributes *has_color(block, color)*, *has_shape(block, shape)* and *has_size(block, size)*. The action *move(block, place)* moves a block to a specific place (*table* or on top of another block). In the SM domain, the fluents are the location of *mario* and the *monster* (assuming there is only one monster)— we reason about the former and assume the latter is defined fluent known at all times, i.e., the inertial fluent is *loc(agent, block)*. Mario can move to the left or the right by one position, or jump to the left or right by up to three positions, which are represented as actions *move(mario, dir)* and *jump(mario, dir, numpos)* with direction (*left*, *right*) and number of positions (1, 2, 3) as arguments. Statics describe block attributes, e.g., *has_material(block, material)*, and location attributes, e.g., *right_of(block, block)*.

For the BW domain, the dynamics are defined in terms of causal laws such as:

$$move(B, L) \text{ \textbf{causes} } on(B, L)$$

state constraints such as:

$$\neg on(B, L_2) \text{ \textbf{if} } on(B, L_1), \ L_1 \neq L_2$$

and executability conditions such as:

$$\textbf{impossible} \ move(B_2, L) \text{ \textbf{if} } on(B_2, L), \ B_1 \neq B_2$$

The SM domain's dynamics are defined in a similar manner, using causal laws such as:

$$move(mario, right) \textbf{ causes } loc(mario, B_2),\ right\_of(B_2, B_1),\ loc(mario, B_1)$$

state constraints such as:

$$\neg loc(mario, B_2) \textbf{ if } loc(mario, B_1),\ B_1 \neq B_2$$

and executability conditions such as:

$$\textbf{impossible } move(mario, right) \textbf{ if } loc(mario, B_1),\ right\_of(B_2, B_1),$$
$$has\_material(B_2, spike)$$

The recorded history of a dynamic domain is usually a record of (a) fluents observed to be true at a time step $obs(fluent, boolean, step)$, and (b) the occurrence of an action at a time step $hpd(action, step)$. Our prior architecture expanded on this view by allowing histories to contain (prioritized) defaults describing the values of fluents in their initial states [2, 32]. For instance, we can represent a default statement of the form "blocks are usually on the table or on another block that is on the table" and elegantly encode exceptions to such default knowledge.

The domain representation is translated into a program $\Pi(\mathscr{D}, \mathscr{H})$ in CR-Prolog, a variant of Answer Set Prolog (ASP) that supports representation and reasoning with defaults and their direct and indirect exceptions [33]. This program is a collection of statements describing domain objects and relations between them, and incorporates consistency restoring (CR) rules in ASP [11][2]. ASP is based on stable model semantics and non-monotonic logics, and includes *default negation* and *epistemic disjunction*, e.g., unlike $\neg a$ that implies *a is believed to be false*, *not a* only implies that *a is not believed to be true*, and unlike "$p \lor \neg p$" in propositional logic, "p or $\neg p$" is not tautologous. ASP can represent recursive definitions, defaults, causal relations, and constructs that are difficult to express in classical logic formalisms. The ground literals in an *answer set* obtained by solving Π represent beliefs of an agent associated with Π; statements that hold in all such answer sets are program consequences. Algorithms for computing the entailment of CR-Prolog programs, and for planning and diagnostics, reduce these tasks to computing answer sets of CR-Prolog programs. Π consists of causal laws of $\mathscr{D}_H$, inertia axioms, closed world assumption for defined fluents, reality checks, and records of observations, actions, and defaults from $\mathscr{H}$. Every default is turned into an ASP rule and a CR rule that allows the robot to assume, under exceptional circumstances, that the default's conclusion is false, so as to restore program consistency—see [2, 32] for formal definitions of states, entailment, and models for consistent inference. Although not discussed here, the ASP program representing the current beliefs of the robot also supports other capabilities such as jointly explaining unexpected action outcomes and partial descriptions extracted from sensor inputs—see [1] for more details.

---

[2] We use the terms "ASP" and "CR-Prolog" interchangeably in this paper.

It is challenging to provide and encode all the knowledge corresponding to any given complex domain. For instance, some of the domain axioms may be unknown or may change over time, and the plans created using this incomplete knowledge may not succeed. Consider a scenario in the BM domain in which the goal is to stack three of four blocks placed on the table. Figure 5(a) shows a possible goal configuration that could be generated based on the available domain knowledge. The corresponding plan (starting with all four blocks on the table) has two steps: $move(b_1, b_0)$ followed by $move(b_2, b_1)$. The robot expects to use this plan to stack the blocks as desired. Unknown to the robot, it is not possible to stack any block on top of a prism-shaped block in this domain, and execution of this plan results in failure that cannot be explained—specifically, action $move(b_1, b_0)$ does not result in the configuration shown in Fig. 5(b). In this paper, we focus on discovering previously unknown executability conditions that can prevent such actions from being executed.

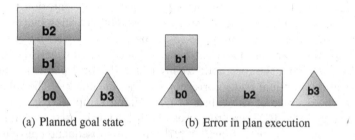

(a) Planned goal state   (b) Error in plan execution

Fig. 5. Illustrative example of (a) planned goal state; and (b)error in a plan execution step.

3.2   Relational RL for Discovering Axioms

Our approach for incremental and interactive discovery of domain axioms differs from previous work by us and other researchers. The proposed approach:

- Explores the existence of previously unknown axioms only when unexpected action outcomes cannot be explained by reasoning about exogenous actions [1].
- Uses RRL and decision tree regression for improving the computational efficiency of identifying candidate axioms, and for generalizing from specific axioms.
- Focuses on the discovery of unknown axioms by generalizing across multiple MDPs, instead of using RRL for planning, which limits generalization to a specific MDP.

Generalization and computational efficiency are key considerations for incremental and interactive learning. For instance, in the BW domain, discovery of the axiom "a red cube should not be placed on a blue prism" does not help when the tabletop has a *red prism* and *blue cube*, unless the agent realizes that the axiom it has discovered is a specific instance of the general axiom "no block should be placed on a prism-shaped block".

A sequence of steps is used to identify and generalize from candidate axioms. First, when a specific plan step fails, the corresponding state is considered the goal state in a RL problem, with the objective of finding state-action pairs that are most likely to lead to this error state. The RL problem uses an MDP formulation and the tuple $\langle S, A, T, R \rangle$, where:

- S: set of states.
- A: set of actions.
- $T : S \times A \times S' \rightarrow [0, 1]$ is the state transition function.
- $R : S \times A \times S' \rightarrow \Re$ is the reward function

Popular RL algorithms such as Q learning or SARSA, which estimate $Q(s, a)$, the Q-values of state-action pairs, become computationally intractable as the state space increases in size and do not generalize to relationally equivalent states and actions. The second step uses a relational representation to support generalization. After a few episodes (i.e., iterations) of Q-learning (with eligibility traces) for a specific goal state, all state-action pairs that have been visited, along with their Q-values, are used to construct a binary (i.e., logical) decision tree (BDT). The path from the root node to any leaf node corresponds to one state-action pair, and individual nodes correspond to specific fluents—the value at the leaf node is the average of the values of all training samples that are grouped under that node. The BDT created after one iteration is used to compute the policy (based on a soft-max function [27]) in the subsequent episode. When the learning is terminated after convergence of the Q-values or after a specific number of episodes, the BDT relationally represents the experiences of the robot. Figure 6 illustrates a subset of a BDT constructed for the BW domain.

The method described above only considers generalization within a specific MDP. To truly identify general domain axioms, the third step of our approach simulates similar errors (to the one actually encountered due to plan step execution failure) and considers the corresponding MDPs as well. The Q-value of a state-action pair is now the weighted average of the values across different MDPs. The weight assigned to a particular state-action pair in a specific MDP is inversely proportional to the shortest distance between the state and the goal state of the corresponding MDP based on the optimal policy for that MDP:

$$w_i = \frac{1/d_i}{\sum_{j=0}^{N} 1/d_j}$$

where w_i is the weight of the state-action pair of MDP_i, d_i is the distance from the state to the goal state of MDP_i and N is the number of MDPs considered. Note that these similar MDPs are currently chosen randomly—future work will use the information encoded in the CR-Prolog program to direct attention to objects and attributes more relevant to the observed failure.

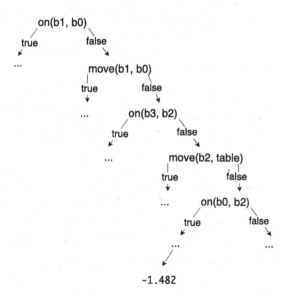

Fig. 6. Illustrative example of a subset of the binary decision tree for a specific scenario in the BW domain.

The fourth step identifies candidate executability constraints. The head of such an axiom has a specific action, and the body contains attributes that influence (or are influenced by) the action. We construct training samples by considering each such possible action and the corresponding attributes based on the BDT constructed as described above. These training samples are used to construct a decision tree whose root node corresponds to non-occurrence of the action, intermediate nodes correspond to attributes of object involved in the action, and the leaf nodes are the average of the values of the training samples grouped under that node. Each path from the root node to a leaf is a candidate axiom with a corresponding value. Figure 7 illustrates a subset of such a tree for a specific action.

The final step considers all candidate axioms (for different actions), and uses the K-means algorithm to cluster these candidates based on their value. The axioms that fall within the cluster with the largest mean are added to the CR-Prolog program and used in the subsequent reasoning steps.

4   Experimental Setup and Results

The proposed architecture and algorithms were grounded and experimentally evaluated in the Blocks World domain and the Simple Mario domain. We describe the performance in illustrative execution scenarios in these domains. We also compare the rate of convergence of the proposed algorithm for discovering axioms, henceforth referred to as "Q-RRL", with that of traditional Q-learning.

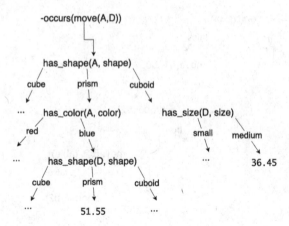

Fig. 7. Illustrative example of a decision tree constructed to represent candidate axioms related to a specific action in the BW domain.

4.1 Blocks World

As stated in Sect. 3, the robot's objective in the BW domain was to stack the blocks in a specified configuration. Consider the experimental trials in which the robot did not know that it was not possible to move any block on top of a prism-shaped block. We considered different scenarios with blocks of different shapes and colors (but the same size). For instance, one scenario had the following four blocks: $b0$ (Red Prism); $b1$ (Red Cube); $b2$ (Blue Cuboid); and $b3$ (Blue Prism). All blocks were initially on the table, i.e., $on(b0, table)$, $on(b1, table)$, $on(b2, table)$, and $on(b3, table)$. We provided the goal state description as $(on(b0, table), on(b1, b0), on(b2, b1), on(b3, table))$, i.e., the objective was to stack three of the four blocks on the table. The plan obtained by solving the ASP program had actions $move(b1, b0)$ and $move(b2, b1)$. The action $move(b1, b0)$ fails, as expected. During Q-RRL and Q-Learning, the agent experiences a reward of $+100$ when it reaches goal state and a negative reward (i.e., cost) of -1.5 otherwise (i.e., for all other actions).

As stated earlier, RRL is triggered when executing plan steps to stack the blocks results in an unexpected and unexplained outcome. When such an error occurs, different related scenarios are simulated to generate the training samples for generalization. Figure 8 shows the rate of convergence of the average Q-value obtained using Q-RRL and Q-learning. The Q-RRL algorithm converges much faster, i.e., the optimal policy is computed in a much fewer number of iterations. Note that the rate of convergence is the performance measure in these experiments—it does not matter whether the actual average Q-values of one algorithm are higher (or lower) than the other algorithm. The following are some axioms identified during the various iterations:

$$\neg occurs(move(A, D), I) \leftarrow has\_shape(D, prism), has\_shape(A, cuboid),$$
$$has\_color(D, blue)$$

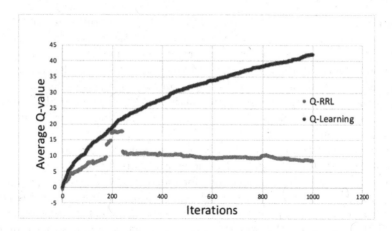

Fig. 8. Comparing the rate of convergence of Q-RRL with that of Q-learning in a specific scenario in the BW domain—Q-RRL converges much faster.

$$\neg occurs(move(A, D), I) \leftarrow has\_shape(D, prism), has\_shape(A, cube),$$
$$has\_color(D, blue), has\_color(A, red)$$
$$\neg occurs(move(A, D), I) \leftarrow has\_shape(D, prism), has\_shape(A, prism),$$
$$has\_color(A, red), has\_color(D, blue)$$

$$\neg occurs(move(A, D), I) \leftarrow has\_shape(D, prism), has\_shape(A, cube),$$
$$has\_color(D, red)$$

As the robot explores different scenarios, there are fewer and fewer errors because actions that are impossible are no longer included in the plans that are generated. Furthermore, the robot is able to incrementally generalize from the different specific axioms to finally add an axiom to the CR-Prolog program:

impossible $move(A, D)$ **if** $has\_shape(D, prism)$ (action language)
$\neg occurs(move(A, D), I) \leftarrow has\_shape(D, prism)$ (CR-Prolog statement)

In other experimental trials, the proposed architecture and algorithms resulted in the successful discovery of other such domain axioms.

4.2   Simple Mario

In the SM domain, the agent "mario" has to travel to a specific destination, "flag", from a starting position. As described at the beginning of Sect. 3, moving actions move mario one position away from the current position, while jumping actions attempt to move up to three positions away. If an obstacle prevents the agent from moving to a certain location, it lands on the closest (open) position available. Collision with any angry monster in the domain terminates the episode. Furthermore, blocks in the domain are made of different materials—*brick* blocks are harmless, whereas materials such as *spike* or *air* will result in the termination of the episode. The objective is to pick actions that will not result in episode termination—any such unexpected termination that cannot be explained triggers RRL for discovering axioms.

To evaluate the ability to efficiently discover generic domain axioms in the SM domain, scenarios related to the one causing an error (e.g., with different block attributes, and different locations for *mario* and monsters) are simulated (see Sect. 3.2). These simulated scenarios provide the training samples necessary for generalizing from the specific axioms discovered. For instance, in one scenario, three positions that would result in episode termination were used to trigger RRL. The first and second positions involve movement to blocks with *spike* material, while the third position involves collision with an angry monster. Figure 9 compares the rate of convergence of Q-RRL with that of Q-learning as a function of the number of episodes. Similar to the results obtained in the BW domain, Q-RRL converges significantly faster than Q-learning. Over a set of episodes, the following are some generalized axioms discovered:

$$\neg occurs(move(mario, left), I) \leftarrow loc(mario, B_1), \quad left\_of(B_2, B_1),$$
$$has\_material(B_2, spike)$$
$$\neg occurs(move(mario, right), I) \leftarrow loc(mario, B_1), \quad right\_of(B_2, B_1),$$
$$has\_material(B_2, spike)$$

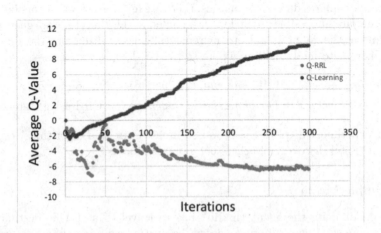

Fig. 9. Comparing the rate of convergence of Q-RRL with that of Q-learning in a specific scenario in the SM domain—Q-RRL converges much faster.

$$\neg occurs(jump(mario, left, 1), I) \leftarrow loc(mario, B_1), \; left\_neighbor(B_2, B_1),$$
$$has\_material(B_2, spike)$$
$$\neg occurs(jump(mario, right, 1), I) \leftarrow loc(mario, B_1), \; right\_neighbor(B_2, B_1),$$
$$has\_material(B_2, spike)$$

These axioms specify that *mario* cannot execute a move or jump action if this action will lead it to a block with *spike* material. Similar performance was observed in other scenarios that resulted in the failure of the corresponding plans, with the successful discovery of the corresponding domain axioms.

5   Conclusion

Robots collaborating with humans in complex domains frequently need to represent, reason with, and learn from different descriptions of incomplete domain knowledge and uncertainty. The architecture described in this paper combines the complementary strengths of declarative programming and relational reinforcement learning to discover previously unknown axioms governing domain dynamics. We illustrated the capabilities of this architecture in some simulated domains, with promising results. Future work will explore the ability to discover other kinds of axioms in more complex domains. We will also compare the performance of our algorithm with other popular relational reinforcement learning algorithms. Furthermore, we will conduct experimental trials on a mobile robot after including some probabilistic models of the uncertainty in perception on robots.

Acknowledgments. This work was supported in part by the US Office of Naval Research Science of Autonomy award N00014-13-1-0766. All opinions and conclusions in this paper are those of the authors alone.

References

1. Colaco, Z., Sridharan, M.: What happened and why? A mixed architecture for planning and explanation generation in robotics. In: Australasian Conference on Robotics and Automation (ACRA), 2–4 December 2015, Canberra, Australia (2015)
2. Zhang, S., Sridharan, M., Gelfond, M., Wyatt, J.: Towards an architecture for knowledge representation and reasoning in robotics. In: Beetz, M., Johnston, B., Williams, M.-A. (eds.) ICSR 2014. LNCS (LNAI), vol. 8755, pp. 400–410. Springer, Heidelberg (2014). doi:10.1007/978-3-319-11973-1_41
3. Zhang, S., Sridharan, M., Wyatt, J.: Mixed logical inference and probabilistic planning for robots in unreliable worlds. IEEE Trans. Robot. **31**(3), 699–713 (2015)
4. Sridharan, M.: Towards an architecture for knowledge representation, reasoning and learning in human-robot collaboration. In: AAAI Spring Symposium on Enabling Computing Research in Socially Intelligent Human-Robot Interaction, 21–23 March 2016, Stanford, USA (2016)

5. Sridharan, M., Rainge, S.: Integrating reinforcement learning and declarative programming to learn causal laws in dynamic domains. In: Beetz, M., Johnston, B., Williams, M.-A. (eds.) ICSR 2014. LNCS (LNAI), vol. 8755, pp. 320–329. Springer, Heidelberg (2014). doi:10.1007/978-3-319-11973-1_33
6. Sridharan, M., Gelfond, M.: Using knowledge representation and reasoning tools in the design of robots. In: IJCAI Workshop on Knowledge-Based Techniques for Problem Solving and Reasoning (KnowProS), 10 July 2016, New York, USA (2016)
7. Bai, H., Hsu, D., Lee, W.S.: Integrated perception and planning in the continuous space: a POMDP approach. Int. J. Robot. Res. **33**(8), 1288–1302 (2014)
8. Hoey, J., Poupart, P., Bertoldi, A., Craig, T., Boutilier, C., Mihailidis, A.: Automated handwashing assistance for persons with dementia using video and a partially observable markov decision process. Comput. Vis. Image Underst. **114**(5), 503–519 (2010)
9. Galindo, C., Fernandez-Madrigal, J.A., Gonzalez, J., Saffioti, A.: Robot task planning using semantic maps. Robot. Auton. Syst. **56**(11), 955–966 (2008)
10. Varadarajan, K.M., Vincze, M.: Ontological knowledge management framework for grasping and manipulation. In: IROS-2011 Workshop on Knowledge Representation for Autonomous Robots, 25 September 2011 (2011)
11. Gelfond, M., Kahl, Y.: Knowledge Representation, Reasoning and the Design of Intelligent Agents. Cambridge University Press, Cambridge (2014)
12. Balduccini, M., Regli, W.C., Nguyen, D.N.: An ASP-based architecture for autonomous UAVs in dynamic environments: progress report. In: International Workshop on Non-Monotonic Reasoning (NMR), 17–19 July 2014, Vienna, Austria (2014)
13. Chen, X., Xie, J., Ji, J., Sui, Z.: Toward open knowledge enabling for human-robot interaction. J. Hum. Robot Interact. **1**(2), 100–117 (2012)
14. Erdem, E., Patoglu, V.: Applications of action languages in cognitive robotics. In: Erdem, E., Lee, J., Lierler, Y., Pearce, D. (eds.) Correct Reasoning. LNCS, vol. 7265, pp. 229–246. Springer, Heidelberg (2012). doi:10.1007/978-3-642-30743-0_16
15. Laird, J.E.: Extending the soar cognitive architecture. In: International Conference on Artificial General Intelligence, 1–3 March 2008, Memphis, USA (2008)
16. Talamadupula, K., Benton, J., Kambhampati, S., Schermerhorn, P., Scheutz, M.: Planning for human-robot teaming in open worlds. ACM Trans. Intell. Syst. Technol. **1**(2), 14:1–14:24 (2010)
17. Kaelbling, L., Lozano-Perez, T.: Integrated task and motion planning in belief space. Int. J. Robot. Res. **32**(9–10), 1194–1227 (2013)
18. Saribatur, Z., Erdem, E., Patoglu, V.: Cognitive factories with multiple teams of heterogeneous robots: hybrid reasoning for optimal feasible global plans. In: International Conference on Intelligent Robots and Systems, Chicago, USA, pp. 2923–2930 (2014)
19. Hanheide, M., Gretton, C., Dearden, R., Hawes, N., Wyatt, J., Pronobis, A., Aydemir, A., Gobelbecker, M., Zender, H.: Exploiting probabilistic knowledge under uncertain sensing for efficient robot behaviour. In: International Joint Conference on Artificial Intelligence (IJCAI), 16–22 July 2011, Barcelona, Spain (2011)
20. Hanheide, M., Gobelbecker, M., Horn, G., Pronobis, A., Sjoo, K., Jensfelt, P., Gretton, C., Dearden, R., Janicek, M., Zender, H., Kruijff, G.J., Hawes, N., Wyatt, J.: Robot task planning and explanation in open and uncertain worlds. Artificial Intelligence (2015). http://dx.doi.org/10.1016/j.artint.2015.08.008
21. Richardson, M., Domingos, P.: Markov logic networks. Mach. Learn. **62**(1–2), 107–136 (2006)

22. Milch, B., Marthi, B., Russell, S., Sontag, D., Ong, D.L., Kolobov, A.: BLOG: probabilistic models with unknown objects. In: Getoor, L., Taskar, B. (eds.) Statistical Relational Learning. MIT Press, Cambridge (2006)
23. Halpern, J.Y.: Reasoning about Uncertainty. MIT Press, Cambridge (2003)
24. Sanner, S., Kersting, K.: Symbolic dynamic programming for first-order POMDPs. In: AAAI Conference on Artificial Intelligence, 11–15 July 2010, Atlanta, USA, pp. 1140–1146 (2010)
25. Baral, C., Gelfond, M., Rushton, N.: Probabilistic reasoning with answer sets. Theory Pract. Logic Program. 9(1), 57–144 (2009)
26. Lee, J., Wang, Y.: A probabilistic extension of the stable model semantics. In: AAAI Spring Symposium on Logical Formalizations of Commonsense Reasoning, March 2015)
27. Sutton, R.L., Barto, A.G.: Reinforcement Learning: An Introduction. MIT Press, Cambridge (1998)
28. Dzeroski, S., Raedt, L.D., Driessens, K.: Relational reinforcement learning. Mach. Learn. 43, 7–52 (2001)
29. Tadepalli, P., Givan, R., Driessens, K.: Relational reinforcement learning: an overview. In: Relational Reinforcement Learning Workshop at the International Conference on Machine Learning (2004)
30. Blockeel, H., Raedt, L.D.: Top-down induction of first-order logical decision trees. Artif. Intell. 101(1–2), 285–297 (1998)
31. Otero, R.P.: Induction of the effects of actions by monotonic methods. In: Horváth, T., Yamamoto, A. (eds.) ILP 2003. LNCS (LNAI), vol. 2835, pp. 299–310. Springer, Heidelberg (2003). doi:10.1007/978-3-540-39917-9_20
32. Sridharan, M., Gelfond, M., Zhang, S., Wyatt, J.: A refinement-based architecture for knowledge representation and reasoning in robotics. Technical report, Unrefereed CoRR abstract, August 2015. http://arxiv.org/abs/1508.03891
33. Balduccini, M., Gelfond, M.: Logic programs with consistency-restoring rules. In: AAAI Spring Symposium on Logical Formalization of Commonsense Reasoning, pp. 9–18 (2003)

Simultaneous Optimization and Sampling of Agent Trajectories over a Network

Hala Mostafa[1]([⊠]), Akshat Kumar[2], and Hoong Chuin Lau[2]

[1] United Technologies Research Center, East Hartford, CT, USA
mostafh@utrc.utc.com
[2] Singapore Management University, Singapore, Singapore
{akshat,hclau}@smu.edu.sg

Abstract. We study the problem of optimizing the trajectories of agents moving over a network given their preferences over which nodes to visit subject to operational constraints on the network. In our running example, a theme park manager optimizes which attractions to include in a day-pass to maximize the pass's appeal to visitors while keeping operational costs within budget. The first challenge in this combinatorial optimization problem is that it involves quantities (expected visit frequencies of each attraction) that cannot be expressed analytically, for which we use the Sample Average Approximation. The second challenge is that while sampling is typically done prior to optimization, the dependence of our sampling distribution on decision variables couples optimization and sampling. Our main contribution is a mathematical program that *simultaneously* optimizes decision variables and implements inverse transform sampling from the distribution they induce. The third challenge is the limited scalability of the monolithic mathematical program. We present a dual decomposition approach that exploits independence among samples and demonstrate better scalability compared to the monolithic formulation in different settings.

1 Introduction

The diffusion of entities or phenomena over networks, be they social, physical or information networks, has been studied in areas as diverse as disease control [8], targeted advertising [5,14] and traffic management. Initial efforts were more concerned with building different diffusion models applicable under different assumptions [6,7,9,12,18,19,21]. Armed with a model, the natural next step is optimization in the context of the learned model. The goal is typically to find the set of actions that result in a diffusion process with certain desirable properties subject to operational constraints [9,11,17]. Applications include disease control (which nodes to vaccinate to curb the spread of disease) and advertising (which nodes to target to encourage the adoption of a product).

The decision problems addressed in the literature involve actions that either do not change the diffusion process, or change it only by altering the network over which diffusion takes place. For example, in influence maximization the goal is to determine the set of nodes to target (e.g. with free samples of a product)

© Springer International Publishing AG 2016
N. Osman and C. Sierra (Eds.): AAMAS 2016 WS, Visionary Papers, LNAI 10003, pp. 50–66, 2016.
DOI: 10.1007/978-3-319-46840-2_4

to maximize the spread of a given phenomenon (e.g. purchase of the product) using a generalization of the Independent Cascade Model [9]. Network design tries to find the set of nodes whose addition to/removal from the network maximizes/minimizes the expected number of cascades that reach/infect a target set of nodes subject to constraints on the cost of adding/removing nodes [13,17].

We consider a more challenging optimization problem where **actions affect the parameters of the diffusion process**. Specifically, we consider a setting where agents at a start node diffuse by following random walks drawn from given conditional transition probability distributions. The parameters of the diffusion process (the transition probability distributions) depend on a combination of the agents preferences and decisions made by a network manager.

As a motivating example, we consider the problem of deciding which attractions to include in a theme park day-pass to maximize its "appeal" while keeping operational costs within budget. Park attractions are modeled as nodes in a network. Park visitors "diffuse" along network edges based on both their inherent preferences and the attractions included in the pass. We use a simple notion of appeal as the expected number of visits to each attraction in the pass. Our focus is not on the economics of bundle pricing and profit estimation (e.g., [1]) but rather on the optimization problem of designing a pass that maximizes visit frequencies when visitor dynamics depends on their preferences and pass contents (visitors are more likely to visit attraction they have already paid for as part of the pass).

We model agent diffusion in the network using conditional distributions P_{uv} that specify the probability of visiting attraction v after u is visited. This is a modification of the Independent Cascade model [9] where probabilities of visiting the different neighbors of a given node add up to 1 (unlike the case of a disease spreading to multiple neighbors of a node, for example). Diffusion starts at a start node (e.g., park entrance) and at each time step, each agent samples from the distribution of its current attraction to determine its next attraction. Each trajectory is therefore a random walk through the network. We highlight that it is a simple but widely applicable model that can describe diffusion processes where flow is conserved, such as traffic movement. We also use a simple model of how bundle contents affect this distribution and note that our model respects the independence of irrelevant alternatives [16], an axiom in decision and social sciences.

The first challenge is that our optimization problem is stochastic; it involves quantities (e.g. expected visit frequencies to park attractions) that depend probabilistically on the decision variables and cannot be expressed analytically in closed form. We address this challenge using Sample Average Approximation (SAA) which creates a deterministic version of the problem that approximates expected quantities by evaluating them on a set of samples [10].

The second challenge is that because the decisions of which attractions are in the pass affect diffusion probabilities, we cannot generate samples offline before the optimization step. To address this, our main contribution is a mathematical program that simultaneously optimizes the decision variables and implements inverse transform sampling on-the-fly from the diffusion distributions induced by the decision variables.

Implementing inverse transform sampling introduces a large number of variables which limit the scalability of the monolithic mathematical program. We present a dual decomposition approach that exploits independence among samples and demonstrate better scalability compared to the monolithic formulation in different settings.

2 Related Work

The body of work concerned with modeling diffusion phenomena spans numerous efforts that vary in the assumptions they make and the kind of model they aim to learn. For example, researchers have addressed the challenging problems of learning disease diffusion dynamics with missing observations where the infected/uninfected status of some nodes is unknown [21], as well as situations where only aggregate diffusion observations are available [19].

NETINF is an algorithm that addresses a somewhat different problem where the diffusion dynamics are assumed to be known and the goal is to infer/learn the underlying network over which entities propagate by observing node infection times [7]. It builds on the widely used Independent Cascade Model [9], which assumes that the phenomenon propagates from a node to each of its neighbors independently and probabilistically and every node is infected by at most one other node.

Once a model is learned, the next step is decision-making in the context of the learned model. One line of work investigates the influence maximization problem where the goal is to determine the set of nodes to target (e.g. with free samples of a product) to maximize the spread of a given phenomenon (e.g. purchase of the product). A related study considers the decision problem of which nodes in a large water distribution network to equip with sensors to best detect the introduction of contaminants [11].

Another line of work addresses network design problems where the goal is to find the set of nodes whose addition to the network maximizes the expected number of cascades that reach/infect a target set of nodes subject to constraints on the cost of adding nodes [17]. This problem arises in telecommunication networks and supply chain management where operators have the option of purchasing additional nodes to improve routing.

The above decision problems involve actions that either do not change the diffusion process (as in the sensor placement work), or change it only by altering the network over which diffusion takes place. For example, the probability of a node infecting a neighbor in the Independent Cascade Model is assumed independent of the actions we take.

The combinatorial optimization problem we address bears some similarities to the coalition formation problem; in both cases entities join to form a coalition (bundle) and a characteristic function maps each coalition/subset of entities to a cost/reward. In our setting, these entities (park attractions) are passive and a centralized decision maker is interested in finding only 1 coalition that maximizes reward subject to constraints. In coalition formation, on the other hand, the entities are active decision makers trying to maximize their own reward. Bloch and Dutta present a survey that focuses on coalition formation in settings where a grand coalition does not necessarily form [3]. Particularly relevant is the network setting they discuss where each node in a network decides whether to establish a link to a given neighbor. A payoff function maps each graph (formed by the established links) to a payoff vector, with one element per node. While this is similar to our work in its concern with whether a node joins a coalition, the authors examine an individual node's game-theoretic optimization process while we focus on the optimization problem faced by a centralized network manager.

3   A MILP for Online Sampling

We present a Mixed Integer Linear Program (MILP) formulation of the combined optimization and sampling problem when *actions affect parameters of the diffusion process*. Specifically, the diffusion of the agents depend on their inherent preferences and the decisions variables. Throughout the section, we will refer to constraints that make up the MILP in Table 1.

We first present the stochastic program formulation and explain how we model the effects of decisions on diffusion. We then use sample average approximation to determinize the stochastic program. Next, we present our main contribution, a linear formulation of a sampling procedure to plug into the MILP.

3.1   The Stochastic Program

Although we focus on the theme park problem as an example where the optimization involves expectations taken over a distribution that depends on the decision variables, our formulation is applicable to any diffusion model where flow is conserved. In our setting, a park owner wishes to design a fixed-price pass. Revenue per pass is the price minus the total redemption cost of the attractions actually visited. The pass should include popular attractions to increase sales. However, since the owner pays a redemption cost c_u to the operator of an attraction u when a visitor redeems the ticket for this attraction, the pass includes less popular items with low redemption probability to increase revenue[1].

We use a stochastic program formulation to find the pass with maximum expected "appeal" subject to the expected redemption cost being within a budget B. As a surrogate for appeal, we maximize the expected number of times pass attractions are visited.

$$\max_x \sum_u x_u \mathbb{E}_{\tilde{P}}[I_u] \tag{1}$$

$$s.t \sum_u x_u c_u \mathbb{E}_{\tilde{P}}[I_u] \leq B \tag{2}$$

---

[1] This problem is motivated by the authors' interaction with the management of a large theme park in Singapore.

where x_u is the binary decision variable of whether item u is in the pass and I_u is a random variable denoting whether u is visited/redeemed. I_u follows the diffusion distribution $\tilde{P}$ that depends on x as discussed below.

3.2 Original and Modified Diffusion Models

The Original Diffusion Model. We adopt a variant of the Independent Cascade Model [9] where instead of an activated/visited node activating a subset of its neighbors, it activates only 1 neighbor, since each sequence of activations models the trajectory of 1 visitor.

If there is no pass, the diffusion model is given by P_{uv} specifying the probability of a visitor at node u moving to node v. This model can be learned from instances of trajectories [21] and used for optimization [17]. To generate a sample trajectory, we start at the start node and sample from the distributions P_{uv} until either a designated end node is reached (park exit) or we have generated a trajectory of a given length.

It is important to note that we cannot evaluate the expected number of visits to a given node in the context of the original model P, since P does not reflect the effects of decisions of which attractions are chosen. We therefore need to express a modified model $\tilde{P}$ in terms of P and the decision variables. For example, we need to capture the effect of the pass contents on the way visitors move in a park; once a visitor buys a pass, she is more likely to visit attractions included in the pass than those for which she needs to buy additional tickets. However, the visitor's inherent preferences modeled by P will still affect her transition probabilities to some extent.

To highlight the importance of optimizing w.r.t. $\tilde{P}$ rather than P, consider a node v with a high probability of being visited under the original P but is only visited after u. If the cost c_u is too high, the optimal pass may not include u. Optimizing w.r.t. P does not account for the decision of not including u and overestimates the expected number of visits to v. Using $\tilde{P}$ allows us to evaluate a pass in the context of its actual effects on visitor trajectories.

The Modified Distribution $\tilde{P}$. A simple model for how pass contents affect the trajectory of a visitor is to discount the probability of transitioning to an item not in the pass by a factor of $\alpha \in [0, 1]$ and increase the probability of each item in the pass to maintain a legal transition function. If p_{uv} is the original transition probability from u to v, we define the modified probability $\tilde{p}_{uv}$ as:

$$\tilde{p}_{uv} = p_{uv} + x_v d_u - \alpha(1 - x_v)p_{uv} \tag{3}$$

where d_u is the probability mass added to each neighbor of u that is in the pass. $\tilde{p}_{uv}$ is thus the old probability, to which we add d_u if v is in the pass, or subtract a fraction α if v is not in the pass. According to Eq. (3), when $\alpha = 1$, attractions that are not in the pass are removed from a visitor's choice set. We note that our scheme for redistributing probabilities respects the axiom of independence of irrelevant alternatives [16], an axiom of decision theory and social sciences which states that if an alternative x is the most preferred among a set T and is also an element of $S \subseteq T$, then x is the most preferred among S [16]. In other words, removing irrelevant alternatives that were not chosen from a set does not change the relative order of other items in the set. In our case, the removal of items/attractions from a visitor's choice set does not change relative order of probabilities of the remaining items.

Let $\mathcal{N}_u$ be the set of u's neighbors and b_u be the number of neighbors of u that are in the pass. d_u is then given by:

$$d_u = \frac{\alpha \sum_{w \in \mathcal{N}_u} (1 - x_w) p_{uw}}{b_u} \tag{4}$$

The numerator is the total mass removed from neighbors not in the pass. This way of re-distributing probability mass guarantees that $\sum_{w \in \mathcal{N}_u} \tilde{p}_{uw} = 1$.

To linearize the product $x_v * d_u$ in constraint (3), we introduce continuous variables $e_{uv} \in [0, 1]$ to represent the probability mass, if any, to be added to p_{uv}.

$$e_{uv} = x_v * d_u$$

Because x_v is binary, the above can easily be expressed using the linear constraints (11–13) in Table 1.

To linearize constraint (4), we introduce binary variables b_u^m for $m = 1..|\mathcal{N}_u|$ where $b_u^m = 1$ if m of u's neighbors are in the pass. This is enforced by constraint (14). For every value of m, constraints (15) and (16) guarantee that if $b_u^m = 1$, then

$$d_u = \frac{\alpha \sum_{w \in \mathcal{N}_u} (1 - x_w) p_{uw}}{m}$$

Semantics of α. The parameter α models how much p_{uv} depends on the decisions x_u. In our example, α can be a measure of a visitor's unwillingness to purchase additional tickets for items outside the pass. When $\alpha = 0$, $\tilde{p}_{uv} = p_{uv}$ and a visitor's trajectory is independent of the pass (he is willing to purchase additional tickets for attractions not in the pass). At $\alpha = 1$,

$$\tilde{p}_{uv} = x_v \left(p_{uv} + \frac{\sum_{w \in \mathcal{N}_u} (1 - x_w) p_{uw}}{\sum_{w \in \mathcal{N}_u} x_w} \right)$$

So if $x_v = 0$, $\tilde{p}_{uv} = 0$. In this case, the visitor is unwilling to pay extra to visit attractions not in the pass. Defining $\tilde{P}$ in terms of x and α has the desirable property of maintaining the relative ordering among a node's neighbors that are in the pass (the same amount is added to the probability of each). It also maintains the ordering among neighbors not in the bundle (their probabilities are multiplied by the same value).

3.3 Sample Average Approximation

Sample Average Approximation (SAA) [10, 15] is a method for solving stochastic optimization problems by sampling from the underlying distribution to generate

Table 1. MILP for optimization and sampling.

$$\max \frac{1}{N} \sum_i \sum_u S_u^i \qquad (5)$$

$$\text{s.t.} \sum_i \sum_u c_u * S_u^i \le B * N \qquad (6)$$

A. Visit frequency constraints $\forall u, i$

$$S_u^i \le x_u \qquad (7)$$

$$S_u^i \le \sum_t \sum_v I_{vu}^{it} \qquad (8)$$

$$S_u^i \ge x_u + \sum_t \sum_v I_{vu}^{it} - 1 \qquad (9)$$

B. Prob. modification constraints $\forall u, v$

$$\tilde{p}_{uv} = p_{uv} + e_{uv} - \alpha(1 - x_v)p_{uv} \qquad (10)$$

$$e_{uv} \le x_v \qquad (11)$$

$$e_{uv} \le d_u \qquad (12)$$

$$e_{uv} \ge x_v + d_u - 1 \qquad (13)$$

$$\sum_{w \in \mathcal{N}_u} x_w = \sum_{m=1}^{|\mathcal{N}_u|} m * b_u^m \qquad (14)$$

$$\forall u, \forall m = 1..|\mathcal{N}_u|:$$

$$d_u \le 1 + \frac{\alpha \sum_{w \in \mathcal{N}_u}(1 - x_w)p_{uw}}{m} - b_u^m \qquad (15)$$

$$d_u \ge \frac{\alpha \sum_{w \in \mathcal{N}_u}(1 - x_w)p_{uw}}{m} + b_u^m - 1 \qquad (16)$$

C. ITS constraints $\forall i = 1..N, \ u, \ v \in \mathcal{N}_u$

$$g_{uv}^i \ge r_u^i - \sum_{v' \prec v} \tilde{p}_{uv'} \qquad (17)$$

$$g_{uv}^i \le 1 + r_u^i - \sum_{v' \prec v} \tilde{p}_{uv'} \qquad (18)$$

D. Edge activiation constraints

$$\forall i = 1..N, \ u, \ v \in \mathcal{N}_u, \ t = 1..T$$

$$I_{uv}^{it} \le g_{uv}^i \qquad (19)$$

$$I_{uv}^{it} \le 1 - g_{uv''}^i \qquad (20)$$

$$I_{uv}^{it} \le \sum_{w \ne v} I_{wu}^{i(t-1)} \qquad (21)$$

$$I_{uv}^{it} \le 1 - \sum_{t' < t} \sum_w I_{wv}^{it'} \qquad (22)$$

$$I_{uv}^{it} \ge g_{uv}^i + 1 - g_{uv'}^i + \sum_{w \ne v} I_{wu}^{i(t-1)}$$

$$+ 1 - \sum_{t' < t} \sum_w I_{wv_j}^{it'} - 3 \qquad (23)$$

$$x_u, b_u^m, g_{uv}^i \in \{0,1\}, I_{uv}^{it} \in \{0,1\} \text{ for } t = 1, u = 1.$$

a finite number of scenarios and reducing the stochastic optimization problem to a deterministic analogue.

In lieu of evaluating $\mathbb{E}_{\tilde{P}}[I_u]$ analytically, which can be hard or impossible depending on how x affects $\tilde{P}$, we use SAA to approximate the expectation as the average over N sample trajectories $\{\xi^i\}_{i \in 1..N}$ drawn from $\tilde{P}$.

$$\mathbb{E}_{\tilde{P}}[I_u] = \frac{1}{N} \sum_{i=1}^N \sum_v I_{vu}^i \qquad (24)$$

where I_{uv}^i is an indicator variable of whether trajectory ξ^i includes a move from v to u. If $I_{vu}^i = 1$, we say that edge vu is *active* in trajectory ξ^i.

The objective function (1) and budget constraint (2) can now be expressed in terms of edge activation variables and linearized by the introduction of variables S_u^i. If $x_u = 0$, $S_u^i = 0 \ \forall i$. If $x_u = 1$, S_u^i indicates whether ξ^i visits u.

The definition

$$S_u^i = x_u * \sum_t \sum_v I_{vu}^{it}$$

is linearized in constraints (7)–(9). We explain the need for the time index t below.

3.4 Inverse Transform Sampling

Our optimization problem has a circularity whereby decisions are evaluated based on samples drawn from $\tilde{P}$ while $\tilde{P}$ itself depends on the decisions. This is different from previous applications of SAA and similar determinization methods (e.g. [17,20,21]) where the samples are generated offline prior to solving the optimization problem.

Our main technical contribution is breaking this circularity by formulating linear constraints that implement Inverse Transform Sampling (ITS) [4] and including them in our MILP, thereby allowing simultaneous optimization and sampling. We first explain ITS then show how we use it in our setting.

In the general case, to perform ITS from a distribution $p(X)$, we uniformly generate a number $r \in [0,1]$. The value of the sample is the largest number x for which $p(-\infty \le X \le x) \le r$. For categorical distributions, where the notion of "largest" number does not hold, an arbitrary order is imposed on the categories which is used to convert the category probabilities into a cumulative distribution function (CDF). For category c, $\text{CDF}(c) = \sum_{c' \prec c} p(c')$, where $\prec$ denotes precedence in the arbitrary order. For a uniformly drawn value r, ITS returns the unique category c for which r is in the interval

$$\left[\sum_{c' \prec c} p(c'), \ \sum_{c' \prec c} p(c') + p(c) \right]$$

In other words, r must lie in the probability range of the returned category.

In our setting, a trajectory consists of a linear path of *active edges* starting at the start node. Sampling a trajectory is therefore the process of deciding, for each edge, whether it is active in this trajectory. To apply ITS to sampling trajectories from our conditional distribution $\tilde{P}$, we uniformly sample a value $r_u^i \in [0,1]$ for every node u and every sample ξ^i. Again, we impose an arbitrary order on the neighbors of u and determine which neighbor's probability range r_u^i falls within. The probability range of a neighbor v of node u is given by:

$$\left[\sum_{v' \prec v} \tilde{p}_{uv'}, \ \sum_{v' \prec v} \tilde{p}_{uv'} + \tilde{p}_{uv} \right]$$

Time-Indexed Variables. Note that if an edge uv is active, then r_u^i falls within the probability range of neighbor v of u. The converse is *not necessarily* true, since we disallow edge activations that result in cyclic trajectories. We disallow cycles by using time-indexed binary activation variables I_{uv}^{it} indicating whether edge uv is traversed at time t in ξ^i.

To show how I_{uw}^{it} depends on r_u^i, consider a node u with neighbors v, w and z and an arbitrary order $\{v, w, z\}$. For node w, we impose constraints that activate edge uw at time t in trajectory ξ^i if 4 conditions hold (i.e., we force I_{uw}^{it} to be the AND of 4 binary conditions): (1) $r_u^i \geq$ the lower limit of w's probability range; (2) $r_u^i <$ the upper limit of w's probability range; (3) u was visited at time $t-1$; and (4) w was not visited at any time $t' < t$.

To enforce the first 2 conditions, we create binary variables g_{uv}^i for each neighbor v of each node u indicating whether r_u^i is greater than the lower limit of v's probability range in sample ξ^i. Constraints (17) and (18) enforce

$$g_{uv}^i = 1 \ \text{iff} \ r_u^i \geq \sum_{v' \prec v} \tilde{p}_{uv'}$$

Constraints (19) and (20) guarantee that r_u^i falls in v's probability range (v'' is the node that directly follows v in the order). Constraint (21) forces I_{uv}^{it} to be 0 if u was not visited at time $t-1$. Constraint (22) forces I_{uv}^{it} to be 0 if v was previously visited. Constraint (23) completes the set of constraints that guarantee that I_{uv}^{it} is the AND (product) of the 4 conditions.

Because by definition of probability ranges, r_u^i will fall within the range of exactly 1 of u's neighbors, it is not possible for 2 edges out of a single node to be activated. And because the constraints disallow cycles, if the uniformly sampled random numbers for a trajectory give rise to a cycle 1-2-3-2, for example, the constraints will only activate edges 1-2 at time 1, and 2-3 at time 2. Some trajectories will therefore be shorter than others.

Extension to Non-linear Diffusion. We have so far shown how ITS can be used to sample linear trajectories through a network. The same methodology can also be used to generate cascades from an Independent Cascade Model where an active node can infect/activate multiple of its neighbors at multiple points in time. In this case, we need a set of uniformly sampled numbers per time step and activation is defined per node rather than per edge. The probability modification constraints will relax the requirement that $\sum_v p_{uv} = 1$, since activations of different neighbors are independent. We leave a thorough exploration of this extension to future work.

Binary Variables. The last line in Table 1 shows the set of binary variables, with all other variables being continuous. It is well known that the difficulty of solving a MILP increases as we increase the number of binary variables. We observe that only the activation variables for edges emanating from the start node u at $t = 1$ need to be specified as binary; the constraints ensure that the rest will only take on 0/1 values.

4   Dual Decomposition Approach

The auxiliary variables introduced by linearization and ITS result in a MILP whose size does not scale well with the number of samples. However, the independence of the sampling process across samples strongly favors a decomposition into a set of subproblems, each responsible for the constraints implementing ITS for a subset of samples. We create local copies of the decision variables x and each subproblem optimizes its local copy. We show how Lagrangian relaxation provides a principled way of exploiting this independence among samples.

4.1   Lagrangian Relaxation

For N samples, we create M subproblems each involving N/M samples. For ease of exposition, we assume $M = N$. Subproblem i involves a local copy of the decision variables (denoted x^i) as well as purely local variables $S_u^i, g_{uv}^i, I_{uv}^{it}$. Each subproblem has the form of the MILP in Table 1, but reduced to the sample(s) it is responsible for and augmented with *consistency constraints* $x_u^i = G_u$ $\forall u$ which force decision variables of different subproblems to be equal (to a global vector G).

The two constraints that "tie" the subproblems are the budget constraint and the global consistency constraints. We relax both by dualizing them into the objective function with appropriate Lagrange multipliers. The Lagrangian of the MILP now becomes

$$\mathcal{L} = \frac{1}{N}\sum_{i,u} S_u^i + \sum_{i,u} \mu_u^i(x_u^i - G_u^i) + \gamma(\sum_{i,u} c_u S_u^i - B*N)$$

where μ and γ are Lagrange multipliers of the consistency constraint in subproblem i and the budget constraint, respectively. The dual is

$$q(\mu,\gamma) = \max_{\mathcal{P}} \sum_{i,u} S_u^i + \sum_{i,u} \mu_u^i(x_u^i - G_u^i) + \gamma(\sum_{i,u} c_u S_u^i - B*N)$$

where the maximization is over the set $\mathcal{P}$ of primal variables $(x, g, I...\text{etc.})$. To prevent the dual from being unbounded from below, μ must satisfy

$$\sum_{i=1}^{N} \mu_u^i = 0 \ \forall u$$

and γ must be non-negative. Under these conditions, the global variable G disappears from the dual (it is multiplied by 0) to give

$$q(\mu,\gamma) = \max_{\mathcal{P}} \sum_{i,u} S_u^i + \sum_{i,u} \mu_u^i x_u^i + \gamma \sum_{i,u} c_u S_u^i - \gamma B*N$$

The relaxation and dualization of the coupling constraints allows us to decompose the dual into the sum of subproblem duals:

$$q(\mu, \gamma) = \sum_i q^i(\mu^i, \gamma) - \gamma BN \tag{25}$$

$$q^i(\mu^i, \gamma) = \max_{P^i} \sum_u S_u^i + \sum_u \mu_u^i x_u^i + \gamma \sum_u c_u S_u^i$$

The above decomposition and the separability of the constraints by subproblem allow us to do each minimization independently. The difficulty of solving each subproblem is now independent of the number of the total number of samples. As we show in the experimental results, this addresses the scalability issues of the monolithic MILP.

4.2 Subgradient Method

The question now is how to solve the dual optimization problem

$$\min_{\mu, \gamma} \quad q(\mu, \gamma)$$

$$\text{s.t.} \quad \sum_{i=1}^N \mu_u^i = 0 \ \forall u$$

$$\gamma \geq 0$$

while obtaining quality bounds on the solution. Duality theory tells us that the value of the dual is an upper bound on the value of the primal, as well as the important fact that the dual is always a convex function. The absence of local optima in the dual allows the use of subgradient descent methods to minimize the dual by iteratively updating the values of the Lagrange multipliers [2]. The update rule for γ at iteration k is given by

$$\gamma^k = \max(0, \gamma^{k-1} - \sigma^k \nabla_\gamma q(\mu^{k-1}, \gamma^{k-1}))$$

where σ^k is the step size at iteration k and

$$\nabla_\gamma q(\mu^{k-1}, \gamma^{k-1}) = \sum_{i,u} c_u \bar{S}_u^{i,k-1} - BN$$

is the subgradient of q wrt γ evaluated at the previous point $(\mu^{k-1}, \gamma^{k-1})$. Each vector $\bar{S}^{i,k-1}$ is the value of S^i in the optimal solution to subproblem i at the previous iteration (this is obtained as part of the solution to the maximization in problem i). The max operator projects γ back to satisfy $\gamma \geq 0$.

For each μ^i, the subgradient is given by

$$\nabla_{\mu^i} q(\mu^{k-1}, \gamma^{k-1}) = \bar{x}^{i,k-1}$$

where vector $\bar{x}^{i,k-1}$ is the value of x^i in the optimal solution to subproblem i at the previous iteration. Projecting μ back to the set $\sum_{i=1}^{N} \mu_u^i = 0 \;\forall u$ involves finding the closest point in this set to the updated μ, which is given by

$$\mu_u^{i,k} = \mu_u^{i,k-1} - \sigma^k (\bar{x}_u^i - \frac{\sum_j \bar{x}_u^j}{N})$$

Intuitively, the updates to the Lagrange multipliers encourage the primal variables to take values that satisfy the relaxed constraints. For example, if the previous iteration's budget exceeds the limit $B * N$, γ will decrease, thus penalizing each q^i into finding a solution with lower cost. Similarly, if a subproblem has a value of x_u^i that is above (resp. below) the average value for this variable across subproblems, the multiplier of this variable will increase (resp.decrease) to promote consistency across subproblems.

Step Size: There are a number of recommendations for setting the step size in subgradient method. We use the following rule which has theoretical justifications in [2]:

$$\sigma^k = \lambda \frac{\max_{k'<k} f^{k'} - q(\mu^k, \gamma^k)}{\| \nabla q^k \|^2}$$

where $\max_{k'<k} f^{k'}$ is the maximum primal value seen so far and is used as an approximation to the optimal dual value. The above rule takes larger steps when the duality gap between the best primal and the current dual is large. The constant multiplier λ is recommended to be in $[0,2]$ and we set it to 0.3. $\| \nabla q^k \|^2$ is the squared norm of the gradient evaluated in the current iteration.

Primal Solutions. While the Lagrange multipliers promote consistency across subproblems, in practice converging to complete consistency is often a slow process. After every iteration of the subgradient method, we can use the x^i values to construct a primal solution. A simple scheme used in [13] is to use a majority vote with a consensus threshold θ where for each u, if at least a fraction θ of subproblems agree on the value of x_u, this value is used in the constructed primal. Otherwise, x_u remains a free optimization variable. We then solve the monolithic MILP of Table 1 with the fixed consensus values to obtain a full primal solution. An iteration has no primal solution if: (1) there are too many free variables, so we avoid solving the monolithic MILP; or (2) the fixed variables result in an infeasible MILP if they always violate the budget constraints.

Besides improving scalability, our decomposition offers modeling flexibility where different subproblems can use different values of α. If we know the distribution over the values of α (e.g. ground surveys indicate that 30 % of visitors are very willing to pay for additional tickets), we can set a low value for α in 30 % of the subproblems and a high value for the rest.

5 Experimental Results

We now compare the performance of the monolithic and decomposed formulations in terms of (1) quality of the best solution found; (2) time the best solution was first found and (3) the duality gap (difference between the maximum primal and the minimum dual solutions). We also investigate how our formulations perform as we change (1) the number of samples; (2) the parameter α and (3) the tightness of the budget constraint[2].

Instead of 1 subproblem per sample, we group every 2 samples in a subproblem. This increases the size of each subproblem, but is more conducive to convergence and finding good intermediate primal solutions. We solve the subproblems in parallel. In solving the monolithic MILP, we allow CPLEX to use all available cores.

We use 5 randomly generated instances of a network with 24 nodes. The instances differ in the redemption costs of nodes, the distribution P, and the connectivity (each node is connected to half of the remaining nodes at random). For every instance, we generate the uniformly sampled numbers $r_u^{i=1..N}$ for samples sizes $N \in \{10, 16, 22, 36\}$. We set the maximum trajectory length to 5, so for N samples, the upper bound on the objective function is $N * (5 - 1)$, since the start node does not count towards the objective. Note that because some trajectories are cut short to avoid cycles, this value is not always attainable.

To vary the tightness of the budget, we calculate the average redemption cost per trajectory over 1000 trajectories drawn from the original distribution P. We then set the budget to either 75 % or 100 % of the calculated average to experiment with tight and relaxed budget settings.

Table 2 compares the performance of the two formulations. Boldface entries indicate the decomposed formulation doing as well as or better than the monolithic formulation. Times are in seconds and the final duality gap is calculated as

$$\frac{min(q) - max(f)}{max(f)} * 100\%$$

where q and f are the dual and primal solution values. All runs were terminated after 3600 s except for experiments with 36 samples and $\alpha = 0.3$ at a budget 75 % of the average (shown in the starred row in Table 2) which was run for 5000 s.

Performance at $\alpha = 0$. As explained above, α is a parameter controlling how much the distribution $\tilde{P}$ depends on the decision variables. When $\alpha = 0$, $\tilde{P} = P$ and the size of the MILP is greatly reduced because trajectory sampling can be done offline, eliminating the constraints and variables implementing the inverse transform sampling. Because it is very easy to obtain, we use the solution from setting $\alpha = 0$ as the initial solution (denoted $x_{\alpha=0}$) when solving for larger values of α in both the monolithic and decomposed formulations. This approach can be helpful in finding good solutions early on. However, as the value of α increases, $x_{\alpha=0}$ becomes less valid and indeed may be infeasible. For example, trajectories from the distribution $\tilde{P}$ induced by $x = x_{\alpha=0}$ and $\alpha = 0.9$ have a high redemption cost because $x_{\alpha=0}$ was obtained assuming no increase in the

---

[2] All MILPs solved using IBM CPLEX 12.6 on a 16-core 2.6 GHz machine under a quota of 200G RAM and 24 threads.

Table 2. Comparison of monolithic and decomposed formulations.

N	Monolithic			Decomposed			Result on 3000 samples	
	Best sol.	1st time	Final gap	Best sol.	1st time	Final gap	% over estimate	% budget violation
$\alpha = 0.3$ Budget = 75% of avg.								
10	34	566	0	33.4	**233**	13.4	30.8 %	13.6 %
16	48	753	25.2	**50.2**	1560	14	12.1 %	19.4 %
22	66.8	361	31.8	66.6	1588	24.1	8.44 %	15.3 %
36⋆	106	540	36.3	104	2012	**30.7**	8.85 %	14.3 %
$\alpha = 0.9$ Budget = 75% of avg.								
10	38.4	1721	2.7	37.4	**354**	2.7	10.0 %	12.9 %
16	45.6	603	43.7	**60**	608	3	6.23 %	25.4 %
22	63.2	536	42.2	**80.6**	1519	**5.5**	4.98 %	19 %
36	N/A	N/A	N/A	**129**	1731	11	4.78 %	6.4 %
$\alpha = 0.3$ Budget = 100% of avg.								
10	37	806	3.3	36.2	**110**	5.7	23.3 %	12.4 %
16	53.2	62.7	20.4	**55.4**	2115	**6.1**	15.4 %	13.5 %
22	72.2	100	22	**72.6**	1435	**16.7**	6.49 %	10.8 %
36	120	113	20	115.8	958	20.5	7.53 %	10.2 %
$\alpha = 0.9$ Budget = 100% of avg.								
10	39.4	890	0.5	39	**119**	1.54	11.19 %	8.44 %
16	56.2	1893	15	**60.6**	127	**2.33**	5.00 %	13.4 %
22	78	287	12.9	**83.2**	336	**2.6**	5.05 %	13.5 %
36	129	603.6	12.1	**136.2**	**556**	**3.6**	5.98 %	8 %

probability of visiting an attraction in the pass, which is not true at $\alpha = 0.9$. "Deploying" the solution $x_{\alpha=0}$ when $\alpha = 0.9$ will therefore typically violate the budget constraint because at $\alpha = 0.9$ visitors flock to pass attractions much more than anticipated.

Performance at Larger α. We notice that the pre-processing done by CPLEX is less effective in pruning the monolithic MILP, which makes runs with $\alpha = 0.9$ the most challenging for the monolithic formulation. Combined with a tight budget that makes finding a feasible solution difficult, the setting $\alpha = 0.9$ with $N = 36$ resulted in only 1 instance that could be solved using the monolithic formulation (corresponding average reported as N/A in Table 2).

However, instances with $\alpha = 0.9$ should be the least challenging, since under this setting most solution will achieve a high objective value. In the theme park example, this situation is like having visitors that are completely "malleable", in which case any day-pass will be very popular, achieving an objective value close to the upper bound. Because each subproblem is responsible for only 2 samples, the decomposed formulation is far less affected by CPLEX's inability to prune the MILP during pre-processing, and can find good solutions early on and terminate with a low duality gap. This is clearly reflected in Table 2 where at a high α and relaxed budget, the decomposed formulation scales well with the number of samples.

Figure 1 shows an example of how the value of the best primal solution and the minimum dual value evolve over time in both formulations. Note that in the monolithic formulation, CPLEX is unable to tighten the upper bound on

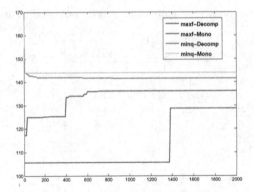

Fig. 1. Average maximum primal and minimum dual values of decomposed and monolithic formulations over time (in seconds). $\alpha = 0.9$, $N = 36$ and relaxed budget.

the objective function beyond the theoretical upper bound of $N(T - 1)$ which for $N = 36$ and maximum trajectory length of 4 is 144. The value of the dual function in our decomposed formulation, on the other hand, falls below that bound. The sharp increase in the best primal value of the monolithic formulation is due to the fact that in some instances, CPLEX was unable to find any feasible solution other than the trivially feasible solution with all $x_u = 0$ with objective value 0. When the first non-trivially feasible solution is found, the average primal value rises sharply.

Effect of Sample Size. Intuitively, the accuracy of the SAA approximation should improve as we use more samples, i.e., the approximate value of a solution should approach the solution's true value. Note that this is different from stating that the value of the optimal solution x_N^* of the determinized version of the stochastic problem will necessarily *improve* as N increases. Rather, the *exact* value $v(x)$ of a solution x will be better approximated by the value $\hat{v}_N(x)$ obtained using N samples as N increases.

In our setting, we do not have access to the exact value $v(x)$ of a solution x; we cannot evaluate x on the set of all trajectories. As a proxy for $v(x)$, we evaluate x on 3000 test trajectories sampled from $\tilde{P}_x$, giving a (better) approximation $\hat{v}_{3000}(x)$. We then compare $\hat{v}_{3000}(x)$ to $\hat{v}_N(x)$ (the optimal value of the objective function in Eq. (5) using N samples) for different values of N. Naturally, $\hat{v}_N(x)$ will tend to be an over-estimate of $\hat{v}_{3000}(x)$. The column "% over estimate" in Table 2 shows the average percentage of this over-estimation for different N. As expected, approximate values obtained using smaller sample sizes tend to be overly optimistic regarding the quality of the solution when applied to the test data. Another notable trend is that this over-estimation is more pronounced at the smaller value of α. The reason is that for larger α, it is not too difficult to score well on the test data, since the modified $\tilde{P}$ will be such that there is a very large probability of visiting items in the pass.

Respecting the Budget Constraint. In addition to performance in terms of visit frequencies of items in the pass, we also calculate how well a solution respects the budget constraint. Any feasible solution for either of our formulations will have an average redemption cost within the specified budget B. However, the cost of an *individual* sample trajectory may be more than B. The last column in Table 2 shows the average percentage budget violation *per sample* when the optimal solution is tested on 3000 sample trajectories. Increasing the number of samples used in the SAA approximation produces solutions that result in lower budget violations when applied to the 3000 test trajectories.

6   Conclusion

In this paper we addressed decision making in settings where movement of agents in a network is affected by both the agents inherent preferences and the actions of the network manager. Using such a notion of simultaneous decision making and trajectory sampling, we addressed the theme park pass design problem in which the objective is to include popular attractions that increase sales while respecting the redemption cost budget. Our key contributions lie in solving the underlying stochastic program that describes the combinatorial optimization problem using sample average approximation. We implement the logic for inverse transform sampling in the language of mixed integer programming, a formulation which can be leveraged in other optimization settings that need to sample from a distribution online. Our mathematical program simultaneously optimizes the decision variable and generates samples on-the-fly from modified probability distribution. To improve scalability, we developed a Lagrangian relaxation-based decomposition that exploits independence among samples. Experimental results comparing the monolithic and decomposed MILP formulations in different settings show better scalability of the latter and more accurate decision evaluation as sample size increases.

Acknowledgement. This research was funded by the National Research Foundation Singapore under its Corp Lab @ University scheme.

References

1. Armstrong, M.: A more general theory of commodity bundling. J. Econ. Theor. **148**(2), 448–472 (2013)
2. Bertsekas, D.P.: Nonlinear Programming, 2nd edn. Athena Scientific, Belmont (1999)
3. Bloch, F., Dutta, B.: Formation of Networks and Coalitions. In: Benhabib, J., Bisin, A., Jackson, M.O. (eds.) Handbook of Social Economics, vol. 1 (2011)
4. Devroye, L.: Non-uniform Random Variate Generation. Springer, New York (1986)
5. Domingos, P., Richardson, M.: Mining the network value of customers. In: ACM SIGKDD International Conference on Knowledge Discovery and Data Mining, pp. 57–66 (2001)

6. Du, J., Kumar, A., Varakantham, P.: On understanding diffusion dynamics of patrons at a theme park. In: AAMAS (2014)
7. Gomez Rodriguez, M., Leskovec, J., Krause, A.: Inferring networks of diffusion and influence. In: Proceedings of the 16th ACM SIGKDD International Conference on Knowledge Discovery and Data Mining, pp. 1019–1028 (2010)
8. Halloran, M.E., Longini, I., Struchiner, C.: Binomial and stochastic transmission models. Design and Analysis of Vaccine Studies. Statistics for Biology and Health, pp. 63–84. Springer, New York (2010)
9. Kempe, D., Kleinberg, J., Tardos, E.: Maximizing the spread of influence through a social network. In: ACM SIGKDD International Conference on Knowledge Discovery and Data Mining, pp. 137–146 (2003)
10. Kleywegt, A.J., Shapiro, A., Homem-de-Mello, T.: The sample average approximation method for stochastic discrete optimization. SIAM J. Optim. **12**, 479–502 (2002)
11. Krause, A., Leskovec, J., Guestrin, C., VanBriesen, J., Faloutsos, C.: Efficient sensor placement optimization for securing large water distribution networks. J. Water Resour. Plan. Manag. **134**(6), 516–526 (2008)
12. Kumar, A., Sheldon, D., Srivastava, B.: Collective diffusion over networks: models and inference. In: International Conference on Uncertainty in Artificial Intelligence (2013)
13. Kumar, A., Wu, X., Zilberstein, S.: Lagrangian relaxation techniques for scalable spatial conservation planning. In: AAAI Conference on Artificial Intelligence, pp. 309–315 (2012)
14. Leskovec, J., Adamic, L.A., Huberman, B.A.: The dynamics of viral marketing. ACM Trans. Web **1**(1), 5 (2007)
15. Pagnoncelli, B.K., Ahmed, S., Shapiro, A.: Sample average approximation method for chance constrained programming: theory and applications. J. Optim. Theor. Appl. **142**(2), 399–416 (2009)
16. Ray, P.: Independence of irrelevant alternatives. Econometrica **41**(5), 987–991 (1973)
17. Sheldon, D., Dilkina, B., Elmachtoub, A., Finseth, R., Sabharwal, A., Conrad, J., et al.: Maximizing the spread of cascades using network design. In: Conference on Uncertainty in Artificial Intelligence, pp. 517–526 (2010)
18. Sheldon, D., Sun, T., Kumar, A., Dietterich, T.: Approximate inference in collective graphical models. In: International Conference on Machine Learning (2013)
19. Sheldon, D.R., Dietterich, T.G.: Collective graphical models. In: Advances in Neural Information Processing Systems, pp. 1161–1169 (2011)
20. Varakantham, P., Kumar, A.: Optimization approaches for solving chance constrained stochastic orienteering problems. In: Perny, P., Pirlot, M., Tsoukiàs, A. (eds.) ADT 2013. LNCS (LNAI), vol. 8176, pp. 387–398. Springer, Heidelberg (2013). doi:10.1007/978-3-642-41575-3_30
21. Wu, X., Kumar, A., Sheldon, D., Zilberstein, S.: Parameter learning for latent network diffusion. In: International Joint Conference on Artificial Intelligence, pp. 2923–2930, Beijing (2013)

POMDPs for Assisting Homeless Shelters – Computational and Deployment Challenges

Amulya Yadav[1(✉)], Hau Chan[2], Albert Jiang[2], Eric Rice[1], Ece Kamar[3], Barbara Grosz[4], and Milind Tambe[1]

[1] University of Southern California, Los Angeles, CA 90089, USA
{amulyaya,ericr,tambe}@usc.edu
[2] Trinity University, San Antonio, TX 78212, USA
{hchan,xjiang}@trinity.edu
[3] Microsoft Research, Redmond, WA 98052, USA
eckamar@microsoft.com
[4] Harvard University, Cambridge, MA 02138, USA
grosz@eecs.harvard.edu

Abstract. This paper looks at challenges faced during the ongoing deployment of HEALER, a POMDP based software agent that recommends sequential intervention plans for use by homeless shelters, who organize these interventions to raise awareness about HIV among homeless youth. HEALER's sequential plans (built using knowledge of social networks of homeless youth) choose intervention participants strategically to maximize influence spread, while reasoning about uncertainties in the network. In order to compute its plans, HEALER (i) casts this influence maximization problem as a POMDP and solves it using a novel planner which scales up to previously unsolvable real-world sizes; (ii) and constructs social networks of homeless youth at low cost, using a Facebook application. HEALER is currently being deployed in the real world in collaboration with a homeless shelter. Initial feedback from the shelter officials has been positive but they were surprised by the solutions generated by HEALER as these solutions are very counter-intuitive. Therefore, there is a need to justify HEALER's solutions in a way that mirrors the officials' intuition. In this paper, we report on progress made towards HEALER's deployment and detail first steps taken to tackle the issue of explaining HEALER's solutions.

1 Introduction

HIV is a huge problem among homeless youth. Past statistics show that homeless youth are 10X more likely to get infected by HIV compared to stably housed youth [4]. The primary reason behind this is that homeless youth tend to engage in high HIV risk behaviors such as unprotected sex, sharing needles while using drugs, etc., due to an absence of educated parental figures in their life who can advise them against such high-risk activities.

Often, homeless youth do not have access to traditional health care facilities, which makes early detection, treatment and control of HIV especially challenging

© Springer International Publishing AG 2016
N. Osman and C. Sierra (Eds.): AAMAS 2016 WS, Visionary Papers, LNAI 10003, pp. 67–87, 2016.
DOI: 10.1007/978-3-319-46840-2_5

among homeless youth populations. To that end, many homeless shelters provide free HIV testing clinics for homeless youth to promote a habit of getting regular HIV tests among youth. Despite these facilities, homeless youth do not get tested regularly as most of them are not aware of basic information about how HIV spreads and how can it be treated. Therefore, getting regular HIV tests is not a pressing concern for them as they are not aware of the consequences of HIV infection. Thus, there is an urgent need to raise awareness about basic HIV related information among homeless youth.

To address this need, many homeless shelters conduct "intervention camps" among homeless youth to raise general awareness about HIV. These intervention camps consist of day/week long educational sessions in which youth are provided with resources and information about HIV prevention and treatment measures [21]. For example, they are provided emergency contact numbers of newly opened HIV testing centers. Free contraceptives are also distributed among them. However, financial and manpower constraints faced by homeless shelters means that they can only organize a limited number of intervention camps. Moreover, in each camp, the shelters can only manage small groups of youth (∼3–4) at a time (as emotional and behavioral problems of youth makes management of bigger groups difficult). Thus, the shelters prefer a series of small sized camps organized sequentially [20]. Using these interventions, the shelter plans to maximize the spread of awareness (about HIV) among the target population (via word-of-mouth influence). To achieve this goal, the shelter uses the friendship based social network of the target population to strategically choose the participants of their limited intervention camps. Unfortunately, the shelters' job is further complicated by a lack of complete knowledge about the social network's structure [18]. Some friendships in the network are known with certainty whereas there is uncertainty about other friendships.

Thus, the shelters face an important challenge: they need a sequential plan to choose the participants of their sequentially organized interventions. This plan must address four key points: (i) it must deal with network structure uncertainty; (ii) it needs to take into account new information uncovered during the interventions, which reduces the uncertainty in our understanding of the network; (iii) the plan needs to be deviation tolerant, as sometimes homeless youth may refuse to be an intervention participant, thereby forcing the shelter to modify its plan; (iv) the intervention approach should address the challenge of gathering information about social networks of homeless youth, which usually costs thousands of dollars and many months of time [20].

In previous work, the authors presented HEALER [29], an adaptive software agent for solving this problem faced by homeless shelters. HEALER casts this problem as a Partially Observable Markov Decision Process (POMDP) and solves it using HEAL, a novel POMDP planner which quickly generates high-quality recommendations (of intervention participants) for homeless shelter officials. Our results from the previous paper show that HEALER significantly outperforms state-of-the-art techniques in terms of influence spread achieved.

Fig. 1. Computers at Safe Place for Youth where HEALER is deployed

Fig. 2. Emergency resource shelf at Safe Place for Youth

HEALER is currently being deployed in a real-world pilot study, in collaboration with Safe Place for Youth[1], a homeless shelter which provides food and lodging to homeless youth aged 12–25. They provide these facilities for ~55–60 homeless youth every day. They also operate an on-site medical clinic where free HIV and Hepatitis-C testing is provided (Figs. 1, 2 and 3). HEALER was reviewed by officials at Safe Place for Youth and their feedback has mostly been positive. In this paper, we report on preliminary progress made in the deployment of HEALER in our pilot study.

However, despite the shelter officials liking HEALER, and allowing us to conduct this pilot study with their youth, the shelter officials were surprised by HEALER's solutions. This is because HEALER's solutions maximize expected utilities (as explained later), while the homeless shelter officials pick youth for interventions based on their popularity in the network. To that end, we aim to develop a POMDP *explanation system*, which will justify HEALER's solutions to the officials in an intuitive manner. In this paper, we explain first steps taken towards building this POMDP explanation system.

[1] http://safeplaceforyouth.org.

2 Related Work

First, we discuss work related to influence maximization. There are many algorithms for finding 'seed sets' of nodes to maximize influence spread in networks [1,9,13,27]. However, all these algorithms assume *no uncertainty in the network structure* and select a single seed set. In contrast, HEALER selects several seed sets sequentially to select intervention participants. Also, HEALER takes into account uncertainty about the network structure and influence status of network nodes (i.e., whether a node is influenced or not). Finally, unlike [1,9,13,27], we use a different diffusion model as we explain later. Golovin et al. [7] introduced adaptive submodularity and discussed adaptive sequential selection (similar to our problem), and they proved that a Greedy algorithm has a $(1 - 1/e)$ approximation guarantee. However, unlike our work, they assume no uncertainty in network structure. Also, while our problem can be cast into the adaptive stochastic optimization framework of [7], our influence function is not adaptive submodular, because of which their Greedy algorithm loses its approximation guarantees [29]. This loss of adaptive submodularity is partly due to the feedback structure that our real world domain imposes on us.

Next, we discuss literature from *social work*. The general approach to these interventions is to use Peer Change Agents (PCA) (i.e., peers who bring about change in attitudes) to engage homeless youth in interventions, but most studies don't use network characteristics to choose these PCAs [23]. A notable exception is Valente et al. [28], who proposed selecting intervention participants with highest *degree centrality* (the most ties to other homeless youth). However, previous studies [2,30] show that *degree centrality* performs poorly, as it does not account for potential overlaps in influence of two high degree centrality nodes.

Another field of related work is planning for reward/cost optimization. In POMDP literature, a lot of work has been done on offline planning; some notable offline planners include GAPMIN [16] and Symbolic Perseus [26]. However, since online planners scale up much better [15],we only focus on the literature on Monte-Carlo (MC) sampling based online POMDP solvers since this approach allows significant scale-up [22]. A recent paper [30] introduced PSINET-W, a MC sampling based online POMDP planner. As we show later, HEALER scales

Fig. 3. Enrolling homeless youth into pilot study at Safe Place for Youth

up whereas PSINET fails to do so. HEALER's algorithmic approach also offers significant novelties in comparison with PSINET. A recent paper [14] looks at the case that not all nodes in the network are known ahead of time (as opposed to our work where we only assume that some edges are not known ahead of time). However, unlike HEALER, they do not consider sequential selection of node subsets.

The final field of related work is on explanation systems for POMDPs. Khan et al. [10] came up with template based explanation system and introduced the notions of minimal sufficient explanations. Also, Seegebarth et al. [24] presented the hybrid plan explanation framework. However, most of these approaches deal with fully observable Markov Decision Processes. We plan on building on the ideas in these papers to build our POMDP explanation system. Next, we will give a brief overview of HEALER's design.

3 HEALER's Design

We now explain the high-level design of HEALER. It consists of two major components: (i) a Facebook application for gathering information about social networks; and (ii) a DIME Solver, which solves the DIME problem (introduced in Sect. 5). We first explain HEALER's components and then explain HEALER's design.

Facebook Application: HEALER gathers information about social ties in the homeless youth social network by interacting with youth via a Facebook application. We choose Facebook for gathering information as Young et al. [32] show that ∼80 % of homeless youth are active on Facebook. Once a fixed number of homeless youth register in the Facebook application, HEALER parses the Facebook contact lists of all the registered homeless youth and generates the social network between these youth. HEALER adds a link between two people, if and only if both people are (i) friends on Facebook; and (ii) are registered in its Facebook application. Unfortunately, there is *uncertainty* in the generated network as friendship links between people who are only friends in real-life (and not on Facebook) are not captured by HEALER.

Thus, HEALER's Facebook application assists homeless shelters in quickly generating first approximations of these social ties at virtually no cost. Previously, homeless shelters gathered this social network information via tedious face-to-face interviews with homeless youth, a process which cost thousands of dollars and many months of time. HEALER's Facebook application allows homeless shelters to quickly generate a (partial) homeless youth social network at low cost. This Facebook application has been tested rigorously by our collaborating homeless shelter with positive feedback and in this paper, we present some initial results using this Facebook application (see Sect. 9).

DIME Solver: The DIME Solver then takes the approximate social network (generated by HEALER's Facebook application) as input and solves the DIME problem (formally defined in Sect. 5) using HEAL [29]. HEALER provides the

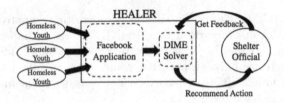

Fig. 4. HEALER's design

solution of this DIME problem as a series of recommendations (of intervention participants) to homeless shelter officials.

HEALER Design: HEALER's design (shown in Fig. 4), begins with the Facebook application constructing an *uncertain* network (as explained above). HEALER has a *sense-reason-act* cycle; where it repeats the following process for T interventions.

It *reasons* about different long-term plans to solve the DIME problem, it *acts* by providing DIME's solution as a recommendation (of intervention participants) to homeless shelter officials. The officials may choose to not use HEALER's recommendation in selecting their intervention's participants. Upon the intervention's completion, HEALER *senses* feedback about the conducted intervention from the officials. This feedback includes new observations about the network, e.g., uncertainties in some links may be resolved as intervention participants are interviewed by the shelter officials (explained more in Sect. 5). HEALER uses this feedback to update and improve its future recommendations.

4 Network Generation

First, we explain our model for influence spread in *uncertain social networks*. Then, we describe how HEALER generates a social network using its' Facebook application.

4.1 Background

We represent social networks as directed graphs (consisting of *nodes* and *directed edges*) where each *node* represents a person in the social network and a *directed edge* between two nodes A and B (say) represents that node A *considers* node B as his/her friend. *We assume directed-ness of edges as sometimes homeless shelters assess that the influence in a friendship is very much uni-directional; and to account for uni-directional follower links on Facebook.* Otherwise friendships are encoded as two uni-directional links. Further, even in the case of a bi-directional friendship, the influence propagation is not symmetric in either direction of the edge and we account for this by maintaining two uni-directional links (each with a different propagation probability) for each bi-directional link.

Uncertain Network: The uncertain network is a directed graph $G = (V, E)$ with $|V| = N$ nodes and $|E| = M$ edges. The edge set E consists of two disjoint subsets of edges: E_c (the set of certain edges, i.e., friendships which we are certain about) and E_u (the set of uncertain edges, i.e., friendships which we are uncertain about). Note that uncertainties about friendships exist because HEALER's Facebook application misses out on some links between people who are friends in real life, but not on Facebook.

To model the uncertainty about missing edges, every uncertain edge $e \in E_u$ has an existence probability $u(e)$ associated with it, which represents the likelihood of "existence" of that uncertain edge. For example, if there is an uncertain edge (A, B) (i.e., we are unsure whether node B is node A's friend), then $u(A, B) = 0.75$ implies that B is A's friend with a 0.75 chance. In addition, each edge $e \in E$ (both certain and uncertain) has a propagation probability $p(e)$ associated with it. A propagation probability of 0.5 on directed edge (A, B) denotes that if node A is influenced (i.e., has information about HIV prevention), it influences node B (i.e., gives information to node B) with a 0.5 probability in each subsequent time step (our full influence model is defined below). This graph G with all relevant $p(e)$ and $u(e)$ values represents an uncertain network and serves as an input to the DIME problem. Figure 5 shows an uncertain network on 6 nodes (A to F) and 7 edges. The dashed and solid edges represent uncertain (edge numbers 1, 4, 5 and 7) and certain (edge numbers 2, 3 and 6) edges, respectively. Next, we explain the influence diffusion model that we use in HEALER.

Influence Model. We use a variant of the independent cascade model [31]. In the standard independent cascade model, all nodes that get influenced at round t get a **single** chance to influence their un-influenced neighbors at time $t + 1$. If they fail to spread influence in this **single** chance, they don't spread influence to their neighbors in future rounds. Our model is different in that we assume that nodes get **multiple** chances to influence their un-influenced neighbors. If they succeed in influencing a neighbor at a given time step t', they stop influencing that neighbor for all future time steps. Otherwise, if they fail in step t', they try to influence again in the next round. This variant of independent cascade has been shown to empirically provide a better approximation to real influence spread than the standard independent cascade model [3, 31]. Further, we assume

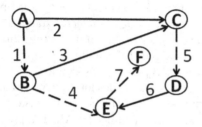

Fig. 5. Uncertain network

that nodes that get influenced at a certain time step remain influenced for all
future time steps. We now explain how HEALER generates an *uncertain social
network*.

4.2 HEALER's Facebook Application

HEALER generates an *uncertain network* by (i) using its Facebook application
to generate a network with no uncertain edges; (ii) using well known link prediction techniques such as KronEM [11] to infer existence probabilities $u(e)$ for
all possible *missing* edges that are not present in the network; (iii) deciding
on a threshold probability τ (in consultation with homeless shelter officials), so
that we *only* add a *missing* edge as an uncertain edge if its inferred existence
probability $u(e) > \tau$; and (iv) asking homeless shelter officials to provide $p(e)$
estimates for network edges.

Choosing τ: Rice et al. [19] show that real-world homeless youth networks are
relatively sparse. Thus, shelter officials choose the threshold probability value τ
such that the number of uncertain edges that get added because of τ does not
make our input uncertain network *overly dense*. Next, we introduce the DIME
problem.

5 DIME Problem

We now provide some background information that helps us define a precise
problem statement for DIME. After that, we will show some hardness results
about this problem statement.

Given the *uncertain network* as input, HEALER runs for T *rounds* (corresponding to the number of interventions organized by the homeless shelter). In
each round, HEALER chooses K *nodes* (youth) as intervention participants.
These participants are assumed to be influenced post-intervention with certainty. Upon influencing the chosen nodes, HEALER '*observes*' the true state of
the *uncertain edges* (friendships) out-going from the selected nodes. This translates to asking intervention participants about their 1-hop social circles, which
is within the homeless shelter's capabilities [19].

After each round, influence spreads in the network according to our influence
model for L *time steps*, before we begin the next round. This L represents the
time duration in between two successive intervention camps. *In between rounds,
HEALER does not observe the nodes that get influenced during L time steps.*
HEALER only knows that explicitly chosen nodes (our intervention participants
in all past rounds) are influenced. Informally then, given an uncertain network
$G_0 = (V, E)$ and integers T, K, and L (as defined above), HEALER finds an
online policy for choosing *exactly* K nodes for T successive rounds (interventions)
which maximizes influence spread in the network at the end of T rounds.

We now provide notation for defining HEALER's policy formally. Let $\mathcal{A} =
\{A \subset V \text{ s.t. } |A| = K\}$ denote the set of K sized subsets of V, which represents
the set of possible choices that HEALER can make at every time step $t \in [1, T]$.

Let $A_i \in \mathcal{A} \forall i \in [1, T]$ denote HEALER's choice in the ith time step. Upon making choice A_i, HEALER 'observes' uncertain edges adjacent to nodes in A_i, which updates its understanding of the network. Let $G_i \forall i \in [1, T]$ denote the uncertain network resulting from G_{i-1} with observed (additional edge) information from A_i. Formally, we define a history $H_i \forall i \in [1, T]$ of length i as a tuple of past choices and observations $H_i = \langle G_0, A_1, G_1, A_2, .., A_{i-1}, G_i \rangle$. Denote by $\mathcal{H}_i = \{H_k \text{ s.t. } k \leq i\}$ the set of all possible histories of length less than or equal to i. Finally, we define an i-step policy $\Pi_i : \mathcal{H}_i \to \mathcal{A}$ as a function that takes in histories of length less than or equal to i and outputs a K node choice for the current time step. We now provide an explicit problem statement for DIME.

Property 1 **DIME Problem.** Given as input an uncertain network $G_0 = (V, E)$ and integers T, K, and L (as defined above). Denote by $\mathcal{R}(H_T, A_T)$ the *expected total number of influenced nodes at the end of round T*, given the T-length history of previous observations and actions H_T, along with A_T, the action chosen at time T. Let $\mathbb{E}_{H_T, A_T \sim \Pi_T}[\mathcal{R}(H_T, A_T)]$ denote the expectation over the random variables $H_T = \langle G_0, A_1, .., A_{T-1}, G_T \rangle$ and A_T, where A_i are chosen according to $\Pi_T(H_i) \forall i \in [1, T]$, and G_i are drawn according to the distribution over uncertain edges of G_{i-1} that are revealed by A_i. The objective of DIME is to find an optimal T-step policy $\Pi_T^* = \text{argmax}_{\Pi_T} \mathbb{E}_{H_T, A_T \sim \Pi_T}[\mathcal{R}(H_T, A_T)]$.

6 DIME POMDP Formulation

DIME is modeled as a POMDP [17] (similar to [29]) because of two reasons. First, POMDPs are a good fit for DIME as (i) we conduct several interventions sequentially, similar to sequential POMDP actions; and (ii) we have *partial observability* (similar to POMDPs) due to uncertainties in network structure and influence status of nodes. Second, POMDP solvers have recently shown great promise in generating near-optimal policies efficiently [25]. We now explain how we map DIME onto a POMDP.

A POMDP is a tuple $\wp = \langle \mathbf{S}, \mathbf{A}, \mathbf{O}, \beta_0, \mathbf{T}, \Omega, \mathbf{R} \rangle$, where $\mathbf{S}$, $\mathbf{A}$ and $\mathbf{O}$ are sets of possible world states, actions and observations respectively; β_0 is the initial belief state (distribution over states); $\mathbf{R}(\mathbf{s}, \mathbf{a}, \mathbf{s}')$ is the reward of taking action $\mathbf{a}$ in state $\mathbf{s}$ and reaching state $\mathbf{s}'$; $\mathbf{T}(\mathbf{s}'|\mathbf{s}, \mathbf{a})$ is the transition probability of reaching $\mathbf{s}'$ by taking action $\mathbf{a}$ in $\mathbf{s}$; $\Omega(\mathbf{o}|\mathbf{a}, \mathbf{s}')$ is the observation probability of observing $\mathbf{o}$, by taking action $\mathbf{a}$ to reach $\mathbf{s}'$. We now explain how we map DIME onto a POMDP.

6.1 States

A POMDP state in our problem is a pair of binary tuples $s = \langle W, F \rangle$ where W and F are of lengths $|V|$ and $|E_U|$, respectively. Intuitively, W denotes the influence status of network nodes, where $W_i = 1$ denotes that node i is influenced and $W_i = 0$ otherwise. Moreover, F denotes the existence of uncertain edges, where $F_i = 1$ denotes that the ith uncertain edge exists in reality, and $F_i = 0$

otherwise (assuming we order the nodes and uncertain edges). For example, in Fig. 5, if *only* node A is influenced, and *only* uncertain edge (A, B) exists, then the POMDP state $s = \langle W, F \rangle$ is given by $W = \langle 1, 0, 0, 0, 0, 0 \rangle$, because only node A is influenced (i.e., $W_1 = 1$) and all other nodes are un-influenced (i.e., $W_i = 0$); and $F = \langle 1, 0, 0, 0 \rangle$ because out of the four uncertain edges in Fig. 5, only (A, B) exists ($F_1 = 1$) and the other uncertain edges don't exist ($F_i = 0$). Thus, the set of all possible POMDP states are all possible combinations of the binary vectors W and F. We denote the set of all possible POMDP states by S.

6.2   Actions

Every choice of a subset of K nodes is a POMDP action. More formally, $A = \{a \subset V s.t. |a| = K\}$. For example, in Fig. 5, one possible action is $\{A, B\}$ (when $K = 2$). We denote the set of all possible POMDP actions by A.

6.3   Observations

Upon taking a POMDP action, we "*observe*" the ground reality of the uncertain edges outgoing from the nodes chosen in that action. Consider $\Theta(a) = \{e \mid e = (\text{x,y}) \text{ s.t. } \text{x} \in a \wedge e \in E_u\} \forall a \in A$, which represents the (ordered) set of uncertain edges that are observed when we take action a. Then, our POMDP observation upon taking action a is defined as $o(a) = \{F_e | e \in \Theta(a)\}$, i.e., the F-values of the observed uncertain edges. For example, by taking action $\{B, C\}$ in Fig. 5, the values of F_4 and F_5 (i.e., the F-values of uncertain edges in the 1-hop social circle of nodes B and C) would be observed. We denote the set of all possible POMDP observations by O.

6.4   Rewards

The reward $R(s, a, s')$ of taking action a in state s and reaching state s' is the number of newly influenced nodes in s'. More formally, $R(s, a, s') = (\|s'\| - \|s\|)$, where $\|s'\|$ is the number of influenced nodes in s'.

6.5   Initial Belief State

The initial belief state is a distribution β_0 over all states $s \in S$. The support of β_0 consists of all states $s = \langle W, F \rangle$ s.t. $W_i = 0 \forall i \in [1, |V|]$, i.e., all states in which all network nodes are un-influenced (as we assume that all nodes are un-influenced to begin with). Inside its support, each F_i is distributed independently according to $P(F_i = 1) = u(e)$. Recall that despite this assumption, there is uncertainty in the influence status of nodes in future time steps, because HEALER does not observe the nodes that have been influenced in between interventions. The only information HEALER has is that explicitly chosen nodes (i.e., our intervention participants in all past rounds) are influenced.

6.6   Transition and Observation Probabilities

Computation of exact transition probabilities $T(s'|s, a)$ requires considering all possible paths in a graph through which influence could spread, which is $\mathcal{O}(N!)$ (N is number of nodes in the network) in the worst case. Moreover, for large social networks, the size of the transition and observation probability matrix is prohibitively large (due to exponential sizes of state and action space).

Therefore, instead of storing huge transition/observation matrices in memory, we follow the paradigm of large-scale online POMDP solvers [5,6,25] by using a generative model $\Lambda(s, a) \sim (s', o, r)$ of the transition and observation probabilities. This generative model allows us to generate on-the-fly samples from the exact distributions $T(s'|s, a)$ and $\Omega(o|a, s')$ at very low computational costs. Given an initial state s and an action a to be taken, our generative model Λ simulates the random process of influence spread to generate a random new state s', an observation o and the obtained reward r. Simulation of the random process of influence spread is done by *"playing"* out propagation probabilities (i.e., flipping weighted coins with probability $p(e)$) according to our influence model to generate sample s'. The observation sample o is then determined from s' and a. Finally, the reward sample $r = (\|s'\| - \|s\|)$ (as defined above). This simple design of the generative model allows significant scale and speed up (as seen in previous work [25] and also in our experimental results section).

Next, we give a high-level overview of HEAL algorithm. For more detailed understanding, please refer to [29].

7   HEAL

HEAL solves the *original POMDP* using a novel *hierarchical ensembling heuristic*: it creates ensembles of imperfect (and smaller) POMDPs at *two* different layers, in a hierarchical manner (see Fig. 6). HEAL's *top layer* creates an ensemble of smaller sized *intermediate POMDPs* by subdividing the original *uncertain network* into several smaller sized *partitioned networks* by using graph partitioning techniques [12]. Each of these partitioned networks is then mapped onto a POMDP, and these *intermediate POMDPs* form our *top layer* ensemble of POMDP solvers.

In the bottom layer, each *intermediate POMDP* is solved using TASP (**T**ree **A**ggregation for **S**equential **P**lanning), our novel POMDP planner, which subdivides the POMDP into another ensemble of smaller sized *sampled POMDPs*. Each member of this *bottom layer* ensemble is created by randomly sampling uncertain edges of the partitioned network to get a sampled network having no uncertain edges, and this sampled network is then mapped onto a *sampled POMDP*. Finally, the solutions of POMDPs in both the *bottom* and *top layer* ensembles are aggregated using novel techniques to get the solution for HEAL's original POMDP.

HEAL uses several novel heuristics. First, it uses a novel two-layered *hierarchical ensembling heuristic*. Second, it uses graph partitioning techniques to partition the uncertain network, which generates partitions that minimize the

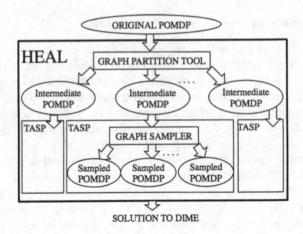

Fig. 6. Hierarchical decomposition in HEAL

edges going across partitions (while ensuring that partitions have similar sizes). Since these partitions are "almost" disconnected, we solve each partition separately. Third, it solves the *intermediate POMDP* for each partition by creating smaller-sized *sampled POMDPs* (via sampling uncertain edges), each of which is solved using a novel tree search algorithm, which avoids the exponential branching factor seen in PSINET [30]. Fourth, it uses novel aggregation techniques to combine solutions to these smaller POMDPs rather than simple plurality voting techniques seen in previous ensemble techniques [30].

These heuristics enable scale up to real-world sizes (at the expense of sacrificing performance guarantees), as instead of solving one huge problem, we now solve several smaller problems. However, these heuristics perform very well in practice. Our simulations show that even on smaller settings, HEAL achieves a 100X speed up over PSINET, while providing a 70 % improvement in solution quality; and on larger problems, *where PSINET is unable to run at all*, HEAL continues to provide high solution quality.

8   Experimental Results

In this section, we analyze HEAL's performance on some settings. Both our experiments are run on a 2.33 GHz 12-core Intel machine having 48 GB of RAM. All experiments are averaged over 100 runs. We use a metric of "*Indirect Influence*" throughout this section, which is number of nodes "*indirectly*" influenced by intervention participants. For example, on a 30 node network, by selecting 2 nodes each for 10 interventions (horizon), 20 nodes (a lower bound for any strategy) are influenced with certainty. However, the total number of influenced nodes might be 26 (say) and thus, the *Indirect Influence* is $26 - 20 = 6$. In all experiments, the propagation and existence probability values on all network edges were uniformly set to 0.1 and 0.6, respectively. This was done based on findings in Kelly et al. [8]. However, we relax these parameter settings later in the section. All experiments are statistically significant under bootstrap-t ($\alpha = 0.05$). For a more comprehensive set of results, please refer to [29].

Baselines: We use two algorithms as baselines. We use PSINET-W as a benchmark as it is the most relevant previous algorithm, which was shown to outperform heuristics used in practice; however, we also need a point of comparison when PSINET-W does not scale. No previous algorithm in the influence maximization literature accounts for uncertain edges and uncertain network state in solving the problem of sequential selection of nodes; in-fact we show that even the standard Greedy algorithm [7,9] has no approximation guarantees as our problem is not adaptive submodular. Thus, we modify Greedy by replacing our uncertain network with a certain network (in which each uncertain edge e is replaced with a certain edge e_0 having propagation probability $p(e_0) = p(e) \times u(e)$), and then run the Greedy algorithm on this *certain network*. We use the Greedy algorithm as a baseline as it is the best known algorithm known for influence maximization and has been analyzed in many previous papers [1,2,7,9,13,27].

Datasets: We use *four real world social networks* of homeless youth, provided to us by our collaborators. All four networks are friendship based social networks of homeless youth living in different areas of a big city in USA (name withheld for anonymity). The first and second networks are of homeless youth living in two large areas (denoted by VE and HD to preserve anonymity), respectively. These two networks (each having ~150–170 nodes, 400–450 edges) were created through surveys and interviews of homeless youth (conducted by our collaborators) living in these areas. The third and fourth networks are relatively small-sized online social networks of these youth created from their Facebook (34 nodes, 120 edges) and MySpace (107 nodes, 803 edges) contact lists, respectively. When HEALER is deployed, we anticipate even larger networks, (e.g., 250–300 nodes) than the ones we have in hand and we also show run-time results on artificial networks of these sizes.

Solution Quality/Runtime Comparison. We compare *Indirect Influence* and run-times of HEAL, HEAL-T and PSINET-W on all four real-world networks. We set $T = 5$ and $K = 2$ (since PSINET-W fails to scale up beyond $K = 2$ as shown later). Figure 7a shows the *Indirect Influence* of the different algorithms on the four networks. The X-axis shows the four networks and the

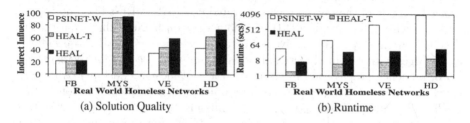

(a) Solution Quality   (b) Runtime

Fig. 7. Solution Quality and Runtime on Real World Networks

Y-axis shows the *Indirect Influence* achieved by the different algorithms. This figure shows that (i) HEAL outperforms all other algorithms on every network; (ii) *it achieves ~70 % improvement over PSINET-W* in VE and HD networks; (iii) it achieves ~25 % improvement over HEAL-T. The difference between HEAL and other algorithms is not significant in the Facebook (FB) and MySpace (MYS) networks, as HEAL is already influencing almost all nodes in these two relatively small networks. Thus, in experiments to come, we focus more on the VE and HD networks.

Figure 7b shows the run-time of all algorithms on the four networks. The X-axis shows the four networks and the Y-axis (in log scale) shows the run-time (in seconds). This figure shows that (i) *HEAL achieves a 100X speed-up over PSINET-W*; (ii) PSINET-W's run-time increases exponentially with increasing network sizes; (iii) HEAL runs 3X slower than HEAL-T but achieves 25 % more *Indirect Influence*. Hence, HEAL is our algorithm of choice that we plan to deploy in our pilot study. Next, we report on initial progress made in the pilot study.

9   Pilot Study with Homeless Youth

We now discuss ongoing efforts towards deploying HEALER in collaboration with Safe Place for Youth in a pilot study. This study will serve as a precursor to a much larger study where we plan to enroll 900 youth into our program. For our pilot study, we have begun generating the network using HEALER's Facebook application.

So far, we have enrolled 60 homeless youth into our pilot study. Over a period of two weeks, each youth that visited Safe Place for Youth was asked about the possibility of them enrolling into our study. Upon their consent, they were explained the goal and reason behind conducting this pilot study - to raise awareness about HIV in their social circles. Each youth was gifted a 20 US dollar gift card for enrolling into the study. They will also be given 25 and 30 US dollar gift cards for showing up after one and three months for follow-up interviews which will be used to assess influence spread. Finally, the youth were also given a three digit personal identification number (PID) using which they will be referred to in the pilot study (as part of an Institutional Review Board requirement to protect the anonymity of homeless youth at all times).

Using this PID, they logged into HEALER's Facebook application and then the social network was generated. Currently, the network is in the process of being refined with suggestions made by officials at Safe Place for Youth. Figure 8 shows a portion of the raw network generated using HEALER's Facebook application. Each node shows the PID of a homeless youth. Note that even though Facebook friendships are mostly bidirectional, we have replaced those bidirectional edges with two unidirectional edges (in order to account for the asymmetry of influence propagation in either direction of most friendships). After this network is refined with suggestions from officials at Safe Place for Youth, link prediction techniques will be used to infer missing or uncertain edges. Once this entire process is over, HEALER will be used to generate recommendations for homeless shelter officials.

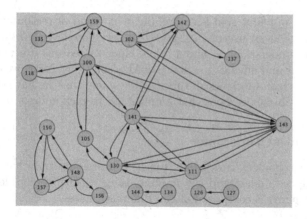

Fig. 8. A portion of the raw network generated using HEALER's Facebook application

10   Explanation System

In our initial talks with homeless shelter officials, we observed that the shelter officials found HEAL's solutions to be very counter-intuitive. This was to be expected since people generally tend to perform bad in situations where multi-step expected utility calculations need to be done in order to find the best action (e.g., sequential planning problems). Since HEAL will be deployed among homeless youth whose welfare is the responsibility of the homeless shelter, we want the shelter officials to be comfortable with solutions provided by HEAL.

Our goal is to be able to justify the solutions of HEAL to the homeless shelter officials in an intuitive manner. This goal is slightly different than the goal of *"explaining"* HEAL's solution to the shelter official. Explaining HEAL's solution would entail telling the official exactly how HEAL calculates its solution, and then explain why HEAL chooses a particular choice of nodes in the network. That is, we would need to give a *"correct"* explanation to the official which would involve maximum expected utility calculations. On the other hand, we just want to justify the solutions of HEAL to the official in an intuitive manner. This means that we want to explain the solution of HEAL in a way that does not go against the official's intuition. In such a case, the official will be much more comfortable in adopting HEAL's solutions.

One possible way of designing this explanation system is to ensure that our system refrains from using MEU (maximum expected utility) calculations to justify HEALER's solutions. Instead, it could explain the solution in terms of concepts that the officials finds believable (or concepts that mirror the officials' intuition). For example, the officials might pick nodes which are centrally located and highly popular in the network. Now, degree centrality is not necessarily an optimal strategy, but if we can explain HEAL's solution in terms of "centrality and popularity" of nodes, then the official might be more willing to agree with the POMDP solution.

To that end, our first goal is to find out what kind of reasoning do officials (or humans in general) use to pick nodes in very simple graph settings. That will give us an understanding about what kinds of reasons are most likely to persuade humans and officials to adopt HEAL's solutions. Next, we describe the details of an Amazon Mechanical Turk (AMT) game that we have developed in order to find the biases/reasons that humans use to pick nodes.

10.1   Mechanical Turk Game

Our Amazon Mechanical Turk game (Fig. 9) collects data from human subjects which will help us understand the reasons using which people select nodes in networks. Our game is comprised of two different phases.

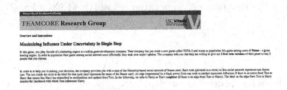

Fig. 9. Instructions Page of AMT Game

First Phase of Game. In the first phase, our game collects data from human subjects by showing them pictures of different graphs and asking them to pick nodes in those graphs. Our game has four different variants, each of which is designed to gauge difficulties faced by humans in different settings. The four settings are as follows:

- **Short + Certain:** In this setting, subjects are asked to select two nodes for a single horizon on 8 different graphs with certain propagation of influence on all edges (Fig. 10).
- **Short + Uncertain:** In this setting, subjects are asked to select two nodes for a single horizon on 8 different graphs with uncertain propagation of influence on all edges (Fig. 11).
- **Long + Certain:** In this setting, subjects are asked to select two nodes for a two rounds on 8 different graphs with certain propagation of influence on all edges (Fig. 12).
- **Long + Uncertain:** In this setting, subjects are asked to select two nodes for a two rounds on 8 different graphs with uncertain propagation of influence on all edges (Fig. 13).

Data collected from these four variants will help us understand where do humans fail. Specifically, it will help us distinguish between whether humans fail at lookahead search (**Long + Certain** and **Long + Uncertain**) or at expected utility calculations (**Short + Uncertain**). At the beginning of the

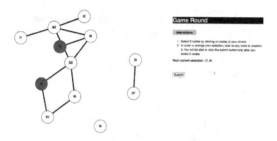

Fig. 10. Short + Certain Variant

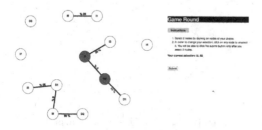

Fig. 11. Short + Uncertain Variant

game, each human subject is randomly assigned to one out of the four possible game variants. He/she is shown the first set of graphs and his responses are recorded.

Second Phase of Game. The second phase of the game collects data on whether people find it easier to verify correct solutions as opposed to coming up with correct solutions (Fig. 14). Recall that in the first phase of our game, each human subject was shown a set of eight different networks and they were asked to select a set of nodes for maximizing influence spread. In the second phase, for each of these eight networks, the human subject is shown four different solutions for that network. The four different solutions are as follows: (i) his own solution from Phase 1; (ii) HEALER's solution; (iii) solution based on Degree Centrality (i.e., nodes picked in order of decreasing degree centrality); (iv) solution based on Betweenness Centrality (i.e., nodes picked in order of decreasing betweenness centrality).

Data collected from the second phase will help us in finding out if people can verify the correct solutions (i.e., HEALER's solutions) even though it might be harder for them to come up with the correct solutions (due to the various difficulties that we test in the first phase of the game). For example, if we find out that people mostly figure out that HEALER's solutions are better than the other solutions, then the need for our POMDP explanation system would be negated. Moreover, if people do not select their own first phase solution in the second phase, that would point to the fact that peoples' biases towards their particular solution are not that strong.

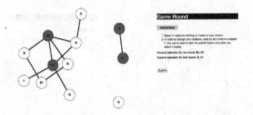

Fig. 12. Long + Certain Variant

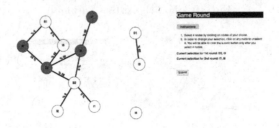

Fig. 13. Long + Uncertain Variant

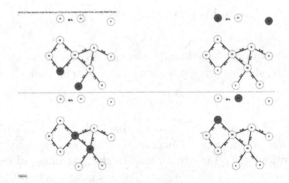

Fig. 14. Second phase of AMT game

Compensation Scheme: Each human subject receives a base compensation of 50 cents and gets a bonus amount proportional to his/her performance on the task (the performance is judged by how close his solution is to the optimal solution). The bonus amount is capped off at one dollar, i.e., if the subject selects the optimal solution on each of the eight networks, he/she gets 1.5 dollars (one dollar bonus + 50 cent base compensation). Data collection using the game is currently underway[2]. In future work, we plan to utilize the collected data to guide the development of our POMDP persuasion system.

---

[2] The game can be played at http://cs-server.usc.edu:16292/.

11   Conclusion

This paper looks at challenges faced during the ongoing deployment of HEALER, a POMDP based software agent that recommends sequential intervention plans for use by homeless shelters, who organize these interventions to raise awareness about HIV among homeless youth. HEALER's sequential plans (built using knowledge of social networks of homeless youth) choose intervention participants strategically to maximize influence spread, while reasoning about uncertainties in the network. In order to compute its plans, HEALER (i) casts this influence maximization problem as a POMDP and solves it using a novel planner which scales up to previously unsolvable real-world sizes; (ii) and constructs social networks of homeless youth at low cost, using a Facebook application. HEALER is currently being deployed in the real world in collaboration with a homeless shelter. Initial feedback from the shelter officials has been positive but they were surprised by the solutions generated by HEALER as these solutions are very counter-intuitive. Therefore, there is a need to justify HEALER's solutions in a way that mirrors the officials' intuition. In this paper, we report on progress made towards HEALER's deployment and detail first steps taken to tackle the issue of explaining HEALER's solutions. Specifically, we build a game on Amazon Mechanical Turk to collect data from human subjects in order to understand biases and reasons that humans use to select nodes in networks. This is the first step towards building our explanation system that will justify solutions of HEALER to homeless shelter officials in an intuitive manner.

Acknowledgements. This research was supported by MURI Grant W911NF-11-1-0332 and NIMH Grant number R01-MH093336.

References

1. Borgs, C., Brautbar, M., Chayes, J., Lucier, B.: Maximizing social influence in nearly optimal time. In: Proceedings of the Twenty-Fifth Annual ACM-SIAM Symposium on Discrete Algorithms, SODA 2014, pp. 946–957. SIAM (2014)
2. Cohen, E., Delling, D., Pajor, T., Werneck, R.F.: Sketch-based influence maximization and computation: scaling up with guarantees. In: Proceedings of the 23rd ACM International Conference on Conference on Information and Knowledge Management, pp. 629–638. ACM (2014)
3. Cointet, J.-P., Roth, C.: How realistic should knowledge diffusion models be? J. Artif. Soc. Soc. Simul. **10**(3), 5 (2007)
4. Council, N.H.: HIV/AIDS among persons experiencing homelessness: risk factors, predictors of testing, and promising testing strategies (2012). www.nhchc.org/wp-content/uploads/2011/09/InFocus_Dec2012.pdf
5. Dibangoye, J.S., Shani, G., Chaib-Draa, B., Mouaddib, A.-I.: Topological order planner for POMDPs. In: International Joint Conference on Artificial Intelligence (IJCAI) (2009)
6. Eck, A., Soh, L.-K.: To ask, sense, or share: ad hoc information gathering. In: Proceedings of the 2015 International Conference on Autonomous Agents and Multiagent Systems, pp. 367–376. International Foundation for Autonomous Agents and Multiagent Systems (2015)

7. Golovin, D., Krause, A.: Adaptive submodularity: theory and applications in active learning and stochastic optimization. J. Artif. Intell. Res. **42**, 427–486 (2011)
8. Kelly, J.A., Murphy, D.A., Sikkema, K.J., McAuliffe, T.L., Roffman, R.A., Solomon, L.J., Winett, R.A., Kalichman, S.C.: Randomised, controlled, community-level HIV-prevention intervention for sexual-risk behaviour among homosexual men in US cities. Lancet **350**(9090), 1500 (1997)
9. Kempe, D., Kleinberg, J., Tardos, É.: Maximizing the spread of influence through a social network. In: Proceedings of the Ninth ACM SIGKDD International Conference on Knowledge Discovery and Data Mining, pp. 137–146. ACM (2003)
10. Khan, O.Z., Poupart, P., Black, J.P.: Minimal sufficient explanations for factored Markov decision processes. Citeseer (2009)
11. Kim, M., Leskovec, J.: The network completion problem: inferring missing nodes and edges in networks. In: Proceedings of the SIAM Conference on Data Mining. SIAM (2011)
12. LaSalle, D., Karypis, G.: Multi-threaded graph partitioning. In: 2013 IEEE 27th International Symposium on Parallel & Distributed Processing (IPDPS), pp. 225–236. IEEE (2013)
13. Leskovec, J., Krause, A., Guestrin, C., Faloutsos, C., VanBriesen, J., Glance, N.: Cost-effective outbreak detection in networks. In: Proceedings of the 13th ACM SIGKDD International Conference on Knowledge Discovery and Data Mining, pp. 420–429. ACM (2007)
14. Marcolino, L., Lakshminarayanan, A., Yadav, A., Tambe, M.: Simultaneous influencing and mapping social networks. In: Proceedings of the Fifteenth International Conference on Autonomous Agents and Multiagent Systems (Short Paper) (AAMAS 2016) (2016)
15. Paquet, S., Tobin, L., Chaib-Draa, B.: An online POMDP algorithm for complex multiagent environments. In: Proceedings of the Fourth International Joint Conference on Autonomous Agents and Multiagent Systems, pp. 970–977. ACM (2005)
16. Poupart, P., Kim, K.-E., Kim, D.: Closing the gap: improved bounds on optimal POMDP solutions. In: International Conference on Automated Planning and Scheduling (2011)
17. Puterman, M.L.: Markov Decision Processes: Discrete Stochastic Dynamic Programming. Wiley, New York (2009)
18. Rice, E.: The positive role of social networks and social networking technology in the condom-using behaviors of homeless young people. Public Health Rep. **125**(4), 588 (2010)
19. Rice, E., Barman-Adhikari, A., Milburn, N.G., Monro, W.: Position-specific HIV risk in a large network of homeless youths. Am. J. Pub. Health **102**(1), 141–147 (2012)
20. Rice, E., Fulginiti, A., Winetrobe, H., Montoya, J., Plant, A., Kordic, T.: Sexuality and homelessness in Los Angeles public schools. Am. J. Pub. Health **102**(2), 200a–201a (2012)
21. Rice, E., Tulbert, E., Cederbaum, J., Adhikari, A.B., Milburn, N.G.: Mobilizing homeless youth for HIV prevention: a social network analysis of the acceptability of a face-to-face and online social networking intervention. Health Educ. Res. **27**(2), 226 (2012)
22. Ross, S., Pineau, J., Paquet, S., Chaib-Draa, B.: Online planning algorithms for POMDPs. J. Artif. Intell. Res. **32**, 663–704 (2008)
23. Schneider, J.A., Zhou, A.N., Laumann, E.O.: A new HIV prevention network approach: sociometric peer change agent selection. Soc. Sci. Med. **125**, 192–202 (2015)

24. Seegebarth, B., Müller, F., Schattenberg, B., Biundo, S.: Making hybrid plans more clear to human users-a formal approach for generating sound explanations. In: Twenty-Second International Conference on Automated Planning and Scheduling (2012)
25. Silver, D., Veness, J.: Monte-Carlo planning in large POMDPs. In: Advances in Neural Information Processing Systems, pp. 2164–2172 (2010)
26. Spaan, M.T., Vlassis, N.: Perseus: randomized point-based value iteration for POMDPs. J. Artif. Intell. Res. **24**, 195–220 (2005)
27. Tang, Y., Xiao, X., Shi, Y.: Influence maximization: near-optimal time complexity meets practical efficiency. In: Proceedings of the 2014 ACM SIGMOD International Conference on Management of Data, pp. 75–86. ACM (2014)
28. Valente, T.W., Pumpuang, P.: Identifying opinion leaders to promote behavior change. Health Educ. Behav. **3**, 881–896 (2007)
29. Yadav, A., Chan, H., Jiang, A., Xu, H., Rice, E., Tambe, M.: Using social networks to aid homeless shelters: dynamic influence maximization under uncertainty - an extended version. In: Proceedings of the Fifteenth International Conference on Autonomous Agents and Multiagent Systems (AAMAS 2016) (2016)
30. Yadav, A., Marcolino, L., Rice, E., Petering, R., Winetrobe, H., Rhoades, H., Tambe, M., Carmichael, H.: Preventing HIV spread in homeless populations using PSINET. In: Proceedings of the Twenty-Seventh Conference on Innovative Applications of Artificial Intelligence (IAAI-15) (2015)
31. Yan, Q., Guo, S., Yang, D.: Influence maximizing and local influenced community detection based on multiple spread model. In: Tang, J., King, I., Chen, L., Wang, J. (eds.) ADMA 2011. LNCS (LNAI), vol. 7121, pp. 82–95. Springer, Heidelberg (2011). doi:10.1007/978-3-642-25856-5_7
32. Young, S.D., Rice, E.: Online social networking technologies, HIV knowledge, and sexual risk and testing behaviors among homeless youth. AIDS Behav. **15**(2), 253–260 (2011)

Summarizing Simulation Results Using Causally-Relevant States

Nidhi Parikh[✉], Madhav Marathe, and Samarth Swarup

Network Dynamics and Simulation Science Lab, Biocomplexity Institute
of Virginia Tech, Virginia Tech, Blacksburg, VA, USA
{nidhip,mmarathe,swarup}@vbi.vt.edu

Abstract. As increasingly large-scale multiagent simulations are being implemented, new methods are becoming necessary to make sense of the results of these simulations. Even concisely summarizing the results of a given simulation run is a challenge. Here we pose this as the problem of simulation summarization: how to extract the causally-relevant descriptions of the trajectories of the agents in the simulation. We present a simple algorithm to compress agent trajectories through state space by identifying the state transitions which are relevant to determining the distribution of outcomes at the end of the simulation. We present a toy-example to illustrate the working of the algorithm, and then apply it to a complex simulation of a major disaster in an urban area.

1 Introduction

Large-scale multiagent simulations are becoming increasingly common in many domains of scientific interest, including epidemiology [9], disaster response [23], and urban planning [22]. These simulations have complex models of agents, environments, infrastructures, and interactions. Often the goal is to study a hypothetical situation or a counter-factual scenario in a detailed and realistic virtual setting, with the intention of making policy recommendations.

In practice, this is done through a statistical experiment design, where a parameter space is explored through multiple simulation runs and the outcomes are compared for statistically significant differences.

As simulations get larger and more complex, however, we encounter two kinds of situations where it is difficult to apply this methodology. First, if a simulation is too computationally intensive to run enough number of times, we don't obtain the statistical power necessary to find significant differences between the cells in a statistical experiment design. Second, if the interventions are not actually known ahead of time, we don't even know how to create a statistical experiment. This can be the case, e.g., when the goal of doing the simulation is actually to find reasonable interventions for a hypothetical disaster scenario.

New methodologies and new techniques are needed for the analysis of such complex simulations. Part of the problem is that large-scale multiagent simulations can generate much more data in each simulation run than goes into the

© Springer International Publishing AG 2016
N. Osman and C. Sierra (Eds.): AAMAS 2016 WS, Visionary Papers, LNAI 10003, pp. 88–103, 2016.
DOI: 10.1007/978-3-319-46840-2_6

simulation, i.e., we end up with more data than we started with. Sense-making in this regime is a challenge.

As a first step towards addressing these kinds of problems, we introduce the problem of simulation summarization. The goal of this problem is to come up with a summary description of a single large multiagent simulation run. The method we introduce is based on a deep theory of causal states in stochastic processes (see Sect. 3). It is simple to implement, which is essential when applying to very large simulations, and is actually more meaningful the larger the simulation, since larger numbers of agents give more statistical power.

The rest of this paper is organized as follows. First we describe the simulation summarization problem and discuss some related work. Then we review the idea of causal states for extracting patterns from time series data. After that we describe how we adapt this idea to the analysis of the results of large-scale simulations. Then we present a toy example to illustrate the effectiveness of our method, before applying it to a large and complex simulation of an improvised nuclear detonation in an urban area. We show how our method finds a number of meaningful causal patterns in the simulation results, while also greatly compressing the results. We end with a discussion of applications and extensions of our method.

2   Problem Description

What constitutes a good summary? This is a question that has been studied in domains such as natural language processing where the goal is to summarize a document or a corpus [16,17], but, as far as we know, is entirely novel for multiagent simulations.

Our perspective on summarizing a multiagent simulation is that the summary representation should capture the causally-relevant states of the simulation. We use the phrase "causally-relevant" instead of causal to side-step the well-known problems with finding causality. There are many efforts aimed at establishing (various forms of) causality in data [11–13,21, e.g.]. Our goal here is not to establish causality, but to compress the simulation results while retaining meaningful states. The intuition is that finding causally-relevant states of the simulation is the most meaningful way to compress it.

In line with this intuition, we adapt the approach of "causal states" that has been developed over the last several years, as reviewed in the next section. By "causally-relevant", in this context, we mean agent states that are maximally informative about outcomes of interest.

Even in simulation scenarios where the set of interventions or cases to study is not known a priori, i.e., simulations which are intended to be exploratory in nature, there is a set of outcomes we care about. For instance, in a disaster simulation we explore in Sects. 6 and 7, the outcome of interest is the health of the agents. Causally-relevant states in this simulation are all the states which have a measurable impact on agent health, even if the impact is delayed. For example in this simulation, being exposed to radiation has an impact on health state only after several hours have passed. The summary should be able to reveal that it is the exposure to radiation that is the causally-relevant state, not the actual change in the agent's health state (since that follows deterministically once exposure has happened).

Next we describe the formalism of causal states which is more broadly applicable to stochastic processes before turning to our approach for simulation summarization.

3   Causal States

Crutchfield and others have developed the theory of minimal causal representations of stochastic processes, termed computational mechanics [7,18]. We briefly review the concepts here before describing how we have adapted them for the summarization problem.

Consider a stochastic process as a sequence of random variables X_t, drawn from a discrete alphabet, $\mathcal{A}$. We will write $\overleftarrow{X}$ to denote the *past* of the sequence, i.e., the sequence $X_{-\infty} \ldots X_{t-2}X_{t-1}X_t$, and $\overrightarrow{X}$ to denote the *future* of the sequence, i.e., the sequence $X_{t+1}X_{t+2}\ldots X_\infty$, following [6,8].

The mutual information between the past and the future of the sequence is termed its excess entropy:

$$\mathbf{E} = I[\overleftarrow{X}; \overrightarrow{X}]. \tag{1}$$

This quantifies the amount of information from the past of the process that determines its future. For example, $\mathbf{E} = 0$ would mean that the future of the process is independent of the past.

Crutchfield and Young [7] suggested a simple method for modeling a stochastic process that captures the information being communicated from $\overleftarrow{X}$ to $\overrightarrow{X}$: group all the histories that predict the same future. This gives rise to a state machine which they call an ϵ-machine, defined in [8]:

$$\epsilon(\overleftarrow{x}) = \{\overleftarrow{x}' \mid Pr(\overrightarrow{X} \mid \overleftarrow{x}) = Pr(\overrightarrow{X} \mid \overleftarrow{x}')\}. \tag{2}$$

In other words, the states of an ϵ-machine correspond to sets of histories that are equivalent in terms of the probability distributions they assign to the future of the process. ϵ-machines have a number of interesting and useful properties. For instance, causal states are Markovian because $\overleftarrow{X}$ is statistically independent of $\overrightarrow{X}$ given the current causal state of the process. They are also optimally predictive because they capture all of the information in $\overleftarrow{X}$ that is predictive of $\overrightarrow{X}$.

Shalizi and Shalizi have presented an algorithm for learning ϵ-machines from time series data, known as *Causal State Splitting Reconstruction* (CSSR) [19]. CSSR learns a function, η, that is *next-step sufficient* and that can be calculated recursively. A next-step sufficient function is a function that can predict the next step of the time series optimally. If it is also recursively calculable, then it can be used to predict the entire future of the time series optimally.

CSSR learns an ϵ-machine as a Hidden Markov Model (HMM) in an incremental fashion. The HMM is initialized with just one state and, as the algorithm processes the time series, more states are added when a statistical test shows that the current set of states is insufficient for capturing all the information in the past of the time series.

Informally, the CSSR algorithm works as follows. It tests the distribution over the next symbol given increasingly longer past sequences. Let L be the length of the past sequences considered so far, and let Σ be the set of causal states estimated so far.

In the next step, CSSR looks at sequences of length $L + 1$. If a sequence of the form ax^L, where x^L is a sequence of length L and $a \in \mathcal{A}$ is a symbol, belongs to the same causal state as x^L, then we would have [19],

$$Pr(X_t \mid ax^L) = Pr(X_t \mid \hat{S} = \hat{\epsilon}(x^L)), \tag{3}$$

where $\hat{S}$ is the current estimate of the causal state to which x^L belongs. This hypothesis can be tested using a statistical test such as the Kolmogorov-Smirnov (KS) test. If the test shows that the LHS and RHS of Eq. 3 are statistically significantly different distributions, then CSSR tries to match the sequence ax^L with all the other causal states estimated so far. If $Pr(X_t|ax^L)$ turns out to be significantly different in all cases, a new causal state is created and ax^L is assigned to it. This process is carried out up to some length L_{max}.

After this, transient states are removed and the state machine is made deterministic by splitting states as necessary. Details of this step can be found in [19] but are not relevant for the present work.

4   Our Approach

Our approach adapts the causal state formalism by treating the trajectory of each agent in the simulation as an instance of the same stochastic process.

In our approach, a multiagent simulation consists of a set of agents, each of which is defined by a k-dimensional state vector $\mathbf{x}(t) = [x_1(t), x_2(t), \ldots x_k(t)]^{\top}$, which evolves over time. Let d_i be the number of possible values x_i can take. The simulation proceeds in discrete time steps from $t = 0$ to $t = T$. Let the number of agents be denoted by N.

We use the term state in a broad sense. It can include, e.g., the action taken by the agent at each time step. It can also include historical aggregations of variables, e.g., it might include a variable that tracks if an agent has ever done a particular action, or the cumulative value of some variable so far.

Our goal is not to learn an ϵ-machine for a simulation, for two reasons. First, the set of states discovered (through CSSR, e.g.), can be hard to interpret. Second, in general, we don't need to predict every step of the simulation. We only care about particular outcomes and the state transitions that are causally-relevant to those outcomes.

Thus, our goal is to compress the trajectory of each agent through state space to a small number of important states that have a significant impact on the outcomes we care about. Let the outcome variable for agent i be denoted by y_i. We assume that y_i is an instance of a random variable Y. Our algorithm for summarization proceeds as follows.

We divide the agent population into a set of clusters, $C(t) = \{C_1(t) \cup C_2(t) \cup \ldots C_m(t)\}$ at each time step. Initially, all the agents are grouped into just one cluster, i.e., $m = 1$ at $t = 0$. At each subsequent time step, the state of each agent changes because at least one of $x_1, \ldots x_k$ changes. The number of ways in which $\mathbf{x}$ can change is $d = d_1 \times d_2 \times \ldots \times d_k$.

Consider an arbitrary cluster of agents, $C_i(t)$. At time step $t + 1$, it can split into up to d groups, based on how each agent's state changes. However, not all of these changes may have a significant impact on the outcome. We treat each group derived from $C_i(t)$ as a candidate cluster, denoted by $CC_{i,j}(t + 1)$, where $j \in 1 \ldots d$. At each step, we compare $Pr(Y|C_i(t))$ with $Pr(Y|CC_{i,j}(t+1))$ using the Kolmogorov-Smirnov (KS) test. Here $Pr(Y|C_i(t))$ is the probability distribution over the final outcomes for all agents that belong to cluster $C_i(t)$ at time step t. If Y is a discrete variable, $Pr(Y = y|C_i(t))$ can be computed as a naive maximum likelihood estimate, i.e., ratio of the number of agents who belong to cluster $C_i(t)$ at time step t and have final outcome $Y = y$ to the number of agents who belong to cluster $C_i(t)$ at time step t. Similarly, $Pr(Y|CC_{i,j}(t+1))$ is the probability distribution over the final outcome for all agents who belong to candidate cluster $CC_{i,j}(t + 1)$ at time step $t + 1$ which is a subset of agents who belong to cluster $C_i(t)$ at time step t and can be computed in a similar fashion. Our null hypothesis (analogous to Eq. 3) is,

$$Pr(Y \mid CC_{i,j}(t + 1)) = Pr(Y \mid C_i(t)). \tag{4}$$

We also introduce a parameter δ, which is a threshold on the "effect size", which we measure as the Kullback–Leibler divergence (KL-divergence) between $Pr(Y \mid C_i(t))$ and $Pr(Y \mid CC_{i,j}(t+1))$. If the null hypothesis is rejected at a level α (say 0.001) and $D_{KL}(Pr(Y \mid C_i(t)) \parallel Pr(Y \mid CC_{i,j}(t+1))) > \delta$, then candidate cluster $CC_{i,j}(t + 1)$ is accepted as a new cluster at time step $t + 1$. The need for the effect size threshold is explained further below. If none of the candidate clusters at time step $t + 1$ are accepted, then $C_i(t)$ is added to the set of clusters for time step $t + 1$.

Thus, the entire simulation is decomposed into a tree structure of agent clusters. Furthermore, each cluster splits only when the corresponding state change is informative about the final outcome of concern.

The trajectory of each agent traces a path through this tree structure. We compress the trajectory by retaining only those time steps at which the cluster to which the agent belongs splits off from its parent cluster. The parameter δ allows us to control how many new clusters are formed at each step, and consequently, how much compression of trajectories we achieve. Setting δ to a high value will retain only the clusters which have a large difference in outcomes from their parent clusters. The summarization algorithm is presented using pseudo-code in Algorithm 1.

The set of compressed agent trajectories ultimately constitutes our summary representation of the simulation. It can be queried for various quantities of

---

Algorithm 1. Simulation Summarization.

---

input   : $\mathbf{x}_i(t), y_i$, where $i \in 1 \ldots N, t \in 0 \ldots T$

output   : $C(t), t \in 0 \ldots T$: a set of clusters for each time step, organized as a tree over
                time

parameters : α: significance level for KS test
                δ: "effect size" threshold on KL-divergence

Initialization: $C(0) \leftarrow$ all agents
for $t \leftarrow 1$ *to* T do
    for $i \leftarrow 1$ *to* $|C(t-1)|$ do
       Generate $CC(t)$, the set of candidate clusters for time step t
       for $j \leftarrow 1$ *to* d do
          Test the null hypothesis (Eq. 4) for each candidate cluster and its parent.
          if *null hypothesis is rejected at level* α *and*
          $D_{KL}(Pr(Y|C_i(t))||Pr(Y|CC_{i,j}(t+1))) > \delta$ then
          | $C(t) \leftarrow CC_{i,j}(t)$
          end
       end
    end
end

---

interest, as will be illustrated in the experiments below. We next present a toy example to illustrate the working of the algorithm, before turning to a large-scale complex disaster scenario simulation.

5   Experiments with a Toy Domain

Here, we present results from a toy example where a set of agents do a random walk on a 5-by-5 grid. There are 100K agents and all of them start at the same location $(2, 2)$ on the grid. At each time step, they move to a neighboring cell (including staying at the same cell) at random. An agent gets a reward when it reaches cell $(5, 5)$. For simplicity, once an agent gets a reward, it does not move.

The condition under which agents obtain reward is unknown to them. Please note that we are not actually learning a policy to maximize the reward. It is just a simple process to illustrate the functioning of our algorithm and to see if it can identify the states that provide information about their chances of getting a reward.

We run this simulation for 30 iterations and about 26500 agents got rewards at the end of the simulation. We tried two different values of KL-divergence threshold, δ: 0.3 and 0.5.

Figures 1a, b, and c show a sample trajectory and corresponding compressed trajectories for δ values 0.3 and 0.5, respectively. The high value of δ (0.5) can only identify states that cause sudden changes in probability distribution over final outcomes and hence identifies cell $(5, 5)$ as the causal state. While the lower δ (0.3) can detect gradual changes and hence identifies neighbors of cell $(5, 5)$ also as once an agent reaches cell $(5, 4)$, it is easy to reach cell $(5, 5)$.

Figure 2 shows the number of clusters vs. iteration for different threshold values. As small values of δ mean identifying gradual changes, the number of clusters are more. As δ increases the number of clusters decreases. Please note that the minimum size of a cluster is constrained to be 30 (so that the number of

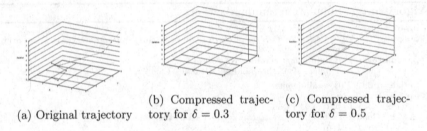

(a) Original trajectory   (b) Compressed trajec- (c) Compressed trajectory for $\delta = 0.3$ tory for $\delta = 0.5$

Fig. 1. A sample trajectory at various levels of compression.

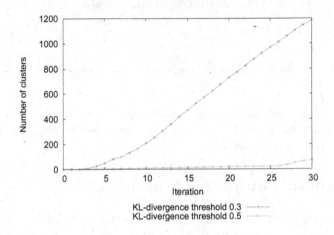

KL-divergence threshold 0.3 ⊢───
KL-divergence threshold 0.5 ──·──

Fig. 2. Number of clusters vs. iteration

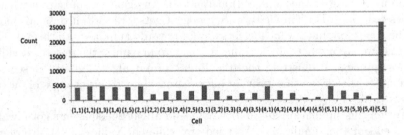

Fig. 3. Frequency distribution for cells in compressed trajectories.

samples in a cluster are enough for performing a statistical test) and this poses a
limit on splitting and hence identifying states that do not appear enough number
of times.

Overall compression defined as ratio of average length of compressed trajectory to length of uncompressed trajectory is 0.051 and 0.0333 for $\delta = 0.3$ and
$\delta = 0.5$, respectively. As expected, higher value of δ leads to higher compression. It also captures the most relevant state (5, 5) (Fig. 3). Figure 3 shows the

number of times a given cell appears in a compressed trajectory for $\delta = 0.5$. Other cells appear in compressed trajectories only in later iterations. These are the cells from which an agent can not reach cell (5, 5) by iteration 30. So the values of state variables (cell here) along with the reward probability give information about state-reward structure.

6   Large-Scale Disaster Simulation

Now, we turn to a very complex multiagent simulation of a human-initiated disaster scenario. Our simulation consists of a large, detailed "synthetic population" [3] of agents, and also includes detailed infrastructure models. We briefly summarize this simulation below before describing our experiments with summarizing the simulation results and the causally-relevant states our algorithm discovers.

6.1   Scenario

The scenario is detonation of 10kT hypothetical improvised nuclear device in Washington DC. The fallout cloud spreads mainly eastward and east-by-northeastward. The area that is studied is called the detailed study area (DSA; Fig. 4) which is the area under the largest thermal effects polygon (circle) and the area under the widest boundary of the fallout contours within DC region county boundaries (which consists of DC plus surrounding counties from Virginia and Maryland).

The blast causes significant damage to roads, buildings, power system, and cell phone communication system. The full simulation uses detailed data about each of these infrastructures to create models of phone call and text message capacity [5], altered movement patterns due to road damage [1], injuries due to rubble and debris, and levels of radiation protection in damaged buildings.

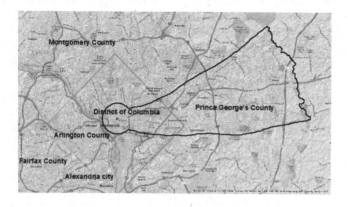

Fig. 4. The detailed study area (DSA).

6.2   Agent Design and Behavior

The scenario affects all people present in DSA at the time of detonation which includes area residents, transients (tourists and business travelers), and dorm students. Health and behavior of an individual depends upon its demographics as well as its location in the immediate aftermath of the event. This information is obtained from synthetic population [2]. Synthetic population is an agent-based representation of a population of a region along with their demographic (e.g., age, income, family structure) and activity related information (e.g. type of activity, location, start time). Detailed description about creating residents, transients, and dorm students can be found in [2,14,15]. There are 730,833 people present in DSA at the time of detonation which is same as the number of agents in the simulation.

Apart from demographics and location (as obtained from synthetic population), agents are defined by a number of other variables like health (modeled on a 0 to 7 range where 0 is dead and 7 corresponds to full health), behavior (described in the next paragraph), whether the agent is out of the affected area, whether the agent is the group leader, whether the agent has received emergency broadcast (EBR), the agent's exposure to radiation, etc.

Each agent keeps track of knowledge about family members' health states which could be unknown, known to be healthy, or known to be injured. This knowledge is updated whenever it makes a successful call to a family member or meets them in person.

Follow-the-leader behavior is also modeled, i.e., once family members encounter each other, they move together from there on. One of them becomes the group leader and others follow him. This kind of behavior is well-documented in emergency situations. Similarly when a person is rescued by someone he travels with him until he reaches a hospital or meets his family members.

Agent behavior is conceptually based on the formalism of decentralized semi-Markov decision process (Dec-SMDP) with communication [10] using the framework of options [20]. Here, high level behaviors are modeled as options, which are policies with initiation and termination conditions. Agents can choose among six options: household reconstitution (HRO), evacuation, shelter-seeking (Shelter), healthcare-seeking (HC-seeking), panic, and aid & assist. High level behavior options correspond to low level action plans which model their dependency with infrastructural systems. These actions are: call, text or move. Whom to call or text and where to move depends upon the current behavior option, e.g., in household reconstitution option, a person tries to move towards a family member and/or call family members while in healthcare-seeking option, a person tries call 911 or move towards a hospital. Details of the behavior model can be found in [14].

7   Experiments

Our goal here is to generate summary for the disaster simulation. Agents and locations that they visit are represented by about 40 variables which could take binary, categorical or continuous values, leading to a very large state space. Hence, here we focus on subsets of these variables for generating summary.

We use data for the first 30 iterations and use the probability distribution over the final health state (in iteration 100, 48 h after the blast) to identify causal states that affect the final health state.

7.1 Effect of Behavior and Emergency Broadcast

In first experiment, we only use two variables to split clusters: if received emergency broadcast (EBR, 1 if received and 0 otherwise) and behavior. Here, apart from the six behavior options mentioned in the previous section, behavior variable also includes two categories indicating if an agent is in healthcare location (in HC loc) and if it is out of area.

We try three different values of δ: 1, 2, and 5. Figure 5 shows number of clusters for different values of threshold. As higher values of δ can only identify sudden changes in the outcomes, $\delta = 5$ only identifies changes when agents die. We compare the causal states identified by other two threshold values next.

We save the compressed trajectories in a database table along with the expected value of final health state. This table can be used to query any subpopulation for the outcome of interest. For example, Identify transitions by iteration 6 (within first hour) where the expected final health state is improved, order by expected improvement in descending order. Top results for $\delta = 2$ and $\delta = 1$ are as shown in Tables 1 and 2, respectively.

Here, $\delta = 2$ shows that being at healthcare location and out of area are important for improving health outcomes. As expected, $\delta = 1$ shows more gradual transitions and shows that evacuation is also important from health perspective. It is evacuation behavior that leads to out of area.

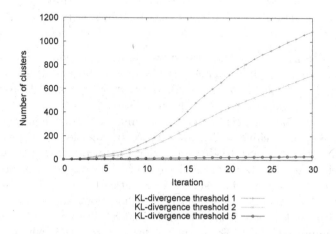

Fig. 5. Number of clusters when considering EBR and behavior only.

Table 1. Effect of EBR and behavior, $\delta = 2$

Rank	Iteration	EBR	Behavior
1	2	0	out of area
2	3	0	out of area
3	5	0	in HC loc
4	6	0	in HC loc

Table 2. Effect of EBR and behavior, $\delta = 1$

Rank	Iteration	EBR	Behavior
1	2	0	out of area
2	3	0	out of area
3	6	0	in HC loc
4	4	1	out of area
5	4	1	in HC loc
6	3	0	evacuation
7	4	0	out of area
8	2	0	evacuation
9	5	0	in HC loc

7.2 Effects of Other Variables

Here, apart from EBR and behavior, we also include current health state, radiation exposure level (with four levels: low, medium, high, and very high), if received treatment, and distance from ground zero (with three levels (based on damage zones as described in [4]): less than 0.6 miles, between 0.6 and 1 mile, and greater than 1 mile). We set $\delta = 5$ and evaluate four queries as below:

Query 1: Identify top 10 transitions by iteration 10 where current health state remains same (so improvement is not due to current health state) but the expected final health state is improved, order by expected improvement in descending order. Top results are as shown in Table 3.

Results show that for agents who are within 1 mile of ground zero, are in health state 4 or 5, reaching healthcare location by iteration 10 helps improving health, even if the exposure level is high. Here, the value of treatment variable is zero which means that these agents have reached healthcare location but have not yet received treatment. This suggests that atleast initially (within first 3 h) there are not long queues at these healthcare locations and so once an agent reaches healthcare location, it is quite likely that it will receive treatment which leads to an improved health. For agents in healthstate 5 to 7, who are far from ground zero though with medium exposure, getting out of area helps. Also, for agents in health state 7, who are far from ground zero, with medium exposure,

Table 3. Top results for query 1.

Rank	Iteration	Health state	EBR	Behavior	Radiation exposure	Treatment	Distance from ground zero
1	8	5	0	in HC loc	high	0	>0.6 mile, <1 mile
2	8	7	1	panic	medium	0	>1 mile
3	10	5	0	out of area	medium	0	>1 mile
4	9	6	0	out of area	medium	0	>1 mile
5	4	4	0	in HC loc	high	0	>0.6 mile, <1 mile
6	7	7	0	out of area	medium	0	>1 mile
7	3	4	0	in HC loc	high	0	>0.6 mile, <1 mile
8	8	7	0	out of area	medium	0	>1 mile
9	8	6	0	out of area	medium	0	>1 mile
10	9	7	0	out of area	medium	0	>1 mile

and panicing, receiving EBR helps (as it provides information about the event and recommends sheltering).

Please note that the algorithm only finds states that affect the final outcomes significantly. Interpretation of the results requires some domain knowledge. For example, it is our knowledge that suggest that reaching healthcare location helps even if the exposure to radiation is high, not receiving high radiation exposure at healthcare location.

Next we identify states that reduce the expected health state by iteration 10.

Query 2: Identify top 10 transitions by iteration 10 where current health state remains same (so reduction is not due to current health state) but the expected final health state is reduced, order by expected reduction in descending order. Top results are as shown in Table 4.

For agents who are currently in a full health, close to ground zero, and have high exposure level, doing household reconstitution (HRO) reduces their expected outcome. Even if the current health state is good, this accounts for the delayed effect of radiation. For people who are already in low health (health state 3), panicing or seeking healthcare (which makes them travel to healthcare location and exposed to more radiation) deteriorates expected health state, even if far from ground zero.

For people who are close to ground zero (within 0.6 mile from ground zero which is a severe damage zone [4]), the likelihood of survival is very low while for people who are further than 1 mile (in light damage zone [4]), though they may have minor injuries, they can survive by themselves. However, survival is more complicated between 0.6 to 1 mile (defined as medium damage zone) and hence next we run queries to see what people who started between 0.6 to 1 mile did that improved or reduced their expected final health.

Table 4. Top results for query 2.

Rank	Iteration	Health state	EBR	Behavior	Radiation exposure	Treatment	Distance from ground zero
1	10	3	0	HC-seeking	low	0	>1 mile
2	9	3	0	HC-seeking	low	0	>1 mile
3	7	7	0	HRO	high	0	<0.6 mile
4	5	3	0	panic	low	0	>1 mile
5	5	3	0	HC-seeking	low	0	>1 mile
6	4	3	0	HC-seeking	low	0	>1 mile
7	9	7	0	HRO	high	0	<0.6 mile
8	8	7	0	HRO	high	0	<0.6 mile
9	4	3	0	panic	high	0	>1 mile
10	7	3	0	panic	high	0	>1 mile

Table 5. Top results for query 3.

Rank	Iteration	Health state	EBR	Behavior	Radiation exposure	Treatment	Distance from ground zero
1	29	5	0	Shelter	medium	0	>0.6 mile, <1 mile
2	24	5	0	Shelter	medium	0	>0.6 mile, <1 mile
3	25	5	0	Shelter	medium	0	>0.6 mile, <1 mile
4	4	4	0	in HC loc	high	0	>0.6 mile, <1 mile
5	21	6	0	Shelter	low	1	>0.6 mile, <1 mile
6	3	4	0	in HC loc	high	0	>0.6 mile, <1 mile
7	14	5	0	Shelter	medium	0	>0.6 mile, <1 mile
8	23	5	0	Shelter	medium	0	>0.6 mile, <1 mile
9	4	5	0	in HC loc	low	0	>0.6 mile, <1 mile
10	3	5	0	in HC loc	medium	0	>0.6 mile, <1 mile

Query 3: For people who started between 0.6 and 1 mile, identify top 10 transitions where current health state remains same and current distance is less than 1 mile (so improvement is not due to current health state or current distance) but the expected final health state is improved, order by expected improvement in descending order. Top results are as shown in Table 5.

Results show that for people who started between 0.6 and 1 mile, reaching healthcare location early on (within first hour) helps improving expected final health, even if moderately injured (health state 4) and have high radiation exposure. For people with minor injury (health state 5) and with medium exposure to radiation, sheltering later on helps. Please not that eventhough our algorithm suggests so, it is not just sheltering in these particular iterations (14, 23, 24, 25

Table 6. Top results for query 4.

Rank	Iteration	Health state	EBR	Behavior	Radiation exposure	Treatment	Distance from ground zero
1	9	3	0	HC-seeking	low	0	>1 mile
2	7	7	0	HRO	high	0	<0.6 mile
3	17	7	0	Aid & assist	high	0	<0.6 mile
4	12	3	0	HC-seeking	low	0	>1 mile
5	4	3	0	HC-seeking	low	0	>1 mile
6	9	7	0	HRO	high	0	<0.6 mile
7	8	7	0	HRO	high	0	<0.6 mile
8	4	3	0	Panic	low	0	>1 mile
9	5	7	0	HRO	high	0	>0.6 mile, <1 mile
10	3	3	0	HC-seeking	low	0	>1 mile

or 29) that helps but it is sheltering for a long period prior to and upto these iterations which improves expected health. This is because currently our algorithm does not detect effects of a sequence of particular actions (e.g., sheltering for a long period of time) and we would like to adapt it in future for detecting effects of sequential actions.

Query 4: For people who started between 0.6 and 1 mile, identify top 10 transitions where current health state remains same (so reduction is not due to current health state) but the expected final health state is reduced, order by expected reduction in descending order. Top results are as shown in Table 6.

For people who started between 0.6 and 1 mile, who are currently in full health (health state 7) and with medium radiation exposure, household reconstitution and aid & assist reduces their expected final health. While for people who are already in low health (health state 3), though with low radiation exposure, panicing or seeking healthcare reduces health. This is because these behavior make them go outside looking for information, family members, other injured people, or nearest healthcare locations, exposing them to further radiation.

We see, in the above queries, that a number of meaningful states have been discovered by the summary.

8   Conclusion

As large-scale and complex simulations are becoming common, there is a need for methods to effectively summarize results from a simulation run. Here, we present a simulation summarization problem as a problem of extracting causal states (including actions) from agents' trajectories. We present an algorithm that identifies states that change the probability distributions over final outcomes. Such causal states compress agent trajectories in such a way that only states that change the distribution of final outcomes significantly are extracted.

These extracted trajectories can be stored in a database and queried. A threshold on effect size is used to specify what change is considered significant. Higher value of this threshold identify states that cause sudden changes in final outcomes while smaller values can identify gradual changes.

We present a toy example to show the effectiveness of our algorithm and then apply it to a large-scale simulation of the aftermath of a disaster in a major urban area. It identifies being in a healthcare location, sheltering, evacuation, and being out of the area as states that improve health outcomes while panic, household reconstitution, and healthcare-seeking as states (behaviors) that worsen health.

There are several directions for future work. Summary representations can be used to compare simulations with different parameter settings to identify if parameter changes result in changes in causal mechanisms. Summary representations can potentially also be used for anomaly detection.

Acknowledgments. We thank our external collaborators and members of the Network Dynamics and Simulation Science Lab (NDSSL) for their suggestions and comments. This work has been supported in part by DTRA CNIMS Contract HDTRA1-11-D-0016-0001, DTRA Grant HDTRA1-11-1-0016, NIH MIDAS Grant 5U01GM070694-11, NIH Grant 1R01GM109718, NSF NetSE Grant CNS-1011769, and NSF SDCI Grant OCI-1032677.

References

1. Adiga, A., Mortveit, H.S., Wu, S.: Route stability in large-scale transportation models. In: Main 2013: The Workshop on Multiagent Interaction Networks at AAMAS 2013, Saint Paul, Minnesota, USA (2013)
2. Barrett, C., Beckman, R., Berkbigler, K., Bisset, K., Bush, B., Campbell, K., Eubank, S., Henson, K., Hurford, J., Kubicek, D., Marathe, M., Romero, P., Smith, J., Smith, L., Speckman, P., Stretz, P., Thayer, G., Eeckhout, E., Williams, M.D.: TRANSIMS: transportation analysis simulation system. Technical report LA-UR-00-1725. An earlier version appears as a 7 part technical report series LA-UR-99-1658 and LA-UR-99-2574 to LA-UR-99-2580, Los Alamos National Laboratory Unclassified Report (2001)
3. Barrett, C., Eubank, S., Marathe, A., Marathe, M., Swarup, S.: Synthetic information environments for policy informatics: a distributed cognition perspective. In: Johnston, E. (ed.) Governance in the Information Era: Theory and Practice of Policy Informatics, pp. 267–284. Routledge, New York (2015)
4. Buddemeier, B.R., Valentine, J.E., Millage, K.K., Brandt, L.D., Region, N.C.: Key response planning factors for the aftermath of nuclear terrorism. Technical report LLNL-TR-512111, Lawrence Livermore National Lab, November 2011
5. Chandan, S., Saha, S., Barrett, C., Eubank, S., Marathe, A., Marathe, M., Swarup, S., Vullikanti, A.K.: Modeling the interactions between emergency communications and behavior in the aftermath of a disaster. In: The International Conference on Social Computing, Behavioral-Cultural Modeling, and Prediction (SBP), 2–5 April 2013, Washington DC, USA (2013)
6. Crutchfield, J.P., Ellison, C.J., Mahoney, J.R.: Time's barbed arrow: irreversibility, crypticity, and stored information. Phys. Rev. Lett. **103**(9), 094101 (2009)

7. Crutchfield, J.P., Young, K.: Inferring statistical complexity. Phys. Rev. Lett. **63**(2), 105–108 (1989)
8. Ellison, C.J., Mahoney, J.R., Crutchfield, J.P.: Prediction, retrodiction, and the amount of information stored in the present. J. Stat. Phys. **136**(6), 1005–1034 (2009)
9. Ferguson, N.M., Cummings, D.A.T., Cauchemez, S., Fraser, C., Riley, S., Meeyai, A., Iamsirithaworn, S., Burke, D.S.: Strategies for containing an emerging influenza pandemic in Southeast Asia. Nature **437**, 209–214 (2005)
10. Goldman, C.V., Zilberstein, S.: Communication-based decomposition mechanisms for decentralized MDPs. J. Artif. Int. Res. **32**(1), 169–202 (2008)
11. Marshall, B.D.L., Galea, S.: Formalizing the role of agent-based modeling in causal inference and epidemiology. Am. J. Epidemiol. **181**(2), 92–99 (2015)
12. Meliou, A., Gatterbauer, W., Halpern, J.Y., Koch, C., Moore, K.F., Suciu, D.: Causality in databases. IEEE Data Eng. Bull. **33**(3), 59–67 (2010)
13. Meliou, A., Gatterbauer, W., Moore, K.F., Suciu, D.: Why so? or why no? Functional causality for explaining query answers. In: Proceedings of the 4th International Workshop on Management of Uncertain Data (MUD), pp. 3–17 (2010)
14. Parikh, N., Swarup, S., Stretz, P.E., Rivers,C.M., Lewis, B.L., Marathe, M.V., Eubank, S.G., Barrett, C.L., Lum, K., Chungbaek, Y.: Modeling human behavior in the aftermath of a hypothetical improvised nuclear detonation. In: Proceedings of the International Conference on Autonomous Agents and Multiagent Systems (AAMAS), Saint Paul, MN, USA, May 2013
15. Parikh, N., Youssef, M., Swarup, S., Eubank, S.: Modeling the effect of transient populations on epidemics in Washington DC. Sci. Rep. **3**, Article no. 3152 (2013)
16. Shahaf, D., Guestrin, C., Horvitz, E.: Metro maps of science. In: Proceedings of the KDD (2012)
17. Shahaf, D., Guestrin, C., Horvitz, E.: Trains of thought: generating information maps. In: Proceedings of the WWW, Lyon, France (2012)
18. Shalizi, C.R., Crutchfield, J.P.: Computational mechanics: pattern and prediction, structure and simplicity. J. Stat. Phys. **104**(3/4), 817–879 (2001)
19. Shalizi, C.R., Shalizi, K.L.: Blind construction of optimal nonlinear recursive predictors for discrete sequences. In: Chickering, M., Halpern, J. (eds.) Proceedings of the Twentieth Conference on Uncertainty in Artificial Intelligence, Banff, Canada, pp. 504–511 (2004)
20. Sutton, R., Precup, D., Singh, S.: Between MDPs and semi-MDPs: a framework for temporal abstraction in reinforcement learning. Artif. Intell. **112**(1–2), 181–211 (1999)
21. Ver Steeg, G., Galstyan, A.: Information transfer in social media. In: Proceedings of WWW (2012)
22. Walloth, C., Gurr, J.M., Schmidt, J.A. (eds.): Understanding Complex Urban Systems: Multidisciplinary Approaches to Modeling. Springer, New York (2014)
23. Wein, L.M., Choi, Y., Denuit, S.: Analyzing evacuation versus shelter-in-place strategies after a terrorist nuclear detonation. Risk Anal. **30**(6), 1315–1327 (2010)

Augmenting Agent Computational Environments with Quantitative Reasoning Modules and Customizable Bridge Rules

Stefania Costantini[1] and Andrea Formisano[2(✉)]

[1] DISIM, Università di L'Aquila, L'Aquila, Italy
[2] DMI, Università di Perugia, GNCS-INdAM, Perugia, Italy
`formis@dmi.unipg.it`

Abstract. There are many examples where large amount of data might be potentially accessible to an agent, but the agent is constrained by the available budget since access to knowledge bases is subject to fees. There are also several activities that an agent might perform on the web where one or more stages imply the payment of fees: for instance, buying resources in a cloud computing context where the objective of the agent is to obtain the best possible configuration of a certain application withing given budget constraints. In this paper we consider the software-engineering problem of how to practically empower agents with the capability to perform such kind of reasoning in a uniform and principled way. To this aim, we enhance the ACE component-based agent architecture by means of a device for practical and computationally affordable quantitative reasoning, whose results actually determine one or more courses of agent's actions, also according to policies/preferences.

1 Introduction

There are many examples where large amount of data might be potentially accessible to an agent, but the agent is constrained by the available budget since access to knowledge bases is subject to fees. There are also several activities that an agent may perform on the web on behalf of an user where one or more stages imply the payment of fees. An important example is that of buying resources in a cloud-computing context, where the objective of the agent is to obtain the best possible configuration for performing certain tasks in the sense of maximizing performance and minimizing costs, that can anyway stay withing given budget constraints. The work [33] identifies the problem that an agent faces when it has limited budget and costly queries to perform. In order to model such situations, the authors propose a special resource-aware modal logic so as to be able to represent and reason about what is possible to do with a certain available budget. The logic can be adapted to reason separately about cost and time limitation, though an integration is envisaged. Interesting as it is, this work constitutes a good starting point but it presents two problems: (i) such kind of modal logic is computationally hard (though this aspect is not discussed in the aforementioned paper) and thus it can hardly constitute the basis for practical tools;

© Springer International Publishing AG 2016
N. Osman and C. Sierra (Eds.): AAMAS 2016 WS, Visionary Papers, LNAI 10003, pp. 104–121, 2016.
DOI: 10.1007/978-3-319-46840-2_7

(ii) the axiomatic system of [33] allows one to prove that something can or cannot be achieved within a certain cost. However, an agent needs, in general, to become aware of how goals might possibly be achieved, and should be enabled to choose the best course of action according to its own policies/preferences.

In this paper we tackle some issues related to this problem. First, we consider the software-engineering problem of how to practically empower agents with the capability to perform such kind of reasoning in a uniform and principled way. Second, we consider the adoption of a reasoning device that enables an agent, which may have several costly objectives, to establish which are the alternative possibilities within the available budget, and to select, based upon its preferences, the goals to achieve and the resources to spend, and finally to implement its choice.

Concerning the first aspect, we enhance the Agent Computational Environment (ACE) framework [13], which is a software engineering methodology for designing intelligent logical agents in a modular way. Therefore, in this paper we refer to agent-oriented languages and frameworks which are rooted in Computational Logic. Modules composing an agent interact, in ACE, via *bridge rules* in the style of the Multi-Context Systems (MCS) approach [7,8,10]. Such rules take the form of conjunctive queries where each conjunct constitutes a sub-query which is posed to a specific module. Thus, the result is obtained by combining partial results obtained from different sources. The enhancements that we propose here for ACE are based upon the flexible agent-tailored modalities for bridge rules application and for knowledge elaboration defined for the DACMACS framework (Data-Aware Commitment-based managed Multi-Agent-Context Systems), which is aimed at designing data-aware multi-agent-context systems [14,15]. There, bridge rules are proactively triggered upon specific conditions and the obtained knowledge is reactively elaborated via a *management function* which generalizes the analogous MCS concept.

Second, we extend ACEs so as to include modules for specialized forms of reasoning, including quantitative reasoning. For this kind of reasoning we suggest to adopt the RASP framework [16,17,19], which is based upon Answer Set Programming (ASP) and hence it is computationally affordable and reasonably efficient. We show the suitability of such approach by discussing a case study, that will constitute the leading example throughout the paper.

A strong innovation that this paper proposes is that, after obtaining from a reasoning module the description of possible courses of actions, bridge rules "patterns" can be specialized and activated so as to put them into action. This feature is made possible by an enhanced flexible ACE semantics.

The resulting framework can be seen as a creative blend of existing technologies, with some relevant formal and practical extensions. Partially specified bridge rules and their dynamic customization and activation is an absolute novelty and constitutes a relevant advance over MCSs versions, applications and extensions: in fact, bridge rules have been so far conceived as predefined, ground and not amenable to any adaptation. Beyond quantitative reasoning, such more general bridge rules may constitute a powerful flexible device in many applications.

The paper is organized as follows. Section 2 presents a case study that will constitute the leading example throughout the paper. In Sect. 3 we discuss the quantitative reasoning device we suggest to exploit. Sections 4 and 5 present the enhanced ACE framework and illustrate, on the case study, the dynamic customization of bridge rules. Section 6 introduces the extended ACE semantics and for completeness we provide in Sect. 7 an actual RASP formalization. Concluding remarks are given in Sect. 8.

2   Specification of the Case Study

In this section we provide the specification of a case study which we will adopt in the rest of the paper for the illustration of the proposed enhancements to the ACE framework. In Sect. 7 we will present a realistic implementation in a specific existing approach for quantitative reasoning, shortly introduced in the next section.

We consider a student, that will be represented by an agent which can be seen as her "personal assistant agent". Upon completing the secondary school, she wishes to apply for enrollment to an US university. Each application has a cost, and the tuition fee will have to be paid in case of admission and enrollment. The student has an allotted maximum budget for both. Thus the agent, on behalf of the student, has to reason about: (i) the universities to which an application will be sent; (ii) the university where to enroll, in case a choice can be made.

Actually, the proposed case study is seen as a prototype of a wide number of situations where two kinds of quantitative reasoning are required:

1. The cost of knowledge, as in practical terms a student applies in order to know whether she is admitted.
2. Reasoning under budget limits, as a student may send an application only if: (i) she can afford the fees related to the application; (ii) in case of admission, she can then afford the tuition fees.

If a solution is found considering her preferences and her budget, she will then be able to apply and, if admitted, to enroll. In case more than an option is available, a choice is required so as to select the "best" one according to some criteria.

Without any pretension to precision, we consider the steps that a student has to undergo in order to apply for admission:

1. Pass the general SAT test.
2. Pass the specific SAT test for the subject of interest (such as Literature, Mathematics, Chemistry, etc.)
3. In case of foreign students, pass the TOEFL test.
4. Fill the general application on the application website (that we call college-org).
5. Send the SAT results to the universities of interest.
6. Complete the application for the universities of interest.

All these steps are subject to the payment of fees, which are fixed (the fee is independent of the university) for steps 1–4 and depend upon the selected university for steps 5–6. In the example we assume that the student has a budget for the application (say 1500 US dollars) and a limit about the tuition fee she is able to pay (say 22000 US dollars per year). However, she has a list of preferred universities, and within such list she would apply only to universities whose ranking is higher than a threshold. Additionally, since she likes basketball, all other things being equal (*ceteris paribus*) she would prefer universities with the best rankings of the basketball team.

3   Resource-Based Reasoning

In the case study, the student's personal assistant agent needs the support of some kind of quantitative reasoning module. Such module should in general be able to provide the agent, given one or more objectives, with a description of the different ways of achieving the objectives while staying within a budget. A desirable property of the reasoner would be that of allowing preferences and constraints to be expressed about objectives to achieve and modalities for achieving them. A mandatory requisite is the ability to perform such reasoning in a computationally affordable way.

In knowledge representation and reasoning, forms of quantitative reasoning are possible, for example, in Linear Logics and Description Logics. For Linear Logic in particular, several programming languages and theorem provers based on its principles exist (cf. [16] for a discussion). In this paper we adopt RASP (Resource-based ASP) [17,19], which has in fact been proven in [18] to be equivalent to an interesting fragment of Linear Logic, specifically, to an empowered Horn fragment allowing for a default negation that Linear Logic does not provide (though still remaining within an NP-complete framework). RASP extends ASP, which is a well-known logic programming paradigm where a program may have several "models", called "answer sets", each one representing a possible interpretation of the situation described by the program (cf., among many, [29]). In particular, RASP explicitly introduces in ASP the notion of *resource*, and supports both formalization and quantitative reasoning on consumption and production of resources. RASP also provides complex preferences about spending resources (and in this it is different from the several approaches to preferences that have been defined for ASP, see e.g., [2,6,11,25] and the references therein). Compared with the "competitors", RASP represents possible different uses of a resource and non-determinism in general by means of different answer sets, rather than exploring the various possibilities via backtracking in a Prolog-like fashion. The RASP inference engine is based upon publicly available ASP solvers [35] that are remarkably well-performing and subject of intensive research and development. After the seminal work of [34] one can mention [1,22,26,28,31,32], among the most recent developments. Specifically, RASP execution is based upon a front-end module called *Raspberry* which translates RASP programs (via a non-trivial process, see [19] for the details) into ASP. The resulting program can be executed by common ASP solvers.

As a side note, we observe that the clasp ASP solver allows one to add external functions to ASP programs. This is done by defining deterministic functions in a scripting language such as lua or python. Relying on this possibility, one might envisage a re-implementation of the RASP framework exploiting such feature of this specific ASP solver, instead of performing a translation from RASP into ASP, as done in Raspberry. Another recently proposed extension of ASP is H-ASP [12], where propositional reasoning is combined with external sources of numerical computation. The main aim of H-ASP is to allow users to reason about a dynamical system by simulating its possible evolutions along a discretized timeline. The external computations are used to compute the system transitions and may involve both continuous and discrete numerical variables. The expressive power of the resulting framework directly depends on the kind of numerical tasks one integrates, and the computational complexity can exceed NP. Clearly, thanks to the generality of ACE, one could integrate modules based on H-ASP in the ACE framework, similarly to what done for RASP. However, in the case of RASP we stay within NP and directly rely on common "pure-ASP" engines without the need of integrating (and encoding) further computational services.

We are not aware of other reasoning frameworks that combine logic and quantitative techniques, apart from the one proposed in [33], which however is not implemented and, as mentioned, in its present form can hardly admit a computationally affordable version. So, there is nowadays no competitor approach to RASP in practical logic-based quantitative reasoning and its applications in agent systems.

4   Enhancing the ACE Framework

The ACE framework as defined in [13] considers an agent as composed of:

(1) the "main" agent program;
(2) a number of Event-Action modules for Complex Event Processing;
(3) a number of external contexts the agent can access in order to gather information.

ACE is therefore a highly modular architecture, where the composing modules communicate via *bridge rules* (to be seen below) in the style of Multi-Context Systems (MCSs) [7,8,10]. MCSs constitute in fact a particularly interesting approach for modeling information exchange among heterogeneous sources because, within a neat formal definition, it is able to accommodate real heterogeneity of sources by explicitly representing their different representation languages and semantics. The same holds for ACEs, where: external contexts are understood as in MCS, i.e., they can be queried but cannot be accessed in any other way; and where "local" agent's modules (main agent program and event-action modules) can be defined in any agent-oriented computational-logic-based programming language, such as, e.g., DALI, AgentSpeak, GOAL, 3APL, METATEM, KGP, etc. (see [3–5,20,21,24,27,30] and the references therein), or also in other logic formalisms such as, e.g., ASP (see [29] and the references therein).

In the present setting, we augment the framework with a set of *Reasoning Modules*, say $R_1, \ldots, R_q$, $q \geq 0$, that we see as specialized modules which are able to perform specific forms of reasoning by means of the best suitable formalism/technique/device. Among such modules we may have quantitative reasoning modules. Therefore, an (enhanced) Agent Computational Environment $\mathcal{A}$ is now defined as a tuple

$$\langle A, M_1, \ldots, M_r, C_1, \ldots, C_s, R_1, \ldots, R_q \rangle$$

where module A is the "basic agent", i.e., an agent program written in any agent-oriented language. The "overall" agent is obtained by equipping the basic agent with the following facilities. The M_is are "Event-Action modules", which are special modules aimed at Complex Event Processing, that allow the agent to flexibly interact with a complex changing environment. The R_js are "Reasoning modules", which are specialized in specific reasoning tasks. The C_ks are contexts in the sense of MCSs, i.e., external data/knowledge sources that the agent is able to query about some subject, but upon which it has no further knowledge and no control: this means that the agent is aware of the "role" of contexts in the sense of the kind of knowledge they are able to provide, but is unable in general to provide a description of their behavior/contents or to affect/modify them in any way.

Interaction among ACE's components occurs via *bridge rules*, inspired by those in MCS. They can be seen as Datalog-like queries where however each sub-query can be posed to a different module. In MCS, bridge rules have, in general, the following form:

$$s \leftarrow (c_1 : p_1), \ldots, (c_j : p_j), not\,(c_{j+1} : p_{j+1}), \ldots, not\,(c_m : p_m).$$

The meaning is that the rule is *applicable* and s can thus be added to the consequences of a module's knowledge base whenever each atom p_r, $r \leq j$, belongs to the consequences of module c_r (that can be a context or an event-action module, or the basic agent), while instead each atom p_w, $j < w \leq m$, does not belong to the consequences of c_w. Practical run-time bridge-rule applicability will consist in posing query p_i to context c_i. In case for some of the c_is the context is omitted, then the agent is querying its own knowledge base. The part $(c_1 : p_1), \ldots, (c_j : p_j)$ is the *positive body* of the rule, while the remaining part is the *negative body*.

We introduce the following restriction on bridge rules bodies: the basic agent A can query any other module (and, clearly, if it is situated in a MAS context it can communicate with other agents according to some kind of protocol). The M_is and the R_is can query external contexts and the basic agent. Contexts can only query other contexts, i.e., they cannot access agent's knowledge. We also assume (for simplicity and without loss of generality) that bridge-rule heads are unique, i.e., there are never two bridge rules with the same head.

In Managed MCSs the conclusion s, which represents the "bare" result of the application of the bridge rule, becomes $o(s)$ where o is a special operator, whose semantics is provided by a module-specific *management function*. The meaning is that the result computed by a bridge rule is not blindly incorporated into the "target" module knowledge base. Rather, it is filtered, adapted, modified and elaborated by an operator that can possibly perform any elaboration, e.g. evaluation, format conversion, belief revision. To the extreme, the new knowledge item can even be discarded if not deemed to be useful.

In the basic agent we adopt, with suitable adaptations, the special agent-oriented modalities introduced in DACMACS. There, bridge-rule activation and management-function application has been adapted to the specific nature of agent systems. First, while bridge rules in MCSs are conceived to be applied whenever applicable (they can be seen, therefore, as a reactive device), DAC-MACS provides a proactive application upon specific conditions. Second, the incorporation of bridge rule results via the management function is separated from bridge-rule application. In particular, bridge-rule application is determined by a *trigger rule* of the form

$$Q \text{ enables } A(\hat{x})$$

where: Q is a query to agent's internal knowledge-base and $A(\hat{x})$ is the conclusion of one of agent's bridge rules. If query Q (the "trigger") evaluates to true, then the bridge rule is allowed to be applied. A trigger rule is proactive in the sense that the application of a bridge rule is enabled only if and when the agent during its operation concludes Q. The bridge rule will be actually applied according to agent's internal control modalities, and will return its results in $\hat{x}$. The result(s) $\hat{x}$ returned by a bridge rule with head $A(\hat{x})$ will then be exploited via a *bridge-update rule* of the following form (where $\beta(\hat{x})$ specifies the operator, management function and actions to be applied to $\hat{x}$):

$$\textbf{upon } A(\hat{x}) \textbf{ then } \beta(\hat{x})$$

We propose a relevant improvement concerning bridge rules. In particular, in MCSs bridge rules are by definition ground, i.e., they do not contain variables: in [9], it is literally stated that [in their examples] they *"use for readability and succinctness schematic bridge rules with variables (upper case letters and '_' [the 'anonymous' variable]) which range over associated sets of constants; they stand for all respective instances (obtainable by value substitution)"* where however such "placeholder" variables occur only in the p_is while instead the c_is (contexts' names) are constants. This is a serious expressive limitation, that we have tackled in related work. In fact, we admit variables in both the p_is in bridge-rule bodies and in the head s, to be instantiated at run-time by the queried contexts. We also admit contexts in the body to be selected from a directory according to their *role*. Here, we propose a further relevant enhancement: we allow contexts occurring in the body of the bridge rules of the main agent A to be instantiated via results returned by ACE's other modules. Such bridge rules will have this form:

$$s \leftarrow (\mathcal{C}_1 : p_1), \dots, (\mathcal{C}_j : p_j), not\,(\mathcal{C}_{j+1} : p_{j+1}), \dots, not\,(\mathcal{C}_m : p_m).$$

where each C_i can be either a plain constant (as before) or an expression of the form $m_i(k_i)$ that we call *context designator*, which is a term where m_i can be seen as a(n arbitrary) meta-function indicating the required instantiation, and k_i is a constant that can be seen as analogous to a Skolem constant. Such term indicates the kind of context to which it must be substituted before bridge-rule execution, so it might be, for instance, *university*(u), *student_data*(sd), *treatment_database*(d), *diagnostic_expert_system*(de). There is no fixed format, rather it is intended as a designation of the required-for knowledge source, that can be either a knowledge repository or a reasoning module.

A bridge rule including context designators will be indicated as a *bridge rule pattern*, as it stands for its versions obtained by substituting the designators with actual contexts' names. Bridge-rule instantiation may be performed by an agent also by means of bridge-update rules, that are in charge of replacing designators with actual suitable knowledge sources. We assume that bridge-update rules' conclusions $\beta(\hat{x})$ are, in general, conjunctions, possibly including actions of the following distinguished forms:

(i) *record*(*Item*), which simply adds *Item* to A's knowledge base; *Item* can be either the "plain" bridge-rule result, or it can be obtained by processing such result via the evaluation of other atoms in $\beta(\hat{x})$;

(ii) *incorporate*(*Item*), which performs some more involved elaboration for incorporating *Item* into A's knowledge base. Notice that *incorporate* is meant as a distinguished predicate, to be defined according to the specific application domain; in particular, it is intended to implement some proper form of belief revision.

(iii) *instantiate*($S, m_i(k_i), L$) which, for every bridge rule ρ with head matching with S, considers the context designator $m_i(k_i)$ and a list L of constants, and generates as many instances of ρ as obtained by substituting $m_i(k_i)$ (wherever it occurs) by elements of L. A bridge rules will be potentially applicable whenever all contexts in its body are constants, i.e., whenever all context designators, if present, have been replaced by actual contexts' names.

(iv) *enable*(S, Q), which enables the application of a potentially applicable bridge rule ρ whose head matches with S and with associated trigger rule of the form Q **enables** S. It does so by generating its trigger, i.e., by adding Q as a new fact.

The combination of the introduction of both context designators and the *instantiate* actions extends the expressiveness of the bridge-rule approach: even allowing variables in place of contexts' names would not allow for the specific customization performed here. The purpose of defining context designators as terms is that of avoiding the requirement of the involved domains to be finite. In fact, context designators can denote values in an infinite domain, where, however, a finite number of *instantiate* actions generates a finite number of customized bridge rules. Notice that the computational complexity of the overall framework depends upon the computational complexity of the involved modules. In [8,9] significant sample cases are reported.

5   Case Study: Bridge Rules Customization and Application

In order to explain the features that we have introduced so far we apply them to the case study. The agent acting on behalf of a prospective college student would for instance include the following trigger rule:

$$wish\_to\_enroll(\textit{Universities}, \textit{Budget})\ \textbf{enables}$$
$$chooseU(\textit{Universities}, \textit{Budget}, \textit{Selected\_UniversitiesL})$$

The meaning is that the agent is supposed to be able to conclude at some stage of its operation $wish\_to\_enroll(\textit{Universities}, \textit{Budget})$, where $\textit{Universities}$ is the list of universities which are of interest for the student, and $\textit{Budget}$ is the budget which is available for completing the application procedure. Whenever this conclusion is reached, the trigger rule is proactively activated, thus enabling a suitable bridge rule. This bridge rule exploits a quantitative reasoning module and might correspond to this simple bridge rule pattern, where however there is the relative context designator $qr\_mod(mymod)$ to be instantiated.

$$chooseU(\textit{Universities}, \textit{Budget}, \textit{Selected\_UniversitiesL}) \leftarrow$$
$$qr\_mod(mymod) : chooseU(\textit{Universities}, \textit{Budget}, \textit{Selected\_UniversitiesL})$$

Let us assume that the agent somehow (dynamically) instantiates this designator, e.g., to the name of a RASP module $rasp\_mod$, thus obtaining:

$$chooseU(\textit{Universities}, \textit{Budget}, \textit{Selected\_UniversitiesL}) \leftarrow$$
$$rasp\_mod : chooseU(\textit{Universities}, \textit{Budget}, \textit{Selected\_UniversitiesL})$$

The RASP module, invoked via a suitable plugin, will return its results in $\textit{Selected\_UniversitiesL}$, that will be a list representing the potential options for sending applications while staying within the given budget. A relevant role is performed by the corresponding bridge-update rule, which may have the form:

upon $chooseU(\textit{Universities}, \textit{Budget}, \textit{Selected\_UniversitiesL})$ **then**
   $preferred\_subject(\textit{Subject})$,
   $instantiate(apply(\textit{Univ}, \textit{ResponseUniv}), myuniv(u), \textit{Selected\_UniversitiesL})$,
   $nearest\_sat\_center(Sc),\ nearest\_toefl\_center(Tc)$,
   $instantiate(general\_tests(\textit{Subject}, R1, R2, R3), sat\_center(sc), [Sc])$,
   $instantiate(general\_tests(\textit{Subject}, R1, R2, R3), language\_center(lc), [Tc])$,
   $enable(general\_tests(\textit{Subject}, R1, R2, R3), enabledgentest)$

By evaluating the sub-queries from left to right, as it is usual in Prolog, this rule will determine the preferred subject $\textit{Subject}$, and via an $instantiate$ action it will create several copies of a bridge rule which finalizes the application (see below), namely one copy for each university included in $\textit{Selected\_UniversitiesL}$. Notice that such bridge rules are not enabled yet. Then, the bridge-update rule finds the contexts' names Sc and Lc of nearest SAT and language-test centers respectively, where the student may perform the tests. The subsequent two *instantiate* actions, together with the *enable* action, will instantiate and trigger a suitable bridge rule pattern (shown below). The trigger part is, in particular:

> *enabledgentest.*
> *enabledgentest* **enables** *general_tests(Subject, R1, R2, R3)*

which, as said, enables a bridge rule obtained by the following bridge rule pattern via its specialization to contexts' names Sc and Lc. This bridge rule will take care of performing the general tests (among which the language certification) and filling the general part of the application:

> *general_tests(Subject, R1, R2, R3)* ← *sat_center(sc) : general_SAT_test(R1)*,
> *sat_center(sc) : specific_SAT_test(R2)*,
> *language_center(lc) : language_certification(R3)*,
> *collegeorg : fill_application*

Each test will return its results, which are then dynamically recorded, whenever available, by the bridge-update rule:

> **upon** *general_tests(Subject, R1, R2, R3)* **then** *record(test_res(R1, R2, R3))*

The recording of test results enables, via the following trigger rule, the application of the bridge rules, one for every selected university *Univ*, each of which will: send test the test results to that university; finalize the university-specific part of the application; wait for the response, returned in *ResponseUniv*.

> **upon** *test_res(R1, R2, R3)* **then** *apply(Univ, ResponseUniv)*

The bridge rule pattern from which such bridge rules are obtained is:

> *apply(Univ, ResponseUniv)* ← *test_res(R1, R2, R3)*,
> *myuniv(u) : send_test_results(R1, R2, R3)*,
> *myuniv(u) : complete_application(ResponseUniv)*

The corresponding bridge-update rules, of the form

> **upon** *apply(Univ, ResponseUniv)* **then** *record(response(Univ, Response))*

will record the responses, to allow a choice to be made among the universities that have returned a positive answer. Finally, enrollment must be finalized (code not shown here). Notice that, in the above bridge rules, some elements in the body implicitly involve the execution of specific actions (such as the payment of fees) that may take time to be executed, and may also involve user intervention (e.g., the student must personally and practically go to perform the SAT and TOEFL tests). Such actions have to be specified in the internal definition of the involved module(s), while user interventions emerge from the interaction between the agent and the user. For lack of space we do not discuss plan revision strategies (that might be needed in case of failure of some of the above steps), to be implemented via agent's reactive and proactive features.

6   Semantics

In order to account for heterogeneity of composing modules, in MCSs and then in DACMACSs and in ACEs each module is supposed to be based upon a specific logic. Reporting from [8], a logic L is a triple $(KB_L; Cn_L; ACC_L)$, where KB_L is the set of admissible knowledge bases of L. A knowledge base is a set of KB-elements, or "formulas". Cn_L is the set of acceptable sets of consequences, whose elements are data items or "facts". Such sets can be called "belief sets" or simply "data sets". $ACC_L : KB_L \rightarrow 2^{Cn_L}$ is a function which defines the semantics of L by assigning to each knowledge-base a set of acceptable sets of consequences.

For any of the aforementioned frameworks, consider an instance $\mathcal{A} = \langle A_1, \ldots, A_h \rangle$ composed of h distinct modules, each of which can be either the basic agents, or an event-action module, or a reasoning module, or an external context. Each module is seen as $A_i = (L_i; kb_i; br_i)$ where L_i is a logic, $kb_i \in KB_{L_i}$ is the module's knowledge base and br_i is a set of bridge rules. A data state of $\mathcal{A}$ is a tuple $S = (S_1, \ldots, S_h)$ such that each of the S_is is an element of Cn_i, i.e. a set of consequences derived from A_i's knowledge base according to the logic in which module A_i is defined.

When modules are not considered separately, but rather they are connected via bridge rules, desirable data states, called *equilibria*, are those where bridge-rule application is considered. In MCSs, equilibria are those data states S where each S_i is acceptable according to function ACC_i associated to L_i, taking however bridge rules application into account. Technically, a data state S is an equilibrium iff, for $1 \leq i \leq n$, it holds that $S_i \in ACC_i(mng_i(app(S), kb_i))$. This means that if one takes the knowledge base kb_i associated to module A_i, considers all bridge rules which are applicable in data state S (i.e., S entails their body), applies the rules, applies the management function, it obtains exactly S_i (or at least S_i is one of the possible sets of consequences). Namely, an equilibrium is a data state that encompasses the application of bridge rules. In dynamic environments however, this does not in general imply that a bridge rule is applied only once, and that an equilibrium, once reached, lasts forever (conditions for reachability of equilibria are discussed in literature, see [23] and the references therein). In fact, contexts are in general able to incorporate new data items, e.g., as discussed in [10], the input provided by sensors. Therefore, a bridge rule is in principle re-evaluated whenever a new result can be obtained, thus leading to evolving equilibria.

As DACMACS and ACEs are frameworks for defining agents and multi-agent systems, the interaction with the external environment and with other agents goes beyond simple sensor input and must be explicitly considered. This is done by assuming, similarly to what is done in Linear Temporal Logic, a discrete, linear model of time where each state/time instant can be represented by an integer number. States $t_0, t_1, \ldots$ can be seen as time instants in abstract terms, though in practice we have $t_{i+1} - t_i = \delta$, where δ is the actual interval of time after which we assume a given system to have evolved.

Consider then a notion of *updates*: for $i > 0$, let $\Pi_i = \langle \Pi_{iA_1}, \ldots, \Pi_{iA_h} \rangle$ be a tuple composed of finite updates performed to each module and let

$\Pi = \Pi_1, \Pi_2, \ldots$ be a sequence of such updates performed at time instants $t_1, t_2, \ldots$. Let $\mathcal{U}_E$, for $E \in \{A_1, \ldots, A_h\}$, be the *update operator* that each module employs for incorporating the new information, and let $\mathcal{U}$ be the tuple composed of all these operators. Notice that each $\mathcal{U}_E$, i.e., each module-specific operator, encompasses the treatment of both self-generated updated and updated coming from interaction with an external environment.

In this more general setting data states evolve in time, where a *timed* data state at time T is a tuple $S^T = (S_1^T, \ldots, S_h^T)$ such that each S_i^T is an element of Cn_i at time T. The timed data state S^0 is an equilibrium according the MCSs definition. Later on however, transition from a timed data state to the next one, and consequently the definition of an equilibrium, is determined both by the update operators and by the application of bridge rules. A bridge rule ρ occurring in each composing module is now *potentially applicable* in S^T iff S^T entails its body. However, in the basic agent a potentially applicable bridge rule is applied only when it has been triggered by a trigger rule of the form seen above, i.e., if for some $T' \leq T$ we have that $S^{T'} \models Q$. In any event-action module M instead, a potentially applicable bridge rule is applied only if the module is *active*, i.e., if $S^{T'} \models tr_M$, where tr_M is an *event expression* which triggers the module evaluation (cf. [13]). Therefore, a timed data state of M at time $T+1$ is an equilibrium iff, for $1 \leq i \leq n$, it holds that $S_i^{T+1} \in ACC_i(mng_i(App(S^T), kb_i^{T+1}))$, where $kb_i^{T+1} = \mathcal{U}_i(kb_i^T, \Pi_T^i)$ and App is the extended bridge-rule applicability evaluation function. The meaning is that an equilibrium is now a data state which encompasses bridge rules applicability (with the new criteria) on the updated knowledge base. So, contexts now evolve in time, where we may say that $A_i^0 = (L_i; kb_i; br_i)$ as before, while $A_i^T = (L_i; kb_i^T; br_i)$. As discussed in [14], if both the update operators and the management functions preserve consistency of modules, then conditions for existence of an equilibrium (at some time T) are unchanged w.r.t. MCSs and DACMACS.

Notice that, for each bridge rule which is triggered (and so is applicable) at time T' the state when it is actually applied is not necessarily T', nor $T' + 1$. In fact, a bridge rule becomes potentially applicable whenever a data state entail its body. So, the actual procedural sequence is the following:

- $S^{T'} \models Q$ for some trigger rule concerning bridge rule with conclusion $A(\hat{x})$, and then such a rule is executed at some time $T'' \geq T'$.
- At time $T \geq T''$ the results will be returned by the modules which are queried in the rule body; the case where $T' = T$, i.e., the bridge-rule body succeeds instantaneously, is an ideal extreme which is hardly the case in practice. In fact, internal and external modules may take some (a priori unpredictable) amount of time for returning their results.
- At time T, bridge-rule results will be elaborated by the management function, in our case implemented by the bridge-update rule.

The important aspect that allows us to smoothly incorporate enhanced ACE features in this semantics is that knowledge base updates in an agent are not necessarily determined from the outside. Rather, (part of) an update can also be the result of proactive self-modification. So, the generality and flexibility of ACE's semantics allows us to introduce advanced features without needing substantial modifications.

In particular, we consider bridge rule patterns as elements of agent's knowledge base. A bridge rule pattern will produce new bridge rules only when its context designators will be instantiated. Such instantiation can be seen as a part of a self-modification, i.e., it can be seen as an update. Therefore, for the main agent we now have $A_i^0 = (L_i; kb_i; br_i)$ and $A_i^T = (L_i; kb_i^T; br_i^T)$, where at each subsequent time the set of bridge rule associated to the module can be augmented by newly generated instances. The other definitions remain unchanged. This limited though effective semantic modifications constitute, in our opinion, a successful result of the research work that we present here. In fact, we obtain more general and flexible systems without significantly departing from the original MCSs' semantics, and this grants our approach a fairly general applicability.

7 Case Study: RASP Implementation

Below we discuss how to represent in RASP the case study discussed in Sect. 2. We do not report the full code, that the reader can find on the web site http://www.dmi.unipg.it/formis/raspberry/ (section "Enrollment") where the solver Raspberry can also be obtained.[1] Our aim is to have a glance at how RASP works, and to demonstrate that the proposed approach is not only a more general architecture than basic ACE, but it has indeed a practical counterpart.

RASP code clearly must include a list of facts defining the universities to which the students is potentially interested, the SAT subjects (in general), and the SAT subjects corresponding to Courses (or Schools) available at each university.

```
% Universities
university(theBigUni).      university(theSmallUni).
university(thePinkUni).     university(theBlueUni).
university(theGreenUni).
% SAT subjects
sat_subject(literature).  sat_subject(mathematics).
sat_subject(chemistry).
% SAT subjects in each University
availableSubject(theBigUni, S) :- sat_subject(S).
availableSubject(theGreenUni, S) :- sat_subject(S).
availableSubject(theSmallUni, mathematics).
availableSubject(thePinkUni,  mathematics).
availableSubject(thePinkUni,  literature).
availableSubject(theBlueUni,  mathematics).
availableSubject(theBlueUni,  chemistry).
```

---

[1] Raspberry, the grounder gringo (v.3.0.5), and the solver clasp (v.3.1.3) are used as follows:

```
raspberry_2.6.5 -pp -13 -n 15000 -i enrollment_pref.rasp > enrollment_pref.asp
gringo-3.0.5 enrollment_pref.asp | clasp-3.1.3 0.
```

Below we then list: the tuition fees and the maximum fee allowed; the university rankings and the minimum required; the basketball team ranking, as it constitutes an additional evaluation factor.

```
% Tuition fees
tuitionFee(theBigUni,   21000).  tuitionFee(theSmallUni, 16000).
tuitionFee(thePinkUni,  15000).  tuitionFee(theBlueUni,  25000).
tuitionFee(theGreenUni, 15000).
% Constraint C1:  Tuition fee cannot exceed this threshold
maxTuition(22000).
% University reputation ranking R
reputation(theBigUni,   100).  reputation(theSmallUni,  90).
reputation(thePinkUni,   80).  reputation(theBlueUni,   75).
reputation(theGreenUni,  60).
% Constraint C2:  R must be higher than this threshold
reputationThrs(70).
% BasketballTeam Ranking
extraRank(theSmallUni, 10).  extraRank(theBigUni,   10).
extraRank(thePinkUni,   8).  extraRank(theBlueUni,   8).
extraRank(theGreenUni,  6).
```

The RASP fact below states that we have 1500 dollars, sum intended here as the budget available for completing applications. In general, symbol '#' indicates that an atom represents a resource. The constant before '#', here 'dollar', indicates the (arbitrary) name of the resource. The number after the '#' indicates an amount. In case of a fact, this amount is available initially, and can be then (in general) either consumed or vice versa incremented, as in RASP resource production can also be modeled.

```
% Budget for the application procedure
dollar#1500.
```

Now, the subject of interest and (if applicable) the status as foreign prospective students are indicated. Concerning the English language, nothing needs to be done if the student is not foreign, otherwise the TOEFL fee must be payed for performing the required test (we remind the reader that this RASP program evaluates the necessary expenses, so it is concerned with fees).

```
% My_subject
my_subject(mathematics).
% Omit the following fact if not foreign:
foreign.
% Language prerequisite
languageReqOK :- not foreign.
languageReqOK :- testTOEFLfee, foreign.
```

The universities where to potentially apply are derived according to the preferred subject, and the constraints concerning the university ranking and tuition fee. The student can apply if some university meeting the required requisites is actually found.

```
% Filtering of Universities
canApply(U,S) :- university(U), my_subject(S), reputation(U, R),
    availableSubject(U, S), reputationThrs(Th), R > Th,
    maxTuition(M), tuitionFee(U, Tu), Tu < M.
canApplyForSubject(Subj) :- canApply(Univ,Subj).
canApply :- canApply(Univ,Subject).
```

We now introduce proper RASP rules that perform quantitative reasoning, specifically by considering the fees for the different kinds of tests. The reader can ignore the prefix [1-1] which means that whenever the rule is applied, or "fired", this is done only once. This specification is not significant here, whereas it is useful in the description of more complex resource production/consumption processes.

```
% 1) General SAT test, fee1 fixed
    [1-1]: testSATfeeGen :- dollar#300, canApply.
% 2) Disciplinary SAT test, fee2 fixed
    [1-1]: testSATfeeSbj(mathematics) :-
            dollar#170, canApplyForSubject(mathematics).
    [1-1]: testSATfeeSbj(literature) :-
            dollar#180, canApplyForSubject(literature).
    [1-1]: testSATfeeSbj(chemistry) :-
            dollar#150, canApplyForSubject(chemistry).
    [1-1]: testSATfeeSbj(physics) :-
            dollar#160, canApplyForSubject(physics).
% 3) For foreign student, TOEFL fee3 fixed
    [1-1]: testTOEFLfee :- dollar#200, foreign, canApply.
% 4) Collegeorg application, fee4 fixed
    [1-1]: testCollegeOrg :- dollar#130, canApply.
```

A general rule with head testGeneralDone then establishes whether all general tests have been considered. If the available budget is too low and so no applications can issued, then no money is actually spent. Otherwise, the costs related to potential applications and the remaining amount (if any) are computed. Clearly, this code (omitted here) performs a quantitative evaluation and does not execute actual actions, which are left to the agent.

At this point, the Raspberry RASP solver can compute all solutions which maximize the number of applications. Solutions can be further customized with respect to the constraints. For instance, the standard #maximize ASP statements allow one to prefer universities with the best ranking and, in case of equivalent solutions, the ones with the best basketball team ranking (see the full code in the web site mentioned earlier, for the details on how to optimize the solution and enforce student preferences).

With the given facts, the best preferred solution provided by Raspberry involves applying to thePinkUni and theBigUni, with a total rating (sum of the two rankings) of 180 for the universities and 18 for the basketball teams.

If omitting maximization, there is a second solution which involves applying to thePinkUni and theSmallUni, with a total rating (sum of the two rankings) of 170 for the universities and 18 for the basketball teams.

The RASP module always returns the remaining (not spent) amount which is 90 dollars in the former case and 120 dollars in the latter one. Then, the agent might in general choose the best solution. However, it might instead choose another one based upon other criteria not expressed in the RASP program, i.e., geographic location or acceptance rates or maybe lesser expense, in case there would be relevant differences.

8   Concluding Remarks

The contribution of this paper is twofold. First, we have demonstrated, also by means of a practical example, how quantitative reasoning can be performed in agent-based frameworks. Second, we have enhanced modular approaches inspired to MCSs with partially specified bridge rules, that can be dynamically customized and activated according to agent's reasoning results. The approach of this paper is fairly general, and can be thus adapted to several application domains and to different agent architectures. Since no significant related work exists, our approach to coping with the cost of knowledge and the cost of action is relevant in a variety of domains, from logistics to configuration to planning, which are particularly well-suited for agents and MAS. An important application that we envisage is planning in robotic environments, where agents are embodied in robots that have limited resources available (first of all energy) and must complete their tasks within those limits, while possibly giving priority to the most important/urgent objectives.

References

1. Alviano, M., Dodaro, C., Faber, W., Leone, N., Ricca, F.: WASP: a native ASP solver based on constraint learning. In: Cabalar, P., Son, T.C. (eds.) LPNMR 2013. LNCS (LNAI), vol. 8148, pp. 54–66. Springer, Heidelberg (2013). doi:10. 1007/978-3-642-40564-8_6
2. Bienvenu, M., Lang, J., Wilson, N.: From preference logics to preference languages, and back. In: Proceedings of KR 2010, pp. 414–424 (2010)
3. Bordini, R.H., Braubach, L., Dastani, M., Fallah-Seghrouchni, A.E., Gómez-Sanz, J.J., Leite, J., O'Hare, G.M.P., Pokahr, A., Ricci, A.: A survey of programming languages and platforms for multi-agent systems. Informatica (Slovenia) 30(1), 33–44 (2006)
4. Bordini, R.H., Hübner, J.F.: BDI agent programming in AgentSpeak using *Jason*. In: Toni, F., Torroni, P. (eds.) CLIMA 2005. LNCS (LNAI), vol. 3900, pp. 143–164. Springer, Heidelberg (2006). doi:10.1007/11750734_9
5. Bracciali, A., Demetriou, N., Endriss, U., Kakas, A., Lu, W., Mancarella, P., Sadri, F., Stathis, K., Terreni, G., Toni, F.: The KGP model of agency for global computing: computational model and prototype implementation. In: Priami, C., Quaglia, P. (eds.) GC 2004. LNCS (LNAI), vol. 3267, pp. 340–367. Springer, Heidelberg (2005). doi:10.1007/978-3-540-31794-4_18
6. Brewka, G., Delgrande, J.P., Romero, J., Schaub, T.: asprin: Customizing answer set preferences without a headache. In: Bonet, B., Koenig, S. (eds.) Proceedings of AAAI 2015, pp. 1467–1474. AAAI Press (2015)
7. Brewka, G., Eiter, T.: Equilibria in heterogeneous nonmonotonic multi-context systems. In: Proceedings of AAAI 2007, pp. 385–390. AAAI Press (2007)
8. Brewka, G., Eiter, T., Fink, M.: Nonmonotonic multi-context systems: a flexible approach for integrating heterogeneous knowledge sources. In: Balduccini, M., Son, T.C. (eds.) Logic Programming, Knowledge Representation, and Nonmonotonic Reasoning. LNCS (LNAI), vol. 6565, pp. 233–258. Springer, Heidelberg (2011). doi:10.1007/978-3-642-20832-4_16

9. Brewka, G., Eiter, T., Fink, M., Weinzierl, A.: Managed multi-context systems. In: Walsh, T. (ed.) Proceedings of IJCAI 2011, pp. 786–791. IJCAI/AAAI (2011)

10. Brewka, G., Ellmauthaler, S., Pührer, J.: Multi-context systems for reactive reasoning in dynamic environments. In: Schaub, T. (ed.) Proceedings of ECAI 2014. IJCAI/AAAI (2014)

11. Brewka, G., Niemelä, I., Truszczyński, M.: Preferences and nonmonotonic reasoning. AI Mag. **29**(4), 69–78 (2008)

12. Brik, A.: Extensions of answer set programming. Ph.D. thesis, University of California, San Diego (2012)

13. Costantini, S.: ACE: a flexible environment for complex event processing in logical agents. In: Baldoni, M., Baresi, L., Dastani, M. (eds.) EMAS 2015. LNCS (LNAI), vol. 9318, pp. 70–91. Springer, Heidelberg (2015). doi:10.1007/978-3-319-26184-3_5

14. Costantini, S.: Knowledge acquisition via non-monotonic reasoning in distributed heterogeneous environments. In: Calimeri, F., Ianni, G., Truszczynski, M. (eds.) LPNMR 2015. LNCS (LNAI), vol. 9345, pp. 228–241. Springer, Heidelberg (2015). doi:10.1007/978-3-319-23264-5_20

15. Costantini, S., De Gasperis, G.: Exchanging data and ontological definitions in multi-agent-contexts systems. In: Paschke, A., Fodor, P., Giurca, A., Kliegr, T. (eds.) Proceedings of RuleML 2015 Challenge. CEUR Workshop Proceedings (2015). CEUR-WS.org

16. Costantini, S., Formisano, A.: Modeling preferences and conditional preferences on resource consumption and production in ASP. J. Algorithms Cogn. Inf. Logic **64**(1), 3–15 (2009)

17. Costantini, S., Formisano, A.: Answer set programming with resources. J. Logic Comput. **20**(2), 533–571 (2010)

18. Costantini, S., Formisano, A.: RASP and ASP as a fragment of linear logic. Journal of Applied Non-Classical Logics **23**(1–2), 49–74 (2013)

19. Costantini, S., Formisano, A., Petturiti, D.: Extending and implementing RASP. Fundam. Inform. **105**(1–2), 1–33 (2010)

20. Costantini, S., Tocchio, A.: A logic programming language for multi-agent systems. In: Flesca, S., Greco, S., Ianni, G., Leone, N. (eds.) JELIA 2002. LNCS (LNAI), vol. 2424, pp. 1–13. Springer, Heidelberg (2002). doi:10.1007/3-540-45757-7_1

21. Costantini, S., Tocchio, A.: The DALI logic programming agent-oriented language. In: Alferes, J.J., Leite, J. (eds.) JELIA 2004. LNCS (LNAI), vol. 3229, pp. 685–688. Springer, Heidelberg (2004). doi:10.1007/978-3-540-30227-8_57

22. Dal Palù, A., Dovier, A., Pontelli, E., Rossi, G.: GASP: answer set programming with lazy grounding. Fundam. Inform. **96**(3), 297–322 (2009)

23. Dao-Tran, M., Eiter, T., Fink, M., Krennwallner, T.: Distributed evaluation of nonmonotonic multi-context systems. JAIR **52**, 543–600 (2015)

24. Dastani, M., van Riemsdijk, M.B., Meyer, J.C.: Programming multi-agent systems in 3APL. In: Bordini, R.H., Dastani, M., Dix, J., Fallah-Seghrouchni, A.E. (eds.) Multi-Agent Programming. Multiagent Systems, Artificial Societies, and Simulated Organizations, vol. 15, pp. 39–67. Springer, New York (2005)

25. Delgrande, J., Schaub, T., Tompits, H., Wang, K.: A classification and survey of preference handling approaches in nonmonotonic reasoning. Comput. Intell. **20**(12), 308–334 (2004)

26. Dovier, A., Formisano, A., Pontelli, E., Vella, F.: A GPU implementation of the ASP computation. In: Gavanelli, M., Reppy, J. (eds.) PADL 2016. LNCS, vol. 9585, pp. 30–47. Springer, Heidelberg (2016). doi:10.1007/978-3-319-28228-2_3

27. Fisher, M.: METATEM: the story so far. In: Bordini, R.H., Dastani, M.M., Dix, J., Fallah Seghrouchni, A. (eds.) ProMAS 2005. LNCS (LNAI), vol. 3862, pp. 3–22. Springer, Heidelberg (2006). doi:10.1007/11678823_1

28. Gebser, M., Kaminski, R., Kaufmann, B., Romero, J., Schaub, T.: Progress in *clasp* series 3. In: Calimeri, F., Ianni, G., Truszczynski, M. (eds.) LPNMR 2015. LNCS (LNAI), vol. 9345, pp. 368–383. Springer, Heidelberg (2015). doi:10.1007/978-3-319-23264-5_31

29. Gelfond, M.: Answer sets. In: Handbook of Knowledge Representation. Elsevier, 2007

30. Hindriks, K.V., Hoek, W., Meyer, J.-J.C.: GOAL agents instantiate intention logic. In: Artikis, A., Craven, R., Kesim Çiçekli, N., Sadighi, B., Stathis, K. (eds.) Logic Programs, Norms and Action. LNCS (LNAI), vol. 7360, pp. 196–219. Springer, Heidelberg (2012). doi:10.1007/978-3-642-29414-3_11

31. Liu, G., Janhunen, T., Niemelä, I.: Answer set programming via mixed integer programming. In: Proceedings of KR 2012 (2012)

32. Maratea, M., Pulina, L., Ricca, F.: A multi-engine approach to answer-set programming. TPLP **14**(6), 841–868 (2014)

33. Naumov, P., Tao, J.: Budget-constrained knowledge in multiagent systems. In: Weiss, G., Yolum, P., Bordini, R.H., Elkind, E. (eds.) Proceedings of AAMAS 2015, pp. 219–226. ACM (2015)

34. Simons, P., Niemelä, I., Soininen, T.: Extending and implementing the stable model semantics. Artif. Intell. **138**(1–2), 181–234 (2002)

35. Web-references. Some ASP solvers. Clasp: www.potassco.sourceforge.net; Cmodels: www.cs.utexas.edu/users/tag/cmodels; DLV: www.dlvsystem.com; Smodels: www.tcs.hut.fi/Software/smodels

Using Awareness to Promote Richer, More Human-Like Behaviors in Artificial Agents

Logan Yliniemi[1(✉)] and Kagan Tumer[2]

[1] University of Nevada, Reno, Reno, NV, USA
logan@unr.edu
[2] Oregon State University, Corvallis, OR, USA
kagan.tumer@oregonstate.edu

Abstract. The agents community has produced a wide variety of compelling solutions for many real-world problems, and yet there is still a significant disconnect between the behaviors that an agent can learn and those that exemplify the rich behaviors exhibited by humans. This problem exists both with agents interacting solely with an environment, as well as agents interacting with other agents. The solutions created to date are typically good at solving a single, well-defined problem with a particular objective, but lack in generalizability.

In this work, we discuss the possibility of using an awareness framework, coupled with the optimization of multiple dynamic objectives, in tandem with the cooperation and coordination concerns intrinsic to multiagent systems, to create a richer set of agent behaviors. We propose future directions of research that may lead toward more-human capabilities in general agent behaviors.

1 Introduction

Agents don't act like humans. To a certain extent, this is a desirable trait. Humans can be seen as irrational, moody, and on occasion downright unpleasant.

The agent-based research community has developed compelling solutions for a wide variety of problems, ranging from systems to catch poachers [50] to robotic soccer [3] to stock trading [4] to air traffic management [46,51], space exploration [33,52], and many others. However, the solutions produced by the agent research community don't tend to resemble the human decision making process.

Research in this matter in the artificial intelligence community has existed for many decades, with a number of different forms. Common sense [27–29], context and awareness [5,13,14,39] and lifelong learning [8,45], are all different instantiations of this concept, which at its core is trying to capture the incredible flexibility and often (apparent) unpredictability of human decision making.

This is not to say that the human way of thinking is somehow superior to agent-based reasoning, but instead is to ask why we cannot achieve this in addition to the advantages that agents have in solving complex problems.

In this work we posit that there may be two prongs which form a very simple answer: first, that the solutions simply do not exist within the paradigm that

© Springer International Publishing AG 2016
N. Osman and C. Sierra (Eds.): AAMAS 2016 WS, Visionary Papers, LNAI 10003, pp. 122–133, 2016.
DOI: 10.1007/978-3-319-46840-2_8

we, as a community, have been using to solve these problems; and second, that rich decision making requires a broader sense of awareness of one's environment and its meaning, which has not yet received research attention.

At their most basic, most papers in the field produce some form of *agent* to solve some *problem*. Over the years, we've created more-and-more impressive *agents* to solve increasingly difficult *problems*. This is the tried and true framework for agent-based research. Find a problem, and specifically tailor an agent-based algorithm to solve this problem.

Despite, or possibly because of these successes, the community has not made significant steps toward the richer set of behaviors that humans exhibit on an everyday basis. Perhaps it is not the pursuit of a particularly impressive agent to solve a particularly difficult task which will lead us toward agents which exhibit these rich behaviors we seek, but instead these behaviors may require a paradigm change.

This type of creative barrier is one that is mirrored in another field: optimization. Many optimization techniques have been developed for a wide variety of optimization problems, but when optimizing a single value, there are only so many behaviors that can be described this way, and thereby discovered by a single-objective optimization. In recent years, complex optimization problems are not solved by an excessively impressive *optimizer* solving a difficult *problem*, but instead, through a different paradigm. Multi-objective optimization offers a much richer set of behaviors that describes a more complete set of desirable behaviors a system may exhibit [30, 34].

To a certain extent, this is a leap that the agent-based research community is and has been making. We've discovered that some of our techniques from single-objective problems are applicable to multi-objective problems [53, 56], and even that creating a multi-objective problem can make the single-objective problems easier to solve [6, 7].

However, in this work we argue that the crux of the issue does not lie in considering agent-based problems as multi-objective problems, as this only addresses a portion of the larger issue. We posit that human decision making can be reasonably modeled by a multi-objective process, with constantly-shifting, dynamic, non-linear priorities. We pose a series of human experiences that illustrate this point, and use these experiences to form a paradigm through which each of these issues can be addressed by the agent-based research community.

The remainder of this work is organized as follows: we begin in Sect. 2 by offering some background on multi-objective optimization, since this is a central tenet of our outlook. We then identify a series of human experiences in Sect. 3 that support the dynamic multi-objective model of a human. In Sect. 4 we begin building an agent-based framework that can reflect this process and identify some portions of the work that are being done. Finally, in Sect. 5, we conclude this work with a challenge to the agent community to reach this vision.

2 Background: Optimization

Within the context of this work, it is important to understand the beginnings of multi-objective optimization (Sect. 2.1), its modern presence Sect. 2.2), and how the form of the reward can change the behavior (Sect. 2.3). However, we begin by discussing the general concept of optimization.

The core concept of single objective optimization is to choose a set of parameters which you have control over, x, such that you can either minimize or maximize a value you can't directly control, y, through some form of functional mapping $y = f(x) . f(x)$ can be nonlinear, discontinuous, stochastic, and difficult or expensive to sample, which form some of the core issues that has kept the field of optimization vibrant and active for many years.

2.1 History of Multi-objective Optimization

Though many concepts in the field of multi-objective problem solving are named after Vilfredo Pareto, we traced the origins of the field beyond Pareto, to Edgeworth [11].

Edgeworth establishes that, given the choice between a large quantity of good A and a small quantity of good B, or a small quantity of good A and a large quantity of good B, an individual might be indifferent to which set of goods he receives. This establishes the concept of an indifference curve (a curve along which one combination of goods is not preferred to another combination also located on the curve), and also to the concept of a preference curve, which lies perpendicular to the indifference curve.

Pareto solidified the study of the field. He discusses a concept that he calls *ophelimity*, which can be roughly associated with economic use or utility, which he defines as follows [31,32]:

> *For an individual, the ophelimity of a certain quantity of a thing, added to another known quantity (it can be equal to zero) which he already possesses, is the pleasure which this quanitity affords him*

Pareto makes a strong case that the goal of an individual is to constantly increase their personal ophelimity as far as is feasible. Combining the works of Edgeworth and Pareto, this involves the individual moving along their personal preference curve, which sits perpendicular from his indifference curve, and may be nonlinear (Fig. 1).

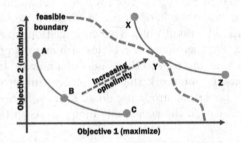

Fig. 1. Curve ABC forms an indifference curve, as does XYZ. Curve XYZ represents an increase in ophelimity from ABC. Since Y is the feasible solution with the highest ophelimity, it will be preferred by the decision maker.

2.2 Multi-objective Optimization

Multi-objective optimization is an extension to the single-objective optimization process, where the formulation instead is to maximize or minimize (or some mixture of the two) a vector of solutions $y = f(x)$. Each individual element of y can be optimized simultaneously in the formulation discussed in the previous section, but the primary challenge in multi-objective optimization is the optimization of all of these quantities simultaneously. This leads to an entire set of solutions which form the Pareto optimal set on the border between the feasible and infeasible portions of the objective space. These Pareto optimal solutions describe the optimal tradeoffs between the objectives.

This expansion of the problem has led to many advances in optimization, and has allowed solution of extremely complex optimization problems, which would be very difficult to pose in a single-objective sense [16, 21, 49].

Methods in multi-objective optimization vary widely. The simplest and possibly widest-used is the linear combination, in which the (often weighted) objectives are simply added together. This is very computationally efficient, but has well-documented drawbacks, and does not provide the richer behavior space we seek [2, 9, 25]. The linear combination can provide these richer behavior spaces if combined with the concept of indifference, and if the objective space is transformed to guarantee specific types of convexity [54, 55].

Other concepts include nonlinear schemes [18, 26], partitioning the search space [36, 37], and population-based methods in which each population member is compared (pairwise) to each of the other population members, to develop some fitness metric [10, 57].

2.3 Rewards Change Behaviors

Imbuing an adaptive agent with a richer set of possible behaviors poses a difficult problem from the reward design standpoint. While we can typically describe in common language what we would like an agent to do, the act of translating this into a reward or evaluation that leads to this behavior is a difficult process, especially when what you want the agent to do changes over time, or uses on a contextual dependence of events that the agent might not have direct awareness of or the capability to sense.

The design of such a framework, in which agents are able to switch between different contexts and weigh different priorities or objectives with different nonlinear weights, which are simultaneously time-varying, is an extremely difficult design problem with the tools that exist to date.

However, in order to develop this richer set of behaviors that captures the flexibility and emergence that are characteristics of human behaviors, we need to develop techniques for designing such time-varying multiple simultaneous rewards, as well as the algorithms that can use these (Fig. 2).

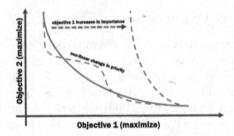

Fig. 2. A curve of indifference (solid) can change shape with time. These changes may be easy to parameterize, or nonlinear and difficult to describe, especially with higher numbers of objectives.

3   Some Human Experiences

In this section we pose a series of cases which identify ways in which the use of contextual clues can promote awareness and a shift of mindset in human behaviors. We also present relatively simple cases which are still best described by a combination of multiple objectives.

3.1   Class Begins

Consider a group of students who have shown up a few minutes before a class is due to begin, so they begin interacting with each other about whichever topics are on their mind. There is some signal given, whether by an external cue or by the instructor, that class is about to begin, and the students quiet and begin to listen to the instruction being delivered. If a small group of students continues to speak after class has begun, they may be quieted by their classmates.

This case serves to show that human awareness can lead to swift changes in priorities, and that communication as well as passive observation can lead to a person changing contexts. While this dynamic and the exact mechanics may change on a classroom-to-classroom basis, there is a nearly universally understood "time for outside of class matters" and "time for instruction", each with very different priorities. The shift between these is rapid and shared among the people involved.

3.2   A Loud Noise

Imagine that you are outdoors in a city center, and suddenly, you hear a loud sound. Not only you, but everyone around you, will turn toward the direction of the noise, to determine whether it was a signal of a context switch. In this situation, Shaw states "Unless the danger is very obvious, people often require secondary or confirmatory data before they will begin to react" [40].

Was it simply a car backfiring? Was it a siren? An auto accident? By gathering additional information, you're able to make an intelligent and rational decision about what to do next. Depending on what the additional information shows, your priorities might rapidly shift back to (i) whatever they were previously, especially if there is no perceived change in context; (ii) flight away from the danger; or (iii) to help those in harm's way.

This case serves to show that human awareness detects changes in the environment which signal broader changes in context, and that a change in context can lead to drastically different priorities, which may vary between individuals. It also serves to show that humans use supporting first-hand observations to verify a possible context switch.

3.3 Socially Appropriate Navigation

Consider the simple act of trying to navigate through a crowded hallway in a way that does not disturb those around you. This Socially Aware Navigation is a problem which humans readily solve on a regular basis [15]. In order to properly address this problem, though, you have many competing objectives. As a sample of a set of possible priorities,

  (i)   you are trying to navigate to your goal as quickly as possible
 (ii)   you are trying not to physically disturb any other person along the way
(iii)   you are trying to avoid walking through groups of people talking with each other
 (iv)   you are trying to expend minimal energy
  (v)   you are trying to stay with your group members
 (vi)   you are preoccupied with your thoughts
(vii)   you are trying to have courteous interactions

Depending on the details of your situation, your priorities are going to be very different.

- *Efficiency*: If you're having a tough day, perhaps you're much more concerned with (i) and (iv) than the remainders.
- *A hall of coworkers*: If the hall is filled with your colleagues, you may prioritize (vii), along with (iii).
- *Late for an important meeting*: (i) may take precedence over (iii), and you might put no priority at all on (iv).
- *Absentminded*: If other events are occupying your thoughts and attention, you may implicitly place a higher priority on (vi), and allow the others to take lower precedence.
- *A foreigner*: If you are in a foreign place and do not speak the language, you might be more inclined to avoid interactions and therefore prioritize (ii), (iii), and (v).
- *A parent with small children*: (v) likely takes very high priority, with a possible side of (ii) and (iii); you might simply acknowledge that (i) and (iv) are not useful priorities.
- *Inconsiderate others*: If the people crowding the hallway are not being considerate of the people making their way through, perhaps (ii) will take a lower priority in your mind.

- *Combination*: These situations are not mutually exclusive, and if you have a combination of these situations, you may have some combination of the priorities of each.

All of these different sets of priorities are completely rational, though they lead to vastly different courses of action. It is an incredibly human trait that we each can look at the same situation, and, based on our previous experiences and current priorities, come to a different conclusion about the actions that should be taken. This is also why it is so easy to think that someone else is making the wrong choice in a situation. If we are weighing their actions and the likely outcomes with our own priorities, then it is extremely likely that they may appear irrational. They could be using a different prioritization of the same objectives that we are considering, but it is possibly more likely that they are trying to optimize an objective that we haven't even considered in the first place.

To compound this problem, interacting within the human environment is an extremely information-limited problem. It is difficult, even with prolonged shared experiences, to completely understand the motivations and past experiences of those around us, which inherently guide their priorities within a situation. Finally, very different mindsets can lead to the same behaviors: an absentminded person could behave similarly to one concerned only with their path efficiency. They have very different motivations, and different priorities as expressed above, but could exhibit similar observable behaviors.

This case serves to show that with different sets of priorities, different action sets can be seen as equally rational and reasonable. Additionally, without thoroughly understanding an individual's priorities, judging the rationality of their actions is extremely difficult.

3.4   Falsely Shouting "Fire" in a Theatre

Consider, for a moment, the concept of a person entering into a crowded theatre and shouting "Fire!" when there is none. For a moment, the theatre goers may briefly be confused, as the exclamation does not fit into the context that they were expecting. Is this a part of the play? Then, after a short time to process, each individual may rapidly change their priorities, from maximizing their enjoyment to minimizing their time inside the theatre. This process can happen rapidly in parallel, creating a mass panic.

In a decision from 1919, the U.S. Supreme court noted that this is one of the (very few) exceptions to free speech under the U.S. constitution. To quote the decision: "The most stringent protection of free speech would not protect a man in falsely shouting fire in a theatre and causing a panic. It does not even protect a man from an injunction against uttering words that may have all the effect of force" [20].

This decision cites that the use of words may have all the effect of force, and the reason for this is the rapid and extreme context switching that would happen for each person sitting in the theatre. It immediately places every person in the theatre in danger from the circumstances that may arise from the mass exodus from the theatre by (reasonably) self-concerned patrons. In fact, simply shouting fire has led to a loss of life in the panic of some situations [35, 48], whereas in other highly dangerous situations that actually involved a large fire, no loss of life occurred [40].

This case serves to show that a human's sense of context can be manipulated by the actions of others, and that the sense of context has a high impact on the actions of others: "all the effect of force".

4   Toward Richer Agent Behaviors

In order to achieve rich behaviors such as these, a possible route is to create a framework which has the same characteristics, both within sensing the context and when it changes, and in the decision making process once a context has been identified.

These characteristics are:
Context sensing

- Independent detection of a context change
- Inter-agent communication to facilitate context switching
- Sensory verification of a communicated context switch

Decision-making

- Event-dependent multiple priorities
- Priorities with nonlinear preference curves
- Varying priorities based on past experiences
- A strong change in behavior corresponding with changes in context

In this section, we identify areas in which the MAS and AI communities have made some steps toward imbuing agents with these characteristics, and some possible future directions of research. This is linked to over 3 decades of work [23, 24] in awareness, long term autonomy, and common sense for artificial intelligence, but in this section we look at the research with an eye toward using multi-objective optimization with dynamically-changing priorities.

4.1   The Detection of Context Changes

Giving an agent awareness of context, which is broader than a simple state representation, is an extremely large research problem. It is possible that contributions to such a detection method this could come from sources like transfer learning [38, 43, 44] anomaly detection [1, 17, 22], the detection of opponent policy switching in non-stationary problems [12, 19, 47] or shared autonomy [41, 42].

Each of these problem types are ones in which the MAS and AI community have many collective years of experience solving. In the particular application of identifying context changes, we propose one avenue: since many candidate priorities must exist for the richer behavior space that we seek, why not constantly track the evaluations of these objectives, and use the past history as a litmus test? If an agent takes an action and can predict a vector of rewards, but receives a vastly different vector, it is very possible that a context change has happened.

4.2 The Use of Context

Once a shift in context has been detected, the agent can suddenly find itself in a world of uncertainty, and there are many research questions to be addressed: how does the agent select its new set of objectives from among the entire set it may consider? How does the agent prioritize these objectives, and with what form of a preference scheme? How can policy information be maintained across changes in context, and still used in a constructive manner?

Again, the MAS and AI community has many collective years of solving these types of problems. The selection of a new set of priorities without excessive regret is in many ways similar to handling a new opponent strategy in a competitive game. The preference scheme can be built up based on what can be achieved within the constraints of the new context. Outside knowledge can be incorporated with reward shaping. Policy information can be maintained through transfer.

The incorporation of any combination of these at once is a large research problem, which requires concerted effort on a community-wide, collaborative level. It requires publishing work that requires the knowledge of multiple subfields to properly review and understand. It requires a level of risk. However, it also provides a substantial reward: a future *agent* that can not only solve a particularly difficult *problem*, but can use a sense of awareness to situate itself within its environment, such that it can potentially solve many problems despite (or due to) many changes in context along the way.

5 Conclusion

In this work we have identified a challenge for the MAS and AI community: the development of agents with a richer set of behaviors, which may be able to mimic the human decision making process. We have identified, through a series of vignettes, some desirable aspects of the human decision making process, and provided a paradigm through which an autonomous agent-based system might be able to mimic these human behaviors, through the incorporation of a sense of *awareness* into the agents. Such agents will be capable of detecting when changes in their environment, their interaction with the environment, or actions of others indicate a change in *context*, and use this to quickly change the set of *priorities* which they consider. These agents will then consider their *priorities* with some form of *non-linear* preference (and indifference), and take actions based on these priorities and preferences. In order to imbue artificial agents with the flexibility and emergence associated with human behaviors, we, as a community, need to develop each of these techniques, with an eye toward integration with each of the others.

References

1. Agogino, A., Tumer, K.: Entropy based anomaly detection applied to space shuttle main engines. In: IEEE Aerospace Conference (2006)
2. Athan, T.W., Papalambros, P.Y.: A note on weighted criteria methods for compromise solutions in multi-objective optimization. Eng. Optim. **27**, 155–176 (1996)
3. Barrett, S., Stone, P.: Cooperating with unknown teammates in complex domains: a robot soccer case study of ad hoc teamwork. In: Proceedings of the Twenty-Ninth AAAI Conference on Artificial Intelligence, January 2015
4. Bloembergen, D., Hennes, D., McBurney, P., Tuyls, K.: Trading in markets with noisy information: an evolutionary analysis. Connection Sci. **27**(3), 253–268 (2015)
5. Brézillon, P.: Context in artificial intelligence: I. a survey of the literature. Comput. Artif. Intell. **18**, 321–340 (1999)
6. Brys, T., Harutyunyan, A., Vrancx, P., Taylor, M.E., Kudenko, D., Nowé, A.: Multi-objectivization of reinforcement learning problems by reward shaping. In: 2014 International Joint Conference on Neural Networks (IJCNN), pp. 2315–2322. IEEE (2014)
7. Brys, T., Taylor, M.E., Nowé, A.: Using ensemble techniques and multi-objectivization to solve reinforcement learning problems. In: ECAI, pp. 981–982 (2014)
8. Carlson, A., Betteridge, J., Kisiel, B., Settles, B., Hruschka Jr., E.R., Mitchell, T.M.: Toward an architecture for never-ending language learning. In: AAAI, vol. 5, p. 3 (2010)
9. Das, I., Dennis, J.E.: A closer look at drawbacks of minimizing weighted sums of objectives for pareto set generation in multicriteria optimization problems. Struct. Optim. **14**, 63–69 (1997)
10. Deb, K., Pratap, A., Agarwal, S., Meyarivan, T.: A fast elitist multi-objective genetic algorithm: NSGA-II. Evol. Comput. **6**, 182–197 (2002)
11. Edgeworth, F.Y., Psychics, M.: An Essay on the Application of Mathematics to Moral Sciences. C. Kegan Paul and Company, London (1881)
12. Elidrisi, M., Johnson, N., Gini, M.: Fast learning against adaptive adversarial opponents. In: Proceedings of the 11th International Conference on Autonomous Agents and Multiagent Systems, November 2012, Valencia, Spain (2012)
13. Erickson, T.: Some problems with the notion of context-aware computing. Commun. ACM **45**(2), 102–104 (2002)
14. Fagin, R., Halpern, J.Y.: Belief, awareness, and limited reasoning. Artif. Intell. **34**(1), 39–76 (1987)
15. Feil-Seifer, D.: Distance-based computational models for facilitating robot interaction with children. J. Hum. Rob. Interact. **1**(1), 55–77 (2012)
16. Flener, P., Pearson, J., Ågren, M., Garcia-Avello, C., Celiktin, M., Dissing, S.: Air-traffic complexity resolution in multi-sector planning. J. Air Transp. Manage. **13**(6), 323–328 (2007)
17. Ghosh, A., Sen, S.: Agent-based distributed intrusion alert system. In: Sen, A., Das, N., Das, S.K., Sinha, B.P. (eds.) IWDC 2004. LNCS, vol. 3326, pp. 240–251. Springer, Heidelberg (2004). doi:10.1007/978-3-540-30536-1_28
18. Giagkiozis, I., Fleming, P.J.: Methods for multi-objective optimization: an analysis. Inform. Sci. **293**, 338–350 (2015)
19. Hernandez-Leal, P., Munoz de Cote, E., Sucar, L.E.: A framework for learning and planning against switching strategies in repeated games. Connection Sci. **26**(2), 103–122 (2014)

20. Holmes Jr., O.W.: U.S. supreme court opinion: Schenck v. United States (1919)
21. Jeyadevi, S., Baskar, S., Babulal, C.K., Iruthayarajan, M.W.: Solving multiobjective optimal reactive power dispatch using modified NSGA-II. Int. J. Electr. Power Energ. Syst. **33**(2), 219–228 (2011)
22. Kaluža, B., Kaminka, G.A., Tambe, M.: Detection of suspicious behavior from a sparse set of multiagent interactions. In: Proceedings of the 11th International Conference on Autonomous Agents and Multiagent Systems, vol. 2, pp. 955–964. International Foundation for Autonomous Agents and Multiagent Systems (2012)
23. Lenat, D.B.: CYC: a large-scale investment in knowledge infrastructure. Commun. ACM **38**(11), 33–38 (1995)
24. Lenat, D.B., Guha, R.V., Pittman, K., Pratt, D., Shepherd, M.: CYC: toward programs with common sense. Commun. ACM **33**(8), 30–49 (1990)
25. Marler, R.T., Arora, J.S.: The weighted sum method for multi-objective optimization: new insights. Struct. Multi. Optim. **41**, 853–862 (2009)
26. Marler, R.T., Arora, J.S.: Survey of multi-objective optimization methods for engineering. Struct. Multi. Optim. **26**, 369–395 (2004)
27. McCarthy, J.: Programs with Common Sense. Defense Technical Information Center, Panama (1963)
28. McCarthy, J.: Generality in artificial intelligence. Commun. ACM **30**(12), 1030–1035 (1987)
29. McCarthy, J.: Artificial intelligence, logic and formalizing common sense. In: Thomason, R.H. (ed.) Philosophical logic and artificial intelligence, pp. 161–190. Springer, Netherlands (1989)
30. Messac, A., Hattis, P.D.: Physical programming design optimization for high speed civil transport (HSCT). J. Aircr. **33**(2), 446–449 (1996)
31. Pareto, V.: Manuale di Economia Politica. Piccola Biblioteca Scientifica, Societa Editrice Libraria (1906)
32. Pareto, V.: Manual of Political Economy. MacMillan Press Ltd., London (1927)
33. Pěchouček, M., Mařík, V.: Industrial deployment of multi-agent technologies: review and selected case studies. Auton. Agent. Multi-Agent Syst. **17**(3), 397–431 (2008)
34. Penn, R., Friedler, E., Ostfeld, A.: Multi-objective evolutionary optimization for greywater reuse in municipal sewer systems. Water Res. **47**(15), 5911–5920 (2013)
35. Powe, L.A.: Searching for the false shout of fire. Const. Comment. **19**, 345 (2002)
36. Sato, H.: Inverted PBI in MOEA/D and its impact on the search performance on multi and many-objective optimization. In: Proceedings of the 2014 Conference on Genetic and Evolutionary Computation, pp. 645–652. ACM (2014)
37. Sato, H.: MOEA/D using constant-distance based neighbors designed for many-objective optimization. In: 2015 IEEE Congress on Evolutionary Computation (CEC), pp. 2867–2874. IEEE (2015)
38. Sen, S., Sekaran, M., Hale, J.: Learning to coordinate without sharing information. In: AAAI, pp. 426–431 (1994)
39. Serafini, L., Bouquet, P.: Comparing formal theories of context in AI. Artif. Intell. **155**(1), 41–67 (2004)
40. Shaw, R.: Don't panic: behaviour in major incidents. Disaster Prev. Manag. Int. J. **10**(1), 5–10 (2001)
41. Tambe, M.: Electric elves: what went wrong and why. AI Mag. **29**(2), 23 (2008)
42. Tambe, M., Scerri, P., Pynadath, D.V.: Adjustable autonomy for the real world. J. Artif. Intell. Res. **17**(1), 171–228 (2002)

43. Taylor, M.E., Kuhlmann, G., Stone, P.: Autonomous transfer for reinforcement learning. In: Proceedings of the 7th International Joint Conference on Autonomous Agents And Multiagent Systems, vol. 1, pp. 283–290. International Foundation for Autonomous Agents and Multiagent Systems (2008)
44. Taylor, M.E., Stone, P.: An introduction to intertask transfer for reinforcement learning. AI Mag. **32**(1), 15 (2011)
45. Thrun, S., Mitchell, T.M.: Lifelong robot learning. In: Steels, L. (ed.) The Biology and Technology of Intelligent Autonomous Agents. NATO ASI Series, vol. 144, pp. 165–196. Springer, Heidelberg (1995)
46. Tumer, K., Agogino, A.: Distributed agent-based air traffic flow management. In: Proceedings of the 6th International Joint Conference on Autonomous Agents and Multiagent Systems, p. 255. ACM (2007)
47. Wang, Z., Boularias, A., Mülling, K., Peters, J.: Balancing safety and exploitability in opponent modeling. In: AAAI (2011)
48. Wendland, M.F.: The calumet tragedy + death of a city in Northern Michigan, 1913–1914. Am. Heritage **37**(3), 39 (1986)
49. Xu, H., Zhang, Z., Alipour, K., Xue, K., Gao, X.Z.: Prototypes selection by multi-objective optimal design: application to a reconfigurable robot in sandy terrain. Ind. Rob. Int. J. **38**(6), 599–613 (2011)
50. Yang, R., Ford, B., Tambe, M., Lemieux, A.: Adaptive resource allocation for wildlife protection against illegal poachers. In: Proceedings of the 2014 International Conference on Autonomous Agents and Multi-agent Systems, pp. 453–460. International Foundation for Autonomous Agents and Multiagent Systems (2014)
51. Yliniemi, L., Agogino, A.K., Tumer, K.: Evolutionary agent-based simulation of the introduction of new technologies in air traffic management. In: Genetic and Evolutionary Computation Conference (GECCO) (2014)
52. Yliniemi, L., Agogino, A.K., Tumer, K.: Multirobot coordination for space exploration. AI Mag. **4**(35), 61–74 (2014)
53. Yliniemi, L., Tumer, K.: Multi-objective multiagent credit assignment through difference rewards in reinforcement learning. In: Dick, G., et al. (eds.) SEAL 2014. LNCS, vol. 8886, pp. 407–418. Springer, Heidelberg (2014). doi:10.1007/978-3-319-13563-2_35
54. Yliniemi, L., Tumer, K.: PaCcET: an objective space transformation to iteratively convexify the Pareto front. In: Dick, G., et al. (eds.) SEAL 2014. LNCS, vol. 8886, pp. 204–215. Springer, Heidelberg (2014). doi:10.1007/978-3-319-13563-2_18
55. Yliniemi L., Tumer, K.: Complete coverage in the multi-objective PaCcET framework. In: Silva, S. (ed.) Genetic and Evolutionary Computation Conference (2015)
56. Yliniemi, L., Wilson, D., Tumer, K.: Multi-objective multiagent credit assignment in NSGA-II using difference evaluations. In: Proceedings of the 2015 International Conference on Autonomous Agents and Multiagent Systems, pp. 1635–1636. International Foundation for Autonomous Agents and Multiagent Systems (2015)
57. Zitzler, E., Laumanns, M., Thiele, L.: SPEA2: improving the strength Pareto evolutionary algorithm. Comput. Eng. **3242**(103) (2001)

Using GDL to Represent Domain Knowledge for Automated Negotiations

Dave de Jonge$^{(\boxtimes)}$ and Dongmo Zhang

Artificial Intelligence Research Group, Western Sydney University,
Penrith, NSW 2751, Australia
{d.dejonge,d.zhang}@westernsydney.edu.au

Abstract. Current negotiation algorithms often assume that utility has an explicit representation as a function over the set of possible deals and that for any deal its utility value can be calculated easily. We argue however, that a more realistic model of negotiations would be one in which the negotiator has certain knowledge about the domain and must reason with this knowledge in order to determine the value of a deal, which is time-consuming. We propose to use Game Description Language to model such negotiation scenarios, because this may enable us to apply existing techniques from General Game Playing to implement domain-independent, reasoning, negotiation algorithms.

Keywords: Automated negotiation · General game playing · Game description language

1 Introduction

Most work on Automated Negotiations focuses purely on the strategy to determine which deals to propose *given* the utility values of the possible deals. Little attention has been given to negotiation settings in which determining the utility value of a deal is itself a hard problem that takes a substantial amount of time. One often assumes the utility value of any deal is known instantaneously, or can be determined by solving a simple linear equation [1]. In such studies the process of evaluating the proposal is almost completely abstracted away and one either assumes that the negotiation algorithms do not require any domain knowledge or reasoning at all, or that all such knowledge is hardcoded in the algorithm. The preferences of the agent's opponents on the other hand, are often assumed to be completely unknown.

In this paper however, we argue that in real negotiations it is very important to have domain knowledge, and a good negotiator must be able to reason about this knowledge. One cannot, for example, expect to make profitable deals in the antique business if one does not have extensive knowledge of antique, no matter how good one is at bargaining. Moreover, a good negotiator should also be able to reason about the desires of its opponents. A good car salesman for example would try to find out what type of car would best suit his client's needs, in order to increase the chances of coming to a successful deal.

© Springer International Publishing AG 2016
N. Osman and C. Sierra (Eds.): AAMAS 2016 WS, Visionary Papers, LNAI 10003, pp. 134–153, 2016.
DOI: 10.1007/978-3-319-46840-2_9

We therefore propose a new kind of negotiation setting in which the agents do not have an explicit representation of their utility functions but instead are presented with domain knowledge in the form of a logic program. Agents will need to apply logical reasoning in order to determine the value of any proposal.

Another point that is rarely taken into account, is that an agent's utility may not always solely depend on the agreements it makes, but may also depend on decisions taken outside the negotiation thread. For example, suppose that you negotiate with a car salesman to buy a car. If you are single and you live in the city then it may be a very good deal to buy a small car which is easy to park and uses little fuel. However, if one year later you get married and decide to start a family, that deal suddenly is not so good anymore because you now require a larger family car. Interestingly, we see that although the deal itself has not changed at all, its utility value certainly has changed as a consequence of some decision taken long after the negotiations had finished.

Moreover, an agent's utility may not only depend on its own actions, but also on actions of other agents, as is typical for business deals. Imagine for example renting a property to open a restaurant in a street with no other restaurants. This might be a good deal until suddenly five other restaurants also open in that same street, giving you so much competition that you can no longer afford the rent.

We note that these properties we are addressing here–applying logical reasoning about the domain, and choosing a proper strategy with respect to your opponents' strategies–are also the main issues in the field of *General Game Playing* (GGP). General Game Playing deals with the implementation of agents that can play *any* kind of game. In contrast to specialized Chess- or Go- computers, which can only play one specific game and are largely based on knowledge provided by human experts, a GGP program cannot apply any game-specific heuristics because it only knows the rules of the games it is playing at run-time.

Therefore, in this paper we propose to use Game Description Language (GDL), which is commonly regarded as the standard language for GGP research [18], to define negotiation domains and we propose to use common techniques from GGP to implement negotiating agents. We investigate to what extent GDL is applicable to the field of automated negotiations and compare its advantages and disadvantages. We conclude that describing negotiation domains in GDL is indeed possible, but that some small adaptations may need to be made to GDL to make it more suitable for negotiations.

Another advantage of using GDL for negotiations, is that it allows us to write protocol-independent agents. Currently, negotiating agents are often implemented for only one specific protocol. By applying GGP techniques we could be able to implement an agent that "understands" any kind of protocol as long as it is specified in GDL. So far we have indeed managed to specify the Alternating Offers protocol in GDL.

The rest of this paper is organized as follows. In Sect. 2 we give an overview of existing work in Automated Negotiations and General Game Playing. In Sect. 3 we explain how we can model a negotiation scenario as a game. In Sect. 4 we give a short description of GDL and in Sect. 5 we explain that for negotiation games specified in GDL we can distinguish between three types of agents.

Then, in Sect. 6 we give a short description of a recently introduced language for strategic reasoning that can be used by negotiating agents to make proposals to each other. Next, in Sect. 7 we discuss some of the issues we encountered when applying GDL to negotiations. In Sect. 8 we present some preliminary results that we have so far obtained, and finally, in Sect. 9, we summarize our conclusions.

2   Related Work

The earliest work on automated negotiations was mainly focused on highly idealized scenarios in which it is possible to formally prove certain theoretical properties, such as the existence of equilibrium strategies. A seminal paper in this area is the paper by Nash [21] in which he shows that under certain axioms the outcome of a bilateral negotiation is the solution that maximizes the product of the players' utilities. Many papers have been written afterwards that generalize or adapt some of his assumptions. A non-linear generalization has been made for example in [7]. Such studies give hard guarantees about the success of their approach, but the downside is that it is difficult to apply those results in real-world settings, since many of the assumptions made do not hold in the real world. A general overview of such game theoretical studies is made in [26].

In later work focus has shifted more towards heuristic approaches. Such work focuses on the implementation of negotiation algorithms for domains where one cannot expect to find any formal equilibrium results, or where such equilibria cannot be determined in a reasonable amount of time. It is usually not possible to give hard guarantees about the success of such algorithms, but they are more suitable to real-world negotiation scenarios. Important examples in this area are [5,6]. They propose a strategy that amounts to determining for each time t which utility value should be demanded from the opponent (the *aspiration level*). However, they do not take into account that one first needs to find a deal that indeed yields that aspired utility level. They simply assume that such a deal always exists, and that the negotiator can find it without any effort.

In general, these heuristic approaches still often make many simplifying assumptions. They may for example assume there is only a small set of possible agreements, or that the utility functions are linear additive functions which are explicitly given or which can be calculated without much computational cost. All these assumptions were made for example in the first four editions of the annual Automated Negotiating Agent Competition (ANAC 2010–2013) [1].

Recently, more attention has been given to more realistic negotiation settings in which the number of possible deals is very large so that one needs to apply search algorithms to find good deals to propose, and where utility functions are non-linear, for example in [12,19,20]. Although their utility functions are indeed non-linear over the vector space that represents the space of possible deals, the value of any given deal can still be calculated quickly by solving a linear equation. Even though in theory any non-linear function can indeed be *modeled* in such a way, in real-world settings utility functions are not always *given* in this way (e.g. there is no known closed-form expression for the utility function over the set of all possible configurations of a Chess game). In order to apply their method one would first need to transform the given expression of the utility function into the expression required by their model, which may easily turn out to be an unfeasible task.

Therefore, the idea of complex utility functions was taken a step further in [14], where the utility functions were not only non-linear, but determining the value of any deal was actually an NP-hard problem. Another important example of negotiations where determining utility values involves a hard combinatorial problem is the game of Diplomacy. In this game negotiations are even more complex because the utility values of the players are not directly defined in terms of the agreements they make, but more indirectly through the moves they make in the game. The players negotiate with one another about which moves each will make, which in turn influences the outcome of the game in a non-trivial manner. Determining the effect of an agreement on the player's final utility is a very hard problem that involves Game Theory and Constraint Satisfaction. Pioneering work on negotiations in Diplomacy was presented in [17,24]. New interest in Diplomacy as a test-bed for negotiations has arisen with the development of the DipGame platform [4], which makes the implementation of Diplomacy agents easier for scientific research. Several negotiating agents have been developed on this platform [3,8,13].

General Game Playing is a relatively new topic. Although earlier work has been done, it really started to draw widespread attention in the AI community after the introduction of GDL [18] and the organization of the annual AAAI GGP competition since 2005 [10].

Common techniques applied by GGP players are minimax [22], alpha-beta pruning [15] and Monte Carlo Tree Search (MCTS) [16]. All these techniques generate a search tree in which each node ν represents a certain state w_ν of the game and a certain player α_ν. The root node represents the initial state, and for each node the edges to its child nodes represent the actions that are legal in the state w_ν, for player α_ν. Each time a new node ν is added to the tree, the algorithm parses the game rules, which are written in GDL, to determine which actions are legal for player α_ν in the state w_ν and, if w_ν is a terminal state, which utility value each player receives.

FluxPlayer [25], the winner of the 2006 AAAI GGP competition applies an iterated deepening depth-first search method with alpha-beta pruning, and uses Fuzzy logic to determine how close a given state is to the goal state. Cadia Player [9], the winner in 2007, 2008, and 2012, is based on MCTS extended with several heuristics to guide the playouts so that they are better informed and hence give more realistic results. Furthermore, also the winner of 2014, Sancho[1], as well as the winner of 2015, Galvanise[2] apply variants of MCTS.

---

[1] http://sanchoggp.blogspot.co.uk/2014/05/what-is-sancho.html.
[2] https://bitbucket.org/rxe/galvanise_v2.

3   Negotiation Games

Since GDL is a language to describe games, in this section we explain how a negotiation scenario can be described as a game.

Game theory can be related to negotiations in two possible ways. Firstly, the negotiation protocol can be modeled as a game. This approach is for example taken in Nash' famous paper [21] and is the common approach taken when one intends to formally prove properties of a negotiation scenario. In this case the moves made by the players consist of making proposals and accepting proposals, and the utility functions are directly given as a function over the space of possible outcomes of the negotiation protocol.

However, in this paper we follow a new approach in which not only the protocol, but also the utility functions are defined by means of a Game Theoretical model. That is: players receive utility by making certain moves in some game G, and on top of that they are allowed to negotiate about the moves they will make in that game according to some negotiation protocol N. A typical example of such a negotiation scenario is the game of Diplomacy. In this case there are two types of moves: negotiation-moves (i.e. making proposals, accepting proposals or rejecting proposals) and game-moves (the moves defined in the game G). The proposals that players make or accept are proposals about which game-moves they will make. The utilities of the players are only determined by the game-moves. However, since the agreements they make during the negotiations will partially restrict their possible game-moves, the utility values obtained by the players indirectly do depend on the negotiated agreements.

We will first define the concept of a *protocol*, and then define the concepts of a *negotiation protocol* and of a *game*, which are two different extensions of the concept of a protocol. Next, we will define a *negotiation game*, which is a combination of a negotiation protocol and a game.

Definition 1. *A **protocol** P is a tuple*
$\langle Ag, \mathcal{A}, W, w_1, T, L, u \rangle$, *where:*

- *Ag is the set of **agents** (or **players**):*
  $Ag = \{\alpha_1, \alpha_2, \ldots \alpha_n\}$
- *$\mathcal{A}$ is a tuple $(\mathcal{A}_1, \mathcal{A}_2, \ldots \mathcal{A}_n)$ where each $\mathcal{A}_i$ is the set of **actions** (or **moves**) of agent α_i.*
- *W is a non-empty set of **states**.*
- *$w_1 \in W$ is the **initial** state.*
- *$T \subset W$ is the set of **terminal** states.*
- *L is a tuple $(L_1, L_2, \ldots L_n)$, where each L_i is the **legality** function for α_i, which assigns to each non-terminal state a nonempty set of actions for α_i. $L_i : W \setminus T \to 2^{\mathcal{A}_i}$.*
- *$u : W \times \mathcal{A}_1 \times \mathcal{A}_2 \cdots \times \mathcal{A}_n \to W$ is the update function that maps each state and action profile to a new state.*

We say an action a is a **legal action** for player α_i in state w iff $a \in L_i(w)$. A tuple $\boldsymbol{a} = (a_1, a_2, \ldots a_n)$ consisting of one action $a_i \in \mathcal{A}_i$ for each player is called an **action profile**. An action profile is called a **legal action profile** in state w iff all actions a_i of that action-profile are legal in w. Given a state w and a legal action profile $\boldsymbol{a}$ the update function u defines the **next state** w' as: $w' = u(w, \boldsymbol{a})$. A **legal history** is a finite sequence of states, $(w_1, w_2, \ldots w_m)$, starting with the initial state w_1 such that for each integer j with $1 \leq j < m$ there exists a legal action-profile $\boldsymbol{a}$ such that $u(w_j, \boldsymbol{a}) = w_{j+1}$.

Note that in this model it is assumed that the agents always take their actions simultaneously. This is not really a restriction because any turn-taking protocol can be modeled as a special case of a simultaneous-move protocol, by adding a special dummy-move, often called 'noop', to the model which has no effect on the next state. Then, one can define the legality functions such that in every state all players except one have only one legal move, which is the 'noop' move. The one player that does have more than one legal move is then called the **active player** of that state.

Definition 2. *A **negotiation protocol** N is a tuple $\langle P, Agr, C, \eta \rangle$, where:*

- *P is a protocol.*
- *Agr is a nonempty set of possible agreements, known as the **agreement space**.*
- *$C : T \to Agr$ is the **commitment function** that maps every terminal state of the protocol to an agreement.*
- *$\eta \in Agr$ is the 'conflict deal'.*

The set Agr can be any set that represents the possible deals the agents can make with each another. The interpretation of C is that if the negotiation protocol ends in a terminal state w then $C(w)$ is the agreement that the agents have agreed upon.[3] The set Agr contains one element η that represents the 'conflict deal' i.e. an element to represent that no deal has been made. So if the agents do not come to any agreement, than the protocol ends in a final state w for which $C(w) = \eta$.

As an example, let us define the alternating offers protocol [23] using this model.

Example 1. Suppose we have two agents negotiating how to split a pie according to an alternating offers protocol over m rounds. The agents are denoted $Ag = \{\alpha_1, \alpha_2\}$. The possible agreements are the real values between 0 and 1, representing the fraction of the pie assigned to player α_1, so: $Agr = [0, 1] \cup \{\eta\}$. The actions of the players are either to propose a division of the pie, or to accept the previous proposal, or to do nothing:

$$\mathcal{A}_1 = \mathcal{A}_2 = \{propose(x) \mid x \in [0, 1]\} \cup \{accept, noop\}.$$

A state is given as a triple: (r, x, b) where r is the round of the protocol, x is the last proposal made, and b is either 'true' ($\top$) or 'false' ($\bot$) indicating whether x has been accepted or not.

$$W = \{(r, x, b) \mid 0 \leq r \leq m, \ x \in Agr, \ b \in \{\top, \bot\}\}$$

---

[3] We could generalize this and allow protocols in which more than one deal can be made. However, we will not do so here for simplicity.

The initial state is: $w_1 = (0, \eta, \perp)$. Terminal states are those states in which either the last round has passed or any of the agents has accepted a proposal:

$$T = \{(r, x, b) \in W \mid r = m \ \lor \ b = \top\}$$

In the even rounds player α_1 is the active player and in the odd rounds α_2 is active. In every state all actions except 'noop' are legal for the active player, except that in the initial state it is also not allowed to play 'accept' (because no proposal has yet been made that could be accepted).
If $r = 0$:

$$L_1(r, x, b) = \mathcal{A}_1 \setminus \{accept, noop\} \quad L_2(r, x, b) = \{noop\}$$

If $r > 0$:
$$L_i(r, x, b) = \mathcal{A}_i \setminus \{noop\} \quad L_j(r, x, b) = \{noop\}$$

with $i = r \ (mod \ 2) + 1$ and $j \neq i$. The update function is defined as follows:

$$u((r, x, \perp), propose(y), noop) = (r + 1, y, \perp)$$
$$u((r, x, \perp), noop, propose(y)) = (r + 1, y, \perp)$$
$$u((r, x, \perp), accept, noop) = (r + 1, x, \top)$$
$$u((r, x, \perp), noop, accept) = (r + 1, x, \top)$$

And finally, the commitment function returns the proposal that was accepted or, if no proposal was accepted, returns the conflict deal:

$$C(r, x, \top) = x \quad C(m, x, \perp) = \eta$$

Note that this definition of the alternating offers protocol can be adapted easily to domains other that split-the-pie, simply by replacing Agr by some other agreement space. Everything else remains the same.

Definition 3. *A* ***game*** *G is a pair $\langle P, U \rangle$ where P is a protocol and U is a tuple $U = (U_1, U_2, \ldots U_n)$ where each U_i is the* ***utility function*** *of player α_i, which assigns a utility value to each terminal state of the protocol: $U_i : T \rightarrow \mathbb{R}^+$.*

The goal of each player α_i is to choose a strategy such that the game ends in a terminal state w_m that maximizes his or her utility $U_i(w_m)$. As an example, let us define the prisoner's dilemma using this model.

Example 2. If G is the prisoner's dilemma then we have the following protocol (c stands for 'confess' and d stands for 'deny'):

- $Ag = \{\alpha_1, \alpha_2\}$
- $\mathcal{A}_1 = \mathcal{A}_2 = \{c, d\}$
- $W = \{w_1, w_{cc}, w_{cd}, w_{dc}, w_{dd}\}$
- $T = \{w_{cc}, w_{cd}, w_{dc}, w_{dd}\}$
- $L_1(w_1) = L_2(w_1) = \{c, d\}$

- $u(w_1, c, c) = w_{cc}, \quad u(w_1, c, d) = w_{cd},$
  $u(w_1, d, c) = w_{dc}, \quad u(w_1, d, d) = w_{dd}$

Here, w_1 is the initial state, w_{cc} is the terminal state that is reached when both players play c, w_{cd} is the terminal state that is reached when α_1 plays c and α_2 plays d, etcetera. The utility functions can, for example, be defined as:

- $U_1(w_{cc}) = U_2(w_{cc}) = 2$
- $U_1(w_{cd}) = U_2(w_{dc}) = 10$
- $U_1(w_{dc}) = U_2(w_{cd}) = 0$
- $U_1(w_{dd}) = U_2(w_{dd}) = 8$

Definition 4. *Given a game G, a **strategy** σ for player α_i is a map that maps every non-terminal state of that game to a nonempty set of legal moves for that player. Thus, σ is a map:*

$$\sigma : W \setminus T \to 2^{A_i}$$

*such that for each $w \in W \setminus T$ we have $\sigma(w) \neq \emptyset$ and $\sigma(w) \subseteq L_i(w)$. A **complete strategy** is a strategy such that $|\sigma(w)| = 1$ for all $w \in W \setminus T$, and a **partial strategy** is a strategy that is not complete. A tuple $(\sigma_1, \sigma_2 \ldots \sigma_n)$ consisting of one strategy for each player is called a **strategy profile**.*

In the following, we use a superscript G or N to indicate that something is a component of the game G or of the negotiation protocol N. For example P^G is the protocol of G, and W^N is the set of world states of N.

We will next define a negotiation game NG to be a combination of a negotiation protocol N and a game G. The interpretation of NG is that it is a game that consists of two stages: a negotiation stage followed by an action stage. In the action stage the players play the game G, while in the preceding negotiation stage the players negotiate about which strategies they will apply during the action stage. These agreements are considered binding, therefore, if the players come to an agreement they will have less legal moves during the action stage than they would have in the pure game G.

We say a negotiation protocol N is compatible with a game G if it has the same set of agents as G, and the set of agreements Agr consists purely of strategy profiles for the game G. This means that N is designed for the agents of G to negotiate the strategies they will play in the game G.

Definition 5. *A negotiation protocol N is **compatible** with a game G, if both of the following hold:*

- $Ag^N = Ag^G$.
- *If $x \in Agr^N$ then x is a strategy profile for G.*

The interpretation here, is that if the negotiators agree on some strategy profile $(\sigma_1, \ldots \sigma_n)$ then each player α_i has promised, for any state w of G, to only choose its action from $\sigma_i(w)$. Specifically, if σ_i is a *complete* strategy, then α_i has no more free choice in G, and must play in any state w the unique action in $\sigma_i(w)$. Furthermore, the conflict deal of Agr^N corresponds to the strategy profile in which each player still has its full set of legal actions to choose from: $\sigma_i(w) = L_i(w)$. Indeed, if no agreement is made this means that no agent is restricted by any commitments and may therefore choose any legal action in G.

Definition 6. *Given a game G and a negotiation protocol N compatible with G we define the **negotiation game** NG as a game, such that:*

- $Ag = Ag^N = Ag^G$
- *For each player α_i:* $\mathcal{A}_i = \mathcal{A}_i^N \cup \mathcal{A}_i^G$
- *The set of states W is a subset of $W^N \times W^G$.*
  More precisely: $W = W^{nego} \cup W^{act}$ *with:*

$$W^{nego} = W^N \times \{w_1^G\}$$
$$W^{act} = T^N \times W^G$$

- *The initial state is defined as:* $w_1 = (w_1^N, w_1^G)$.
- *The terminal states are defined as:* $T = T^N \times T^G$.
- *The update function is defined as:*

$$u((v,z), \boldsymbol{a}) = (u^N(v, \boldsymbol{a}), z) \quad if\ (v,z) \in W^{nego}$$
$$u((v,z), \boldsymbol{a}) = (v, u^G(z, \boldsymbol{a})) \quad if\ (v,z) \in W^{act}$$

- *The legality functions are defined as:*

$$L_i(v,z) = L_i^N(v) \quad if\ (v,z) \in W^{nego}$$
$$L_i(v,z) = \sigma_i(z) \quad if\ (v,z) \in W^{act}$$

  where $(\sigma_1, \ldots \sigma_n) = C^N(v)$
- *The utility functions are defined as:*

$$U_i(v,z) = U_i^G(z)$$

Here, we have modeled states w of NG as pairs of states $w = (v, z)$ consisting of a protocol-state $v \in W^N$ and a game-state $z \in W^G$. The initial state w_1 of NG is simply the pair of initial states (w_1^N, w_1^G) of N and G.

We have divided the state space W into two subspaces: W^{nego} and W^{act}, which represent the negotiation stage and the action stage respectively. Note that the initial state is in W^{nego} and that the update and legality functions are defined such that any legal history starts with a sequence of states that are all in W^{nego}, followed by a sequence of states that are all in be in W^{act}. In other words: the game starts in the negotiation stage, until at some point it reaches a state in the action stage, after which the game remains in the action stage.

During the negotiation stage the update function u only acts on the protocol-state, and acts on it according to the update function u^N of N, while during the action stage u only acts on the game-state, according to u^G. In other words: during the negotiation stage the game follows the protocol P^N, while during the action stage the game follows the protocol P^G.

Similarly, during the negotiation stage the legality functions L_i are simply the legality functions L_i^N of the negotiation protocol. Therefore, during this stage the agents can make proposals and accept proposals. During the action stage the legality function of an agent α_i allows it only to take those actions it was committed to during the negotiation stage. Note that indeed, if $(v, z) \in W^{act}$ then v is a terminal state of N, and therefore $C^N(v)$ is some agreement from the agreement space Agr^N of N. Furthermore, since N is compatible with G, we know that $C^N(v)$ is a strategy profile of G. In other words: if during the negotiation stage the agents have agreed to on the strategy profile $C^N(v) = (\sigma_1, \ldots \sigma_n)$ then during the action stage each agent α_i is committed to play according to the strategy σ_i.

Example 3. If G is the Prisoner's Dilemma, and N is the alternating offers protocol compatible with G, then the **Negotiating Prisoner's Dilemma** NG begins with a negotiation stage in which the prisoners may negotiate which strategies they will play. The prisoners may propose any strategy-pair (σ_1, σ_2). Since there is only one non-terminal state in the Prisoner's Dilemma, a strategy is defined by its value $\sigma_i(w_1^G)$ on that non-terminal state w_1^G. That is, σ_i can be either $\sigma_i(w_1^G) = \{c\}$ or $\sigma_i(w_1^G) = \{d\}$ or $\sigma_i(w_1^G) = \{c, d\}$. If the prisoners are rational, then one of them will propose the strategy profile $(\{d\}, \{d\})$ and the other will accept that proposal. In the action stage they are then both committed to play the action d.

Note that this example, in which the players agree to play $(\{d\}, \{d\})$, is in fact a subgame perfect equilibrium of the Negotiating Prisoner's Dilemma.[4] This is interesting, because the outcome strictly dominates the outcome (c, c) which is the Nash-equilibrium of the pure Prisoner's Dilemma. Therefore, in a sense, we can say that we have 'solved' the Prisoner's Dilemma by giving the players the opportunity to negotiate and make binding agreements about their actions.

Finally, we would like to remark that in the definition of a Negotiation Game as presented in this section the players only have one opportunity to negotiate, before they play the game G. However, we could also consider more general models in which, for example, the players have a new opportunity to negotiate before each new turn of the game G. We will not do this however, to keep the discussion simple.

4   Game Description Language

In this section we will give a short introduction to GDL. For more details we refer to [11].

GDL is logical language that was designed to describe games. In principle, it can describe any game G defined according to Definitions 1 and 3. GDL is

---

[4] We should stress here that we have assumed agreements are *binding*. Without this assumption this statement would not be true.

similar to Datalog [2], but it defines the following relation symbols:[5] *init, true, next, legal, goal, terminal, does,* which have a special meaning related to games.

In GDL a state w of a game is represented as a set of atomic formulas, which we will here denote as $V(w)$. These atoms are all of the form $true(p)$, where p can be any ground term. For example, in Tic-Tac-Toe the state in which the center cell contains the marker X and the left upper cell contains the marker O could be represented as:

$$V(w) = \{\ true(cell(2, 2, X))\ ,\ \ true(cell(1, 1, O))\ \}$$

A GDL **rule** is an expression of the following form:

$$s_1 \wedge s_2 \wedge \ldots s_n \rightarrow h$$

where each s_i is a positive or negative literal, and h is a positive literal. The atom h is called the *head* of the rule and the s_i's are called the *subgoals* of the rule. The conjunction of subgoals is called the *body* of the rule. The body of a rule may be the empty conjunction, in which case the rule is also referred to as a *fact*, which we denote as $\rightarrow h$.

A game description is then nothing more then a set of GDL rules. For example, if the game description contains the following rule:

$$true(p) \wedge does(\alpha_i, a) \rightarrow next(q)$$

it means that if the game is in a state w for which $true(p) \in V(w)$ and player α_i plays action a then in the next round the game will be in a state w' for which $true(q) \in V(w')$ holds. Similarly:

$$true(p) \rightarrow terminal$$

means that any state w for which $true(p) \in V(w)$ holds is a terminal state. The fact

$$\rightarrow init(p)$$

means that for the initial state w_1 we have $true(p) \in V(w_1)$. The rule

$$true(p) \rightarrow legal(\alpha_i, a)$$

means that for any state in which $true(p) \in V(w)$ holds it is legal for player α_i to play the move a.

$$true(p) \rightarrow goal(\alpha_i, 100)$$

means that in any state w for which $true(p) \in V(w)$ holds α_i receives a utility value of 100.

GDL uses what is known as negation-by-failure. This means that a negative literal $\neg p$ is considered true if and only if there is no rule from which one can derive the truth of p. GDL can only describe games of full information without

---

[5] GDL defines more relations, but these are not relevant for this paper.

randomness. However, an extension to GDL exists, called GDL-II [27] which does allow for randomness and private information.

The Game Manager is a server application specially designed for General Game Playing. It allows you to start a game with a game description written in GDL, and allows game playing agents to connect and start playing. Once connected, the server sends the game description to the players. The players then need to parse the description and determine for themselves which moves they can make, and what the consequences are. Every round, each player is supposed to send a message back with the move it desires to play. If a player fails to send this message, or if it chooses an action that is illegal in the current state, the server will instead pick a random move for that player. Next, the server sends a message back to all players, informing each player which moves have been made by the other players. From this information the players can then compute the next state, and determine which moves they can make in that new state. This continues until a terminal state is reached.

5   General Negotiation Games

Not only does GDL allow us to define complex negotiation games, it also allows us to write domain-independent negotiation algorithms. With this we mean that the agents do reason about the domain, but they only receive information about the domain at run-time, just like in GGP.

We can now distinguish between three types of agents:

- **Completely generic agents**: agents that are able to interpret any negotiation protocol N and any game G provided at run-time, as long as they are specified in GDL.
- **Protocol-specific agents**: agents that are designed only for one specific negotiation protocol N, but that can interpret any game G provided at run-time, as long as it is specified in GDL.
- **Game-specific agents**: agents that are able to interpret any negotiation protocol N provided at run-time, as long as it is specified in GDL, but that are designed only for one specific game G.

Agents that are completely generic are essentially just GGP agents. Since they can handle any negotiation protocol N and any game G they can handle in principle anything specified in GDL, including games that have nothing to do with negotiations. This, however, also means that when such an agent is playing a negotiation game, it is very hard (if not impossible) for this agent to exploit that fact, and be better at negotiating than any standard GGP algorithm. Therefore, we think that this kind of agent is less interesting for Automated Negotiations research.

We think that protocol-specific agents are more interesting. Such an agent is less generic than a GGP player, but it has the advantage that when implementing it we may incorporate algorithms specific for negotiations. In order to assess the values of the proposals it negotiates it would need to apply advanced reasoning algorithms for GGP, which makes it more interesting than the agents developed for classical negotiation domains.

Another interesting option is to implement game-specific agents. This would allow us to do research on negotiation algorithms that are independent of the negotiation protocol.

6   A Language to Define Strategies

As explained, the proposals made during the negotiation stage of a Negotiation Game are in fact strategy profiles. For example, in the Negotiating Prisoner's Dilemma, player α_1 may propose:

$$(\sigma_1, \sigma_2) = (\{c, d\}, \{d\})$$

Here, σ_1 is the partial strategy in which player α_1 has the choice to play either c or d, and σ_2 is the strategy in which α_2 plays d (of course this is a highly unprofitable deal for α_2 so if α_2 is rational he or she will not accept it).

In the case of the Prisoner's Dilemma a strategy can be represented simply as the set of possible actions in the only non-terminal state. However, in other games, such as Diplomacy, the number of possible actions and states can be extremely large. Therefore, expressing a strategy explicitly as a set of actions for every non-terminal state in such games is infeasible.

Instead, we propose to use Strategic Game Logic: a recently introduced logical language specifically defined to describe game-strategies. SGL is in fact an extension of GDL. While GDL is used to describe the *rules* of a game, SGL can be used to describe *strategies* of a game. We will here only briefly discuss the basic ideas. For a detailed description we refer to [28].

A logical formula ϕ in SGL may represent a set of states, or a set of state-action pairs. For example: $\phi = true(p) \wedge true(q)$ would represent the set of states:

$$\{w \in W \mid true(p) \in V(w) \text{ and } true(q) \in W\}$$

while $\phi = true(p) \wedge does(a)$ represents the set of state-action pairs:

$$\{(w, a) \in W \times \{a\} \mid true(p) \in V(w)\}$$

We say that w satisfies ϕ if w is in the set of states represented by ϕ, and we say that (w, a) satisfies ϕ if (w, a) is in the set of state-action pairs represented by ϕ.

Note that a set S of state-action pairs can be seen as a strategy, defined by $a \in \sigma_i(w)$ iff $(w, a) \in S$. Therefore, negotiators may make proposals of the form $propose(\phi_1, \phi_2)$ where ϕ_1 is an SGL formula that represents a strategy for player α_1 and ϕ_2 is an SGL formula that represents a strategy for player α_2.

SGL defines a number of new operators on top of GDL. That is, if a is an action and ϕ and φ are formulas, then SGL defines the following expressions: $[a]\phi$, $\lfloor a \rfloor \phi$, and $\langle \varphi \S \phi$.

Let ϕ be any formula representing a set of states, and a be any action. If w satisfies ϕ, then by definition $u(a, w)$ satisfies $[a]\phi$. That is: $[a]\phi$ represents the set of states that result from the action a being played in a state that is represented by ϕ. Furthermore, w satisfies ϕ if and only if (w, a) satisfies $\lfloor a \rfloor \phi$.

For the last operator we have that $\langle\varphi\rangle\phi$ is satisfied only if ϕ is satisfied under a new protocol where the legality relation of the original protocol is replaced by the strategy φ. For example, suppose that we have a state w in which it is legal for player α_i to play either action a or action b. Then the formulas $\phi_1 = legal(\alpha_i, a)$ and $\phi_2 = legal(\alpha_i, b)$ are both satisfied by w. Furthermore, let φ be a strategy in which α_i plays action b in state w. Then we have that w satisfies $\langle\varphi\rangle\phi_2$, but not $\langle\varphi\rangle\phi_1$.

Using these new operators SGL defines two more operators that allow to combine any two strategies into a new strategy. Firstly, SGL defines *prioritized disjunction*:

$$\phi \oslash \varphi = \phi \vee (\varphi \wedge \bigwedge_{c \in \mathcal{A}_i} \lfloor c \rfloor \neg \phi)$$

which has the interpretation of *"play strategy ϕ if applicable, otherwise play strategy φ"*. Secondly, SGL defines *prioritized conjunction*:

$$\phi \oslash \varphi = \phi \wedge ((\bigvee_{c \in \mathcal{A}_i} \lfloor c \rfloor (\phi \wedge \varphi)) \rightarrow \varphi)$$

Which is a strategy with the interpretation: *"apply both ϕ and φ if both are applicable; otherwise, apply ϕ only"*.

7 Applying GDL to Negotiations

In this section we will discuss some technical issues that we encountered when using GDL to describe negotiation games.

7.1 Enforcement of Commitments

One problem we need to take care of is the question how to enforce that agents obey their agreements. Although in some domains (such as Diplomacy) there simply is no mechanism at all to force agents to obey agreements, in many existing domains one does require agreements to be enforced. We suggest two possible solutions.

The first option would be to write a game description that includes all rules for the negotiation protocol N, the game G and all rules necessary to guarantee agreement obedience. That is, they would contain rules of the form "If players α_1 and α_2 make the agreement that α_1 will play action a_1 and α_2 will play action a_2, then those actions will be the only legal actions". For example, if the original game G contains the rule

$$true(p) \rightarrow legal(\alpha_i, a)$$

then the negotiation game NG would instead contain the rules:

$$committed(\alpha_i, a) \wedge a \neq b \rightarrow excluded(\alpha_i, b)$$
$$true(p) \wedge \neg excluded(\alpha_i, a) \rightarrow legal(\alpha_i, a)$$

where the first rule specifies that whenever a player gets committed to an action a, then all other actions are excluded. The second rule is an adaptation of the original rule, with the extra premise added that an action a can only be legal if it has not been excluded by the commitments.

The second option would be to write a new game server that forbids the players to make moves that are incompatible with their agreements. In that case we see the negotiation protocol N and the game G as two separate games with each its own game description. If a player gets committed to action a but tries to play the action b the server will not allow it, even though b is legal according to the rules of the pure game G.

The advantage of the first option is that it is completely compatible with existing GGP standards. A negotiation game NG is just another game that can be described in GDL. Any existing GGP player should therefore be able to participate in such a negotiation game. However, the problem is that one would need to write rules that take all possible commitments into account. After all, a commitment may not simply be a single action, as in this example, but could be a disjunction of actions, or it could be conditional (e.g. if you play a I will play b in the next round, or if you play b then I will play a). It would be very complicated to write rules that are generic enough to cover all possible commitments, especially if we allow the full SGL language to specify agreements. Furthermore, it seems rather redundant to explicitly write rules to enforce commitments, if it is obvious that agreements must be obeyed.

We therefore think it might be more practical to choose the second option and implement a special General Negotiation server that handles rule enforcement. Moreover, it also has the advantage that it would allow us to re-use any existing game specification and freely combine it with any negotiation protocol specified in GDL. There is no need to adapt the rules of the game.

7.2   Very Large Spaces

Currently, many GGP algorithms are not able to handle domains where the number of possible actions is very large. The reason is that they apply *grounding*: they try to generate a list that explicitly contains all possible actions. Of course, if there are millions of possible proposals such as in the domain of the ANAC 2014 competition, this approach will not work.

However, we have managed to implement a GDL specification of a domain like in ANAC 2014, where we avoid this problem with a little trick. In this domain the negotiators propose contracts that consist of 10 properties, and each property can have 10 different values, so that there are 10^{10} possible contracts.

Instead of mapping each possible proposal to an action, we have written the description such that making a proposal requires making several actions.

More precisely: apart from the three standard types of action: 'propose', 'accept' and 'noop' from Example 1, we have added a fourth action called 'setValue'. The setValue action takes two parameters: a property-index and a value. By playing a number of setValue actions the player creates a contract, in which the indicated properties have the indicated values. For example, if an agent plays the following three actions:

$$setValue(1, 5), \quad setValue(2, 9), \quad setValue(4, 2)$$

it creates a contract in which the first property has value 5, the second property has value 9 and the fourth property has value 2. All other properties will by default have value 0. Then, after generating the contract the negotiator can propose it by playing the action 'propose'. In this way there are only 103 possible actions, instead of 10^{10}.

7.3   Continuous Time

In GDL it is assumed that games take place over discrete rounds. The duration of each round can be specified in the server. However, in negotiations it is not uncommon to assume that negotiations take place in continuous time. In the ANAC 2014 domain for example, although the agents did take turns, each agent could take as much time as it wanted to make a proposal. In principle, this is not a problem, because we can simple allow agents to make a 'noop' move representing the 'action' of not making an action, and make sure that the other agent only gets the turn after the first agent makes a proposal.

There is however a small technical problem with this, namely that each agent must take care that it indeed submits the 'noop' action before the deadline of the round passes. If it does not manage to do this in time (for example because it is doing heavy calculations that take up all its resources) then the server will automatically pick a random action for that agent. Of course, this is undesirable because the server may choose a highly unprofitable proposal which may then be accepted by the opponent.

We think that, in the context of negotiations in continuous time, it would be better to have a server that by default picks the 'noop' move if you fail to play any action within the time limits.

7.4   Hidden Utilities

In GDL it is not possible to specify games with hidden information. This means that you cannot only determine your own utility values, but also your opponents' utility values. This is fine for most games, but in the field of Automated Negotiations it is often assumed that utility values are hidden.

Again, in order to solve this problem we could write an alternative game server that does not send information to the players about their opponents' utility functions, or alternatively we might use GDL-II to keep information about utility functions hidden.

Another option, is to simply re-interpret the semantics of GDL. That is, we could interpret the goal-values specified in the game descriptions not as utility values, but rather as values that only indicate a preference *order*. For example, suppose we have the following two rules:

$$true(p) \rightarrow goal(\alpha_1, 100)$$
$$true(q) \rightarrow goal(\alpha_1, 50)$$

The classical interpretation of this is the following: "if p is true, then α_1 receives a utility of 100, and if q is true then α_1 receives a utility of 50." However, we could re-interpret this as only meaning the following: "α_1 prefers states in which p is true over states in which q is true". In this second interpretation the values 50 and 100 do not really have any meaning any more. They only serve to establish an ordering between terminal states, while the true utility values remain private information.

8   Results

We have managed to specify the Negotiating Prisoner's Dilemma of Example 3 in GDL, in which the negotiation stage was modeled as a turn-taking protocol with three rounds in which prisoner 1 is first allowed to make a proposal, next prisoner 2 is allowed to either accept that proposal or make a counter proposal, and finally prisoner 1 may accept the last proposal made by prisoner 2.

We have implemented a straightforward minimax algorithm for GGP, and when we let two instances of this algorithm play the Negotiating Prisoner's Dilemma they indeed successfully negotiate and agree to both play 'deny'. This is very interesting, because this algorithm is *not* a negotiation algorithm. It is simply a general game-playing algorithm that may just as well play Tic-Tac-Toe or any other simple game. The reason that it is able to negotiate successfully is that the negotiation scenario was described in GDL.

Moreover, we have implemented a domain similar to ANAC 2014 in which the agents negotiate according to the alternating offers protocol over a space with 10^{10} possible contracts. Since this is a very large domain over many rounds a naive minimax does not work. To be able to handle such domains we need to apply more state-of-the-art GGP techniques. We leave this as future work. Also it would be interesting to see whether any of the top existing GGP players is able to handle this domain.

9   Conclusions

We conclude that GDL is in essence a good option for the description of general negotiation scenarios because it allows us to write complex negotiation domains that require reasoning and logic, and for which assessing the value of a proposal requires thinking ahead about your future actions, as well as the opponents' future actions. Moreover, GDL allows us to write domain-independent agents, in the sense that they only receive domain-knowledge at run-time.

However, there are a number of aspects specific to automated negotiations that are not handled well by GDL and the existing GGP server. Therefore, we think that it is necessary to write a new server application, specific for negotiations. This server will handle rule enforcement and should be able to verify whether any action is compatible with any strategy defined as a formula in SGL.

We have shown that a simple Negotiating Prisoner's Dilemma can be described correctly in GDL, as well as the more complex domain of ANAC 2014. Furthermore, we have shown that it is indeed possible for a GGP algorithm to successfully negotiate in the Negotiating Prisoner's Dilemma even though it is not designed for negotiations. For the larger ANAC 2014 domain we still need to find out whether existing GGP techniques are able to handle it.

Acknowledgments. This work was sponsored by an Endeavour Research Fellowship awarded by the Australian Government, Department of Education.

References

1. Baarslag, T., Hindriks, K., Jonker, C.M., Kraus, S., Lin, R.: The first automated negotiating agents competition (ANAC 2010). In: Ito, T., Zhang, M., Robu, V., Fatima, S., Matsuo, T. (eds.) New Trends in Agent-based Complex Automated Negotiations. SCI, vol. 383, pp. 113–135. Springer, Heidelberg (2010)
2. Ceri, S., Gottlob, G., Tanca, L.: What you always wanted to know about datalog (and never dared to ask). IEEE Trans. Knowl. Data Eng. **1**(1), 146–166 (1989)
3. Fabregues, A.: Facing the challenge of automated negotiations with humans. Ph.D. thesis, Universitat Autònoma de Barcelona (2012)
4. Fabregues, A., Sierra, C.: DipGame: a challenging negotiation testbed. Eng. Appl. Artif. Intell. **24**, 1137–1146 (2011)
5. Faratin, P., Sierra, C., Jennings, N.R.: Using similarity criteria to make negotiation trade-offs. In: International Conference on Multi-Agent Systems, ICMAS 2000, pp. 119–126 (2000)
6. Faratin, P., Sierra, C., Jennings, N.R.: Negotiation decision functions for autonomous agents. Robot. Auton. Syst. **24**(3–4), 159–182 (1998). Multi-AgentRationality. http://www.sciencedirect.com/science/article/pii/S0921889098000293
7. Fatima, S., Wooldridge, M., Jennings, N.R.: An analysis of feasible solutions for multi-issue negotiation involving nonlinear utility functions. In: Proceedings of The 8th International Conference on Autonomous Agents and Multiagent Systems, AAMAS 2009, vol. 2. pp. 1041–1048. International Foundation for Autonomous Agents and Multiagent Systems, Richland, SC (2009). http://dl.acm.org/citation.cfm?id=1558109.1558158
8. Ferreira, A., Lopes Cardoso, H., Paulo Reis, L.: DipBlue: a diplomacy agent with strategic and trust reasoning. In: 7th International Conference on Agents and Artificial Intelligence (ICAART 2015), pp. 398–405 (2015)
9. Finnsson, H.: Simulation-based general game playing. Ph.D. thesis, School of Computer Science, Reykjavik University (2012)
10. Genesereth, M., Love, N., Pell, B.: General game playing: overview of the AAAI competition. AI Mag. **26**(2), 62–72 (2005)

11. Genesereth, M.R., Thielscher, M.: General Game Playing. Synthesis Lectures on Artificial Intelligence and Machine Learning. Morgan & Claypool Publishers, San Rafael (2014)
12. Ito, T., Klein, M., Hattori, H.: A multi-issue negotiation protocol among agents with nonlinear utility functions. Multiagent Grid Syst. **4**, 67–83 (2008). http://dl. acm.org/citation.cfm?id=1378675.1378678
13. de Jonge, D.: Negotiations over large agreement spaces. Ph.D. thesis, Universitat Autònoma de Barcelona (2015)
14. de Jonge, D., Sierra, C.: NB3: a multilateral negotiation algorithm for large, non-linear agreement spaces with limited time. Auton. Agents Multi-Agent Syst. **29**(5), 896–942 (2015). http://www.iiia.csic.es/files/pdfs/jaamas%20NB3.pdf
15. Knuth, D.E., Moore, R.W.: An analysis of alpha-beta pruning. Artif. Intell. **6**(4), 293–326 (1975). http://www.sciencedirect.com/science/article/pii/ 0004370275900193
16. Kocsis, L., Szepesvári, C.: Bandit based Monte-Carlo planning. In: Fürnkranz, J., Scheffer, T., Spiliopoulou, M. (eds.) ECML 2006. LNCS (LNAI), vol. 4212, pp. 282–293. Springer, Heidelberg (2006). doi:10.1007/11871842_29
17. Kraus, S.: Designing and building a negotiating automated agent. Comput. Intell. **11**, 132–171 (1995)
18. Love, N., Genesereth, M., Hinrichs, T.: General game playing: game description language specification. Technical report LG-2006-01, Stanford University, Stanford, CA (2006). http://logic.stanford.edu/reports/LG-2006-01.pdf
19. Marsa-Maestre, I., Lopez-Carmona, M.A., Velasco, J.R., de la Hoz, E.: Effective bidding and deal identification for negotiations in highly nonlinear scenarios. In: Proceedings of The 8th International Conference on Autonomous Agents and Mul-tiagent Systems, AAMAS 2009, vol. 2, pp. 1057–1064. International Foundation for Autonomous Agents and Multiagent Systems, Richland, SC (2009). http://dl. acm.org/citation.cfm?id=1558109.1558160
20. Marsa-Maestre, I., Lopez-Carmona, M.A., Velasco, J.R., Ito, T., Klein, M., Fujita, K.: Balancing utility and deal probability for auction-based negotiations in highly nonlinear utility spaces. In: Proceedings of the 21st International Jont Conference on Artifical Intelligence, IJCAI 2009, pp. 214–219. Morgan Kaufmann Publishers Inc., San Francisco (2009). http://dl.acm.org/citation.cfm?id=1661445.1661480
21. Nash, J.: The bargaining problem. Econometrica **18**, 155–162 (1950)
22. von Neumann, J.: On the theory of games of strategy. In: Tucker, A., Luce, R. (eds.) Contributions to the Theory of Games, pp. 13–42. Princeton University Press, Princeton (1959)
23. Rosenschein, J.S., Zlotkin, G.: Rules of Encounter. The MIT Press, Cambridge (1994)
24. Kraus, S., Lehman, D., Ephrati, E.: An automated diplomacy player. In: Levy, D., Beal, D. (eds.) Heuristic Programming in Artificial Intelligence: The 1st Computer Olympia, pp. 134–153. Ellis Horwood Limited, Chichester (1989)
25. Schiffel, S., Thielscher, M.: M.: Fluxplayer: a successful general game player. In: Proceedings of the AAAI National Conference on Artificial Intelligence, pp. 1191–1196. AAAI Press (2007)
26. Serrano, R.: Bargaining. In: Durlauf, S.N., Blume, L.E. (eds.) The New Palgrave Dictionary of Economics. Palgrave Macmillan, Basingstoke (2008)

27. Thielscher, M.: A general game description language for incomplete information games. In: Proceedings of the Twenty-Fourth AAAI Conference on Artificial Intelligence, AAAI 2010, 11–15 July 2010, Atlanta, Georgia, USA (2010). http://www.aaai.org/ocs/index.php/AAAI/AAAI10/paper/view/1727
28. Zhang, D., Thielscher, M.: A logic for reasoning about game strategies. In: Proceedings of the Twenty-Ninth AAAI Conference on Artificial Intelligence (AAAI 2015), pp. 1671–1677 (2015)

Simulating Urban Growth with Raster and Vector Models: A Case Study for the City of Can Tho, Vietnam

Patrick Taillandier[1]([✉]), Arnaud Banos[2], Alexis Drogoul[3], Benoit Gaudou[4], Nicolas Marilleau[3], and Quang Chi Truong[3,5,6]

[1] UMR IDEES, University of Rouen, Mont-Saint-Aignan, France
patrick.taillandier@univ-rouen.fr
[2] UMR Géographie-cités, CNRS, Paris, France
arnaud.banos@parisgeo.cnrs.fr
[3] UMI 209 UMMISCO, IRD Bondy, Bondy, France
alexis.drogoul@gmail.com, nmarilleau@gmail.com
[4] IRIT, University of Toulouse 1 Capitole, Toulouse, France
benoit.gaudou@ut-capitole.fr
[5] CENRES & DREAM Team, Can Tho University, Can Tho, Vietnam
tcquang@ctu.edu.vn
[6] PDIMSC, University Pierre and Marie Curie/IRD, Paris, France

Abstract. Urban growth has been widely studied and many models (in particular Cellular Automata and Agent-Based Models) have been developed. Most of these models rely on two representations of the geographic space: raster and vector. Both representations have their own strengths and drawbacks. The raster models are simpler to implement and require less data, which explains their success and why most of urban growth models are based on this representation. However, they are not adapted to microscopic dynamics such as, for example, the construction of buildings. To reach such goal, a vector-based representation of space is mandatory. However, very few vector models exist, and none of them is easily adaptable to different case studies. In this paper, we propose to use a simple raster model and to adapt it to a vector representation of the geographic space and processes allowing studying urban growth at fine scale. Both models have been validated by a case study concerning the city of Can Tho, Vietnam.

Keywords: Agent-based simulation · Urban growth · Raster model · Vector model

1 Introduction

Being able to control urban growth has become a major challenge for our society. In this context, the possibilities offered by agent-based and cellular automata models to simulate this phenomena, and thus to evaluate possible outcomes of urban planning policies, are particularly interesting. These last years have seen

N. Osman and C. Sierra (Eds.): AAMAS 2016 WS, Visionary Papers, LNAI 10003, pp. 154–171, 2016.
DOI: 10.1007/978-3-319-46840-2_10

the development of various urban growth models. If many of them are abstract models aiming at underlying the key factors behind the phenomena, only a few aim at reproducing observed urban growth. Concerning this second type of models, most of them are based on Cellular Automata, or at least on a raster representation of space. This representation, consisting in dividing the space in homogeneous (in terms of internal state) space units, has for advantage to require less data (or at least less precise data) and to be simpler to implement, in particular with the numerous platforms that exist today. However, this type of space representation does not allow simulations at fine scale. Moreover, as it was showed by [11] for segregation models, we state that using a vector (GIS) representation for urban growth models would allow to learn new knowledge.

In this paper, we propose to derive a vector model - a model at building scale - from a raster one and to use them to study the urban growth of the Can Tho city in Vietnam. Both models have been implemented using the GAMA platform. GAMA is an open-source modeling and simulation platform for building spatially explicit agent-based simulations [1,14]. It integrates a complete and easy to learn modeling language and supports the definition of large-scale models (up to millions of agents). In addition, it allows a natural integration of GIS data (automatic agentification of data). At last, it integrates some built-in indicators such as the $Fuzzy-KappaSim$ [22] enabling to directly evaluate the simulation results.

This paper is organized as follow: Sect. 2 presents a state of the art of urban growth models. Section 3 is dedicated to the presentation of the case study of Can Tho. Section 4 presents the raster model developed and Sect. 5 the vector model. Section 6 proposes a discussion about the comparison of the two models. At last Sect. 7 concludes and proposes some perspectives.

2   State of the Art of Urban Growth Models

Modeling urban growth has been, since the seventies, one of the most documented domains in disciplines like geography [6,7,9], urbanism [16], or urban economy, and transportation [23,24] (see [2] for a comprehensive review), but also in disciplines not directly connected to urban systems but widely concerned with complex systems in general, such as physics [15,18]. However, despite this huge investment, it is still a challenging issue, especially when it comes to coupling processes and patterns at different geographic scales [25], which could require to use different representations of space.

Many of the first urban growth simulation models were based on a raster representation of space, in particular on square and hexagonal grids. Thus, the '90s have seen the development of many Cellular Automata models such as the ones proposed in [6,10,26].

Even with the multiplication of GIS vector data, this representation of space is still dominant when modeling urban growth. In fact, many recent models still use it (see for instance [17,20,21]). These models cover a large part of the "stylized - particular" axis proposed by [5] to classify models (cf. Fig. 1). Indeed, some of these model are very stylized (e.g. [20]), others are based on a lot of

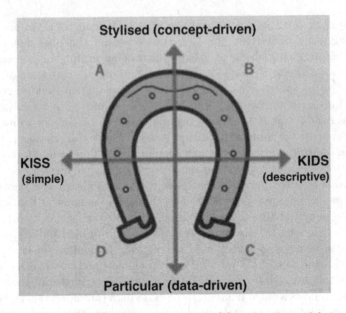

Fig. 1. "Horseshoe" reading template proposed by [5] to classify models in geography.

local pieces of knowledge and are very specific to a case-study such as [3]. In the same way, for the second "axis" "KISS [4] - KIDS [12]", some models are very simple and integrate very few processes (e.g. [20]) while others, that use the possibilities offered by Agent-Based Modeling, integrate many factors (social, economic, human, etc.) (e.g. [3,17]).

Only very few research works have proposed a vector-based model, in particular at the building scale (explicit representation of building geometries). A notable work is [19] that proposes a general framework to build vector urban growth models. This framework is based on the hierarchical decomposition of space in districts, blocks and geographical objects (roads, buildings, etc.). It provides modelers some built-in measures and indicators to help them to define their own dynamics. However, the use of the framework requires a lot of work to adapt it to a given case-study and requires to write Java code.

Our work aims at filling the lack of simple to use and easily adaptable vector models. In particular, we propose a KISS stylized vector-based model, adapted from a raster model, that can be easily implemented for different case-studies.

The Sects. 4 and 5 present respectively the raster model and the vector model.

3   Case Study: The City of Can Tho

3.1   The City of Can Tho

The city of Can Tho is the fourth-largest in Vietnam with 1 200 000 inhabitants and is the largest and fastest growing city in the Mekong Delta.

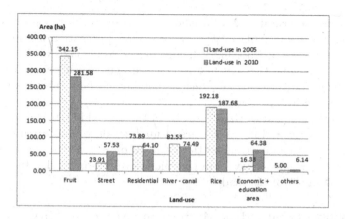

Fig. 2. Evolution of the Land Use between 2005 and 2010 in the An Binh ward. (Source: Generated from the Land Use maps of An Binh ward in 2005 and in 2010)

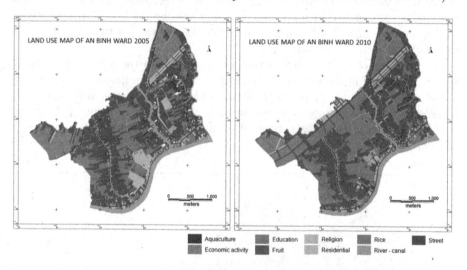

Fig. 3. Map of the Land Use evolution between 2005 and 2010 in the An Binh ward. (Source: Department of Environmental and Natural resources of Can Tho City, Vietnam)

The urbanization of this city shows a very fast growing in Ninh Kieu district, the central district of Can Tho, the agricultural area of this district are quickly replaced by construction area. An Binh ward is only one example for this process. The chart in Fig. 2 shows the rice area of this ward has sharply decreased more than 150 ha while the residential zones, street, economic and education area have increased rapidly. The land-use map in 2005 and in 2010 could explain this shifting (Fig. 3).

As many similar cities in developing countries, it has to face a number of economic, social and ecological challenges linked to this fast growth, such as the colonization of rural and wild-land spaces (and thus the preservation of ecosystems), the social impact (increase of spatial segregation of social groups, spatial fragmentation of labor markets, increase of traffic jams...). But due to its location in the Mekong Delta, it has also to face some specific challenges related to sea level rise (climate change), such as flooding by high tides from the river and canal system in rain season.

It is important to notice that Can Tho being located in the Mekong Delta, it is surrounded by rivers. Inhabitants are located not only along streets but along rivers as they use them for transportation. As a consequence, we have taken into account the importance of rivers in the micro-level vector model. In this model they have the same role as roads.

3.2   The 2020 Local Urban Masterplan of Can Tho City

The Can Tho urban spread is mainly driven by a plan (the last one has been drawn until 2020 and is presented in Fig. 4). It determines which roads should be built or enlarged. It defines also area that will be dedicated to activity or residential buildings. This plan is used to decide investments that will be made in the city in terms of infrastructures.

The interest of models such as the ones presented in the following is (could be) to give some insights to decision-makers about the impacts and efficiency of their plans. It can in particular often be observed in Vietnam a significant difference between plans and actual results, with the consequence of a waste of resources due to the construction of infrastructures that are not adapted or efficient.

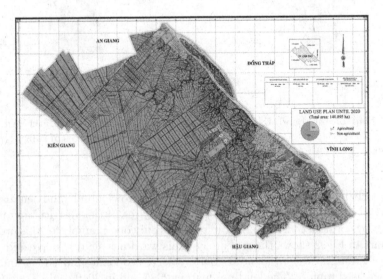

Fig. 4. Plan for Can Tho city in 2020. Red roads will be enlarged and built. Pink and red polygons are planned to become residential buildings. (Color figure online)

3.3   Description of Data

A comprehensive dataset on the evolution of the city shape has been gathered and built by researchers and practitioners.

The dataset contains data at the city level and more precise data for one of the city wards (An Binh ward). This is a ward of the center district (Ninh Kieu) where the urbanisation is very fast:

- Raster map (asc files) of Can Tho in 1999 and 2014 (resolution: 200×200 m). Three possible values for each cell have been defined: urban, non urban and river,
- Shapefile of roads of Can Tho in 2010,
- Shapefile of rivers (and canals) of Can Tho in 2010,
- Shapefile of the district boundaries of Can Tho,
- Vector land use maps (shapefiles) of An Binh ward (Ninh Kieu district) in 2005 and 2010. One type of land use is defined per vector object: river, road, non urban, rice, perennial tree, aquaculture, economic activity, education, religion, residential[1].

Figure 5 shows the dataset. The picture displaying vector data merges shape-files of roads, rivers and buildings.

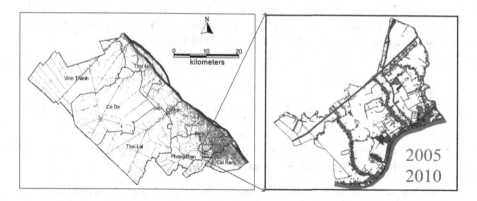

Fig. 5. Raster data (left) of Can Tho city and vector data (right) of An Binh ward, Ninh Kieu district. (Source: Department of Environmental and Natural resources of Can Tho City, Vietnam)

4   Raster Model

4.1   Model Description

As stated in Sect. 2, there are many raster agent-based models. As our goal is to simulate urban growth with minimum local knowledge, we chose to develop

---

[1] We only use the urban-related entities from land use map in the following models.

a KISS stylized raster model that requires a small amount of data. Our model was strongly inspired by the model proposed by [20]. This model proposes two dynamics: the construction of buildings and the construction of roads. The road construction dynamics is not adapted to our application context as its goal is more to study the emergence of classic city patterns than to reproduce real city evolutions. We made then the choice not to integrate the road network construction dynamics, and to consider the construction of roads as part of the input scenario.

As an illustration we use the Can Tho city raster map, aiming at simulating urban growth over 15 years from 1999 to 2014 (with a simulation step duration of 1 year).

In this model, the main agents are `cells` that represent a homogeneous area of space. A cell agent has two attributes:

- `is_built`: is the cell built or not (Boolean value),
- `constructability`: level of constructability of the cell (float value between 0 and 1): 0 means that it is not interesting at all to build on this cell (i.e. to switch the variable `is_built` to true), 1 that it is very interesting.

We have introduced an additional agent, `city_center`, in order to locate the center of the city, i.e. the place that concentrates the administrative activity. In the Can Tho city, we have located it following expert recommendations. In addition this type of agent gives us more flexibility if we want to apply our model on other cities and in particular in polycentric cities.

4.2   Model Dynamics

The general process of the model is based on two steps:

- each cell computes its level of constructability,
- the `nb_build_units` cells with the highest level of constructability are built (which induces that the attribute `is_built` is set to true).

The number of cells built at each simulation step, `nb_build_units`, is one of the parameters of the simulation.

The level of constructability of a cell depends on 3 criteria:

- CR_1: the density of construction in the neighborhood (the highest, the better):

$$CR_1 = \frac{\text{nb of built cells in the neighborhood}}{\text{nb of cells in the neighborhood}} \tag{1}$$

- CR_2: the euclidean distance to the closest road (the closer, the better):

$$CR_2 = 1 - \frac{\text{dist to the closest road}}{\text{max dist to the closest road (among all the cells)}} \tag{2}$$

- CR_3: the distance to the city center using the road network (the closer, the better):

$$CR_3 = 1 - \frac{\text{dist to the city center}}{\text{max dist to the city center (among all the cells)}} \qquad (3)$$

Note that the original model integrated a fourth criteria: the distance to activity. As we chose to minimize the local knowledge required to make the model works, we do not integrate this criteria in our model.

The level of constructability is the weighted average of these 3 criteria:

$$constructability = w_1 * CR_1 + w_2 * CR_2 + w_3 * CR_3 \qquad (4)$$

The three weights (w_1, w_2 and w_3) are parameters of the model.

4.3 Results

Figure 6 illustrates the results of the simulation after 15 steps. It highlights the impact of the three weights and thus of the three processes included in the urban growth model: to this purpose we run experiments with 2 of the 3 weight parameters at 0 and the last one at 1. This gives three different kinds of cities. If only the density criterion is used, the city tends to expand its city center in a homogeneous way. If only the distance to road criterion is used, the construction of buildings reflects the road network. At last, if only the distance to city center criterion is used, the city tends to expand its center following the road network.

4.4 Model Calibration

Finally we looked at the combination of parameters that provides the best simulation results, i.e. results that minimize the error compared to real data. In order to compute the error between two raster images (in our case the real and simulated results) it is easy to simply compare pixel by pixel (cell by cell in our case) the two images; the error is the rate of different pixels. But we consider that this error computation is too strict in our case. In particular because of the random factor in the selection of the cells that will be built among the one with the best constructability, we cannot get exact results. So, instead of this strict comparison between maps, we adopt a fuzzy approach and use the $Fuzzy - KappaSim$ similarity indicator [22]. It does not compute the similarity of cells two by two, but computes the similarity of a cell (in simulated data) with the corresponding cell in the real data and its neighborhood. If the real and simulated cells are different, but there is a similar cell on the neighbourhood, the similarity will be greater than 0.

Using the batch mode of GAMA to find among all the possible combinations of weight values the ones that maximize the $fuzzy - KappaSim$ indicator we get: $w_1 = 0.5$, $w_2 = 1.0$, $w_3 = 1.0$ and a result of $fuzzy - KappaSim = 0.497$. This means that new buildings have to be built along the roads that are close to the city center.

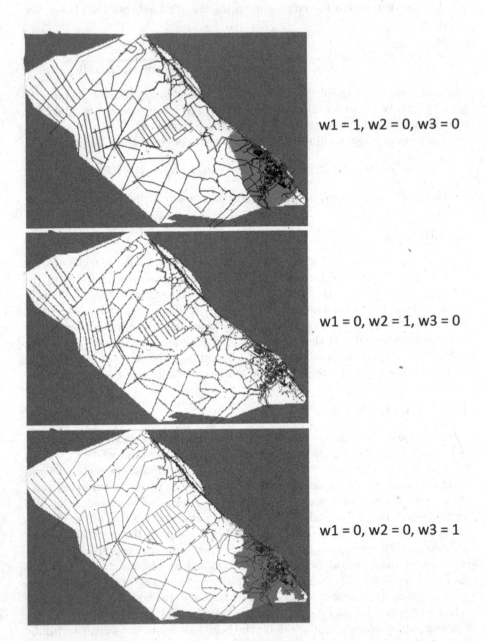

w1 = 1, w2 = 0, w3 = 0

w1 = 0, w2 = 1, w3 = 0

w1 = 0, w2 = 0, w3 = 1

Fig. 6. Results of the raster model in three particular cases: (top) with only the density criterion ($w_1 = 1$, $w_2 = 0$ and $w_3 = 0$); (center) with only the distance to road criterion ($w_1 = 0$, $w_2 = 1$ and $w_3 = 0$); (bottom) with only the distance to city center criterion ($w_1 = 0$, $w_2 = 0$ and $w_3 = 1$). Orange cells represent built cells. (Color figure online)

5   Vector Model

This model is similar in essence to the one based on cellular automata but operates at a finer scale and only uses vector GIS data. In particular, the unit of space and of reasoning is no more the arbitrary defined **cells** but **urban blocks** [8]. In the urban area, urban blocks are blocks containing buildings and delimited by roads and rivers (which are very important for transportation in the Mekong Delta).

Many types of entities have to be taken into account: buildings, roads, rivers, urban blocks. In this model, we chose to represent all them as agents, even when they do not have any dynamic. This choice helps to simplify the interaction process between them and to simplify the description of the model. In our model, simulating urban growth will thus consist in creating new building agents and locating them appropriately.

As an illustration we use the An Binh ward of the Can Tho city, aiming at simulating urban growth over 5 years from 2005 to 2010 (with a simulation step duration of 6 months). The data that will be used are the shapefiles of rivers, roads and land-use of the ward in 2005 to initialize the model. The land-use shapefile in 2010 is used to calibrate the model. Among the land-use shapefile entities, only urban-related ones (i.e. all residential, religion and economic buildings) are used in the model.

5.1   Hypotheses (Based on [20])

We consider that urban blocks (cf. Fig. 7) can be isolated within the ward. An urban block is defined as an urban space delimited by cycling streets or rivers [8]. Each urban block is composed of a set of buildings. Each building has its own function (Residential, Commercial, Education or Religion).

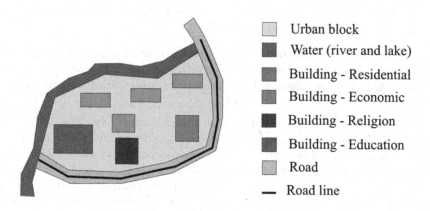

Fig. 7. Illustration of an urban block

New residential buildings are created following 3 rules:

- They tend to be created in blocks with a lot of empty space.
- They tend to be located in blocks not too far away from "services" (non-residential buildings).
- They tend to be located in well-connected blocks (close to roads and rivers).

5.2 Model Description

In this model and due to the capacities of the modeling and simulation platform chosen (GAMA, version 1.6.1) in terms of agentification of GIS data, the model contains agents representing rivers, roads and buildings. These agents are created directly from Can Tho GIS data. They are all characterized by their shape and location. In addition buildings have a type attribute taken its value among residential, commercial, religion and education. The last three types of buildings are considered as services.

Finally the model also contains urban_blocks agents. They are created at the initialization of the model from the existing data. In addition to its shape and location attributes, it contains also the attributes:

- buildings (resp. roads and rivers): it contains the set of building (resp. road and river) agents included in this urban block,
- constructability: this numerical attribute contains the constructability value of the urban block.

5.3 Model Dynamics

The dynamics of the model follows a 2-step process, repeated at every simulation step:

1. The constructability of each urban block is computed,
2. The nb_build_units urban blocks with the highest constructability create nb_new_buildings buildings inside them.

Both steps base their computations on the intensive use of geometrical operations (computation of distances (using road network), intersections, extrusions, etc.). nb_build_units and nb_new_buildings are two parameters of the simulation.

Step 1 - Evaluation of Urban Blocks Constructability. The aim of this first step is to give a mark to each urban block in order to rank them and determine which ones should be constructed first. So for each urban block with enough remaining space to construct a building, we evaluate it given the 3 following criteria: (CV_1) its density of empty space, (CV_2) the quantity of transportation (roads and rivers) inside and around it and (CV_3) its distance to services. The constructability index of each urban block is simply the weighted sum of these three criteria:

$$constructability = w_1 * CV_1 + w_2 * CV_2 + w_3 * CV_3$$

with w_1, w_2 and w_3 the weights associated to each criterion; they are considered as parameters of the simulation. They represent the importance of each of these three attractivenesses (by density, services and transportation) on new buildings. The calibration process will thus aim at finding the weight values for which the simulation results fit the best with real data.

For each urban block, at each simulation step, the three criteria are computed as follows:

- CV_1 is the density of free space, i.e. the rate of free space in the urban block:

$$CV_1 = \frac{\text{area of free space}}{\text{area of the urban block}}$$

- CV_2 is the total area of transportation (roads and rivers) inside and around (at a distance of 1 m) the urban block compared to the area of the urban block:

$$CV_2 = \frac{\text{area of roads \& rivers within a 1 m distance from the urban block}}{\text{area of the urban block}}$$

- CV_3 is the distance of the urban block to services. We consider here as services the educational, religious and commercial buildings. CV_3 thus depends on the distance to the closest educational building ($d_{educational\_building}$), religious building ($d_{religious\_building}$) and commercial building ($d_{commercial\_building}$). It is normalized by the maximum possible distance in the environment ($max\_distance$):

$$CV_3 = 1 - \frac{d_{educational\_building} + d_{religious\_building} + d_{commercial\_building}}{3 * max\_distance}$$

Step 2 - Selection of the nb_build_units Urban Blocks with the Highest Constructability and Creation of nb_new_buildings Buildings Inside Each. Once each urban block has computed its own constructability, the nb_build_units urban blocks with the higher constructability are chosen and nb_new_buildings new buildings are created on them.

To simplify the model, we chose not to create new building shapes. When creating a new building we simply copy the shape of an already existing building. We consider it is a good compromise between the creation of very simple rectangular buildings and of buildings with a random (and thus perhaps not realistic) shape.

In each chosen urban block, a new building is created following the 4 steps (cf. Fig. 8):

1. Choose an existing building in the block or in a neighboring one if none is available,
2. Extrude the shape of its buildings from the block geometry,
3. Erode the resulting shape by the maximum dimension of the chosen building,
4. If the resulting geometry is not empty, choose a random location inside it, create a building at this location (with the shape of the chosen building) and proceed similarly for the next building.

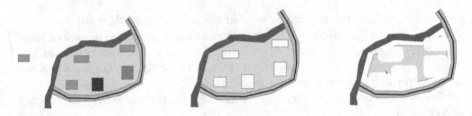

Fig. 8. Steps of the selection of possible locations for a new building. The remaining pink geometry in the right picture represents these possible locations. (Color figure online)

5.4   Results

The Fig. 9 shows preliminary results by considering separately the impact of each criterion. It highlights the impact of the three weights and thus of the three processes included in the urban growth model: to this purpose we run experiments with 2 of the 3 weight parameters at 0 and the last one at 1.

As expected, we get three very different locations for new buildings. If only the density criterion is used, new buildings are created in the empty urban blocks. If only the transportation criterion is used, new buildings are created in area with lot of roads and rivers around. Finally if only the activity criterion is used, new buildings are concentrated in the city center (and a few to another block with several activities).

5.5   Calibration and Validation of the Models on Can Tho Data

The calibration will be the minimization of the distance (i.e. the error) between the simulation results and the data. Contrarily to the raster model where it is easy to compute the error cell by cell, in the vector model we cannot use this grid discretization. As a consequence, the error is computed as the rate of new real buildings that are not intersected (with a given buffer) by buildings obtained by simulation, weighted by their area. As an example in the Fig. 10, the error between real data and simulated data (in 2010) is 0.5. This way of computing error is very close in essence to the fuzzy indicator used in the raster model.

After calibration, the best weights we get are: $w_1 = 0.2$, $w_2 = 1.0$ and $w_3 = 0.0$. The lowest error we get is $error = 0.288$. This means that most of new buildings are in urban blocks with a high density of free space and surrounded by many roads and rivers. This also shows that in the best combination the third criteria (related to the distance to services) does not seem to have an impact.

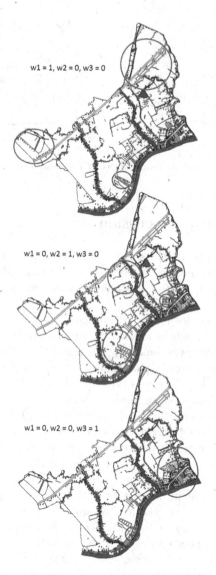

Fig. 9. Results of the vector model in three particular cases: (top) with only the density criterion ($w_1 = 1$, $w_2 = 0$ and $w_3 = 0$); (center) with only the quantity of transportation criterion ($w_1 = 0$, $w_2 = 1$ and $w_3 = 0$); (bottom) with only the distance to services criterion ($w_1 = 0$, $w_2 = 0$ and $w_3 = 1$). Red circles highlight the location of new buildings. Education buildings are in green, religion ones in violet, commercial in orange and residential in gray. (Color figure online)

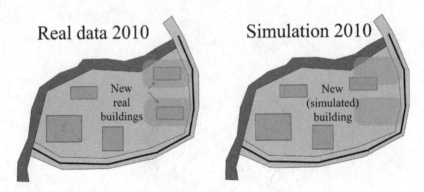

Fig. 10. Computation of the distance between real and simulated data. In this case the distance is 0.5.

6   Comparison and Discussion

The two models are based on the same general process: at each simulation step, the choice of a certain number of cells/blocks to build/densify. However, the difference in space representation has a deep impact on the questions the model can answer.

The raster model has for major advantage to require less data: only landsat data and a shapefile of roads were used in our case study. In addition, the time consumption of the model can be easily controlled through the resolution of the grid. These advantages make it particularly interesting for application context when the data are scare (which was typically the case for the city of Can Tho) and when the city is composed of many buildings.

The vector model requires not only to have a shapefile of roads, but also a shapefile of buildings (eventually with the function of each building). This model allows to simulate with details where buildings are going to be built. It allows as well to precise the function of each new building.

Concerning the comparison of the computational cost of the two models, we carried out an experiment in which we ran the previously presented models for 50 simulation steps on respectively the complete city of Can Tho for the raster model (335×222 cells with a size of $200\,m \times 200\,m$) and the An Binh ward (1037 buildings and 93 urban blocks) for the vector model. The experiment was carried out on an old Macbook computer (early 2011). The average step duration without considering the initialization stage (computation of the distances to roads and to city centers) for the raster model was $1.9\,s$ and $2.4\,s$ for the vector one. These results show that the computation cost is acceptable for both models. Of course, running the vector on the complete city of Can Tho will have increased a lot the computation time, as well as the use of a finer grid (with for example cells with a size of $20\,m \times 20\,m$ that is the average size of buildings in Can Tho). This experiment shows that the raster model is well adapted to be used as city level with a low granularity grid, whereas the vector model is more adapted to be used at ward level.

Concerning this scale level, it is interesting to note that the density criterion is used in an opposite way in the two models: in the raster model the chosen cells are the densest ones, whereas the chosen urban blocks are the less dense ones. We can observe here different forces at different scales. At the city level, there is an attractiveness of the denser area to build the city. But at the ward level, inhabitants prefer to have more free space to build their buildings.

The two models are complementary. An interesting work could be to couple these models in order to be able to use the raster model for the parts of the city where we do not need precise details on building construction, and the vector model for the other parts. Such hybrid model could have for benefits to require less data and be less time consuming than the use of the vector model on the complete city.

7   Conclusion

In this paper, we have presented two complementary KISS urban growth models: a model based on a raster representation at city-scale and a vector one at ward-scale. As discussed in Sect. 6, the two models have their own advantages and drawbacks. The raster model requires less data and can be less time-consuming if the resolution of the grid is not too high. It is well-adapted to simulate urban growth at city scale. In contrary, the vector model allows studying the urban growth at fine scale and simulating the construction of buildings - and thus to answer new questions. This model is well-adapted to simulate the urban growth at district-scale.

Both models have their advantages and drawbacks. They also make sense at different scales: fine scales for the vector-based model, more global ones for the raster-based one. However, coupling these two models within an integrated multi-scale approach is definitely a challenge the research team seeks to address in the next future.

In order to validate the genericity of our two models (and the hybrid one), we plan to test them on other cities.

We plan as well to improve the vector model by adding new criteria in the choice of the urban blocks to densify. In particular, we could add the criterion proposed by [20] concerning the accessibility of the urban blocks toward different activities. Another possible improvement could consist in using a more robust multi-criteria decision-making method to sort the cells/urban blocks. A possibility could be to use the Choquet integral to compute the constructability [13] that allows to take into account the redundancy and synergy between criteria.

Acknowledgements. This work was part of and supported by the Tam Dao Summer School in Social Sciences (JTD) – http://www.tamdaoconf.com/.

References

1. GAMA website (2015). http://gama-platform.org
2. Acheampong, R.A., Silva, E.: Land use-transport interaction modeling: a review of the literature and future research directions. J. Transp. Land Use **8**(3), 1–28 (2015)
3. Arsanjani, J.J., Helbich, M., de Noronha Vaz, E.: Spatiotemporal simulation ofurban growth patterns using agent-based modeling: the case of Tehran. Cities **32**, 33–42 (2013)
4. Axelrod, R.M.: The Complexity of Cooperation: Agent-Based Models of Competition and Collaboration. Princeton University Press, Princeton (1997)
5. Banos, A., Sanders, L.: Modéliser et simuler les systèmes spatiaux en géographie. Modéliser et Simuler-Epistémologies et Pratiques des Modèles et des Simulations, Ebook des éditions Matériologiques, vol. 1, pp. 833–863 (2013)
6. Batty, M., Xie, Y., Sun, Z.: Modeling urban dynamics through GIS-based cellular automata. Comput. Environ. Urban Syst. **23**(3), 205–233 (1999)
7. Benenson, I.: Multi-agent simulations of residential dynamics in the city. Comput. Environ. Urban Syst. **22**(1), 25–42 (1998)
8. Boffet, A., Coquerel, C.: Urban classification for generalisation orchestration. In: 19th International Symposium of Photogrammetry and Remote Sensing (ISPRS 2000), Amsterdam, pp. 16–23, July 2000
9. Caruso, G., Vuidel, G., Cavailhès, J., Frankhauser, P., Peeters, D., Thomas, I.: Morphological similarities between DBM and a microeconomic model of sprawl. J. Geogr. Syst. **13**(1), 31–48 (2011)
10. Clarke, K., Hoppen, S., Gaydos, L.: A self-modifying cellular automaton model of historical. Environ. Plan. B **24**, 247–261 (1997)
11. Crooks, A.T.: Constructing and implementing an agent-based model of residential segregation through vector GIS. Int. J. Geogr. Inf. Sci. **24**(5), 661–675 (2010)
12. Edmonds, B., Moss, S.: From KISS to KIDS – *an 'anti-simplistic' modelling approach*. In: Davidsson, P., Logan, B., Takadama, K. (eds.) MABS 2004. LNCS (LNAI), vol. 3415, pp. 130–144. Springer, Heidelberg (2005). doi:10.1007/978-3-540-32243-6_11
13. Grabisch, M., Labreuche, C.: A decade of application of the Choquet and Sugeno integrals in multi-criteria decision aid. Ann. Oper. Res. **175**(1), 247–286 (2010)
14. Grignard, A., Taillandier, P., Gaudou, B., Vo, D.A., Huynh, N.Q., Drogoul, A.: GAMA 1.6: advancing the art of complex agent-based modeling and simulation. In: Boella, G., Elkind, E., Savarimuthu, B.T.R., Dignum, F., Purvis, M.K. (eds.) PRIMA 2013. LNCS (LNAI), vol. 8291, pp. 117–131. Springer, Heidelberg (2013). doi:10.1007/978-3-642-44927-7_9
15. Haken, H., Portugali, J.: The face of the city is its information. J. Environ. Psychol. **23**(4), 385–408 (2003)
16. Hillier, B., Leaman, A., Stansall, P., Bedford, M.: Space syntax. Environ. Plan. B Plan. Des. **3**(2), 147–185 (1976)
17. Liu, Y., Feng, Y.: A logistic based cellular automata model for continuous urban growth simulation: a case study of the Gold Coast City, Australia. In: Heppenstall, A.J., Crooks, A.T., See, L.M., Batty, M. (eds.) Agent-Based Models of Geographical Systems, pp. 643–662. Springer, The Netherlands (2012)
18. Louf, R., Barthelemy, M.: Modeling the polycentric transition of cities. Phys. Rev. Lett. **111**(19), 198702 (2013)

19. Perret, J., Curie, F., Gaffuri, J., Ruas, A.: A Multi-agent system for the simulation of urban dynamics. In: 10th European Conference on Complex Systems (ECCS 2010), Lisbon (2010)

20. Raimbault, J., Banos, A., Doursat, R.: A hybrid network/grid model of urban morphogenesis and optimization. In: Aziz-Alaoui, M.A., Bertelle, C., Liu, X.Z., Olivier, D. (eds.) Proceedings of the 4th International Conference on Complex Systems and Applications (ICCSA 2014), pp. 51–60, June 2014

21. Torrens, P.M.: Simulating sprawl. Ann. Assoc. Am. Geogr. **96**(2), 248–275 (2006)

22. van Vliet, J., Hagen-Zanker, A., Hurkens, J., van Delden, H.: A fuzzy set approach to assess the predictive accuracy of land use simulations. Ecol. Model. **261**, 32–42 (2013)

23. Waddell, P.: Urbansim: modeling urban development for land use, transportation, and environmental planning. J. Am. Plan. Assoc. **68**(3), 297–314 (2002)

24. Wegener, M.: Overview of land-use transport models. In: Handbook of Transport Geography and Spatial Systems, vol. 5, pp. 127–146. Pergamon/Elsevier Science, Kidlington (2004)

25. White, R.: Modeling multi-scale processes in a cellular automata framework. In: Portugali, J. (ed.) Complex Artificial Environments, pp. 165–177. Springer, Heidelberg (2006)

26. White, R., Engelen, G.: Cellular automata and fractal urban form: a cellular modelling approach to the evolution of urban land-use patterns. Environ. Plan. A **25**(8), 1175–1199 (1993)

Gamification of Multi-agent Systems Theory Classes

J. Baldeón[(⊠)], M. Lopez-Sanchez, I. Rodríguez, and A. Puig

Faculty of Mathematics, Applied Mathematics and Analysis Department,
University of Barcelona, Gran Via, 585, 08007 Barcelona, Spain
{johan.baldeon,maite_lopez,inmarodriguez,annapuig}@ub.edu
http://www.maia.ub.es

Abstract. Traditional theory classroom dynamics suffer from student feedback and interaction. Unfortunately, attendance rates also represent a common problem. In order to mitigate these issues, we propose the inclusion of novel teaching resources. On the one hand, Multi-Agent Systems (MAS) core concepts of distribution, autonomy and interaction can be mapped into collaborative classes, where students can experience theoretical concepts in hands-on activities. On the other hand, class gamification can help to enhance students motivation and engagement. Nevertheless, applying gamification requires the usage of a suitable framework. This paper proposes an extension of the Gamification Model Canvas. This extension includes MAS principles as well as those of Lego Serious Play and Audience Response Systems. Additionally, we illustrate its applicability by means of a case study that designs and gamifies a multi-agent systems class, which has been positively evaluated by students.

Keywords: Gamification · Teaching MAS · LSP · ARS

1 Introduction

Nowadays, learning of multi-agent systems (MAS) concepts is often an individual experience with a unidirectional communication between teachers and students, and where both methodology and environment are those of a traditional classroom. In this context, theory classes are boring, include many abstract concepts [3], and, as a result, students simply do not engage, and there are low attendance rates in theory classes.

But, what about if teachers design MAS classes as if they were multi-agent systems? In this case, teachers and students would work collaboratively, acting as agents that (distributively) interact, and promoting emergent behaviour [1]. In this scenario, both existing knowledge and skills could be put into practice, keeping in mind that this experiential approach would ensure that teaching ideas, principles, and concepts have a lasting value [5].

In addition, if session activities would include emulating MAS applications in this collaborative setting, it would consolidate learned concepts and would

© Springer International Publishing AG 2016
N. Osman and C. Sierra (Eds.): AAMAS 2016 WS, Visionary Papers, LNAI 10003, pp. 172–183, 2016.
DOI: 10.1007/978-3-319-46840-2_11

also enhance students experience [20]. Moreover, these activities would exploit transversal skills such as teamwork, social applications, collective thinking, argumentation and social intelligence [4].

Furthermore, if we gamify these activities, students would become more engaged and motivated. Gamification is the use of game design elements and game mechanics in non-game contexts [6]. In fact, the application of gamification techniques in different contexts has increased in the last years[1].

Specifically, it is a current trend in education since it is used to increase students' engagement and to promote certain learning behaviours on them [7]. Nevertheless, gamification is not a straightforward process and, thus, it should be driven by a formal gamification design framework to prevent failures in the implementation. Gamification Model Canvas[2] (GMC) is a framework which has proven to be an agile, flexible, and a systematic tool that helps to design and to evaluate a gamified system [17]. However, to the best of our knowledge, GMC has been applied only in business contexts rather than in academic ones.

This paper proposes an extension of GMC framework and applies it to gamify a university class. The extension is done at two different levels. On the one hand, at an inner level, we propose the inclusion of a new relevant element within the framework. On the other hand, at an outer level, we consider the addition of external supporting systems, Lego Serious Play (LSP) [8] and Audience Response System (ARS) [13], that help to put into practice the design framework. LSP to generate new ideas (brainstorm) about how to improve theory classes through building models with metaphorical meaning using Lego bricks, and Game-Based ARS to involve all students in a classroom, enhance learning feedback and interactivity within the class. Additionally, we illustrate its applicability through a case study of an undergraduate MAS subject, where students revisit MAS theoretical concepts and design a specific MAS. Moreover, when working collaboratively, MAS principles were somehow mapped into an experiential and immersive design, where students had autonomy to design and play agents themselves and their interaction was key to orchestrate the overall designed system.

2   Related Work

The popularity of gamification in the education field has increased in the last years. Many experiences have introduced gamification into elementary, high school, and even higher education settings, obtaining uneven results in educational attainment and motivation [19]. Usually, unfruitful results can be due to the fact that gamification is being applied by merely adding game rewards to an existing set of learning activities, instead of using gamification design frameworks to make activities more attractive and engaging.

Game designers state that the core of a game for learning should be aligned with those competencies students are aimed to acquire [12]. This should be taken

---

[1] http://www.gartner.com/smarterwithgartner/five-key-trends-in-gartners-2015-digital-marketing-hype-cycle/.

[2] http://www.gameonlab.com/canvas.

into account in order to guarantee the success of a gamified class. Actually, the effective gamification of courses is still a challenge. This is especially the case in the higher education context [11], where students must assimilate high-level concepts in a short period of time.

To the best of our knowledge, few gamified experiences for teaching and learning in computing areas have been proposed in high education. Some of them are encouraging experiences related to teaching MAS concepts. For instance, [1] included role playing games in teaching the content of an MAS, where players understood the basis, were motivated and had fun.

In other experiences, we found the effectiveness of brainstorming driven by LSP, [14] gamified the process of formulating and refining use cases in software development. In general, students who used LSP attained a higher level of skills in the areas of comprehension, application, and analysis. Moreover, the quality of software projects submitted at the end of the course improved, and student engagement increased significantly.

Related to the use of gamification models, other approaches applied design frameworks to introduce Computer Science [15] and C-programming language [10] in introductory courses. Briefly, [15] followed the MDA framework [9] to encourage students to increase participation in social and learning activities by using PeerSpace, an online social network for collaborative learning. As for [10], students achieved higher understanding and engagement in programming in the context of a C-programming language gamified course. Its design was based on Nicholson's theoretical framework [18]. In this engaging experience, most students continued working even after earning the maximum amount of grade points. They also continued mastering unexplored C-programming topics.

Pointing out the encouraging results attained in these experiences, we propose to use both LSP and GMC framework to gamify classes of multi-agent systems, a subject that implies the introduction of theoretical abstract concepts, which may become tiresome and dull to follow.

3   Gamification Model Canvas - GMC

Gamifying effectively an activity is not as straightforward as to use points, medals, and badges to engage users. Therefore, gamification frameworks become a useful guidance for designers [17]. Specifically, GMC constitutes an agile, flexible and systematic instrument that helps to find play-based solutions to develop behaviours in non-game environments. It is based on the MDA game design Framework [9]– which lets collect interests of users about aesthetics and dynamics– and on Business Model Canvas, a tool to design a business model[3].

GMC considers nine ordered elements:[4]

- *Revenues* element describes either the economic or social return of the gamified solution.

---

[3] http://www.businessmodelgeneration.com/canvas.
[4] Note that references to these elements along the paper are highlighted in italics.

- *Players* element focuses on who are the users, how are they, and what are their expectations. They can be considered *newbies*, *masters* or *designers*[5], and each profile involves different Bartle and Marczewski's gamification user types [2,16]. The *newbie* profile is an early user of the system and could be *killer*, *self-seeker*, *consumer* or *exploiter*. The *master* is a regular user who needs more meaningful incentives to become an expert or designer user and could be *explorer*, *achiever* or *socializer*. The *designer* is a very committed user who helps the system and needs self-realization opportunities to develop himself and could be *philanthropist*, *free spirit* or *disruptor*.
- *Behaviours* element describes the behaviours or actions we want to develop in the players in order to get revenues from the project. For example, go to a website, read content, answer a survey, buy something, etc.
- *Aesthetics* element describes the desirable emotional responses elicited in players during the playing experience. For example, challenge (game as an obstacle course), fellowship (game as a social framework), etc.
- *Dynamics* element defines how to create the aesthetics. For example, fellowship aesthetics can be facilitated by means of dynamics that allow sharing information within a group or by tasks (or winning conditions) that cannot be achieved by single players. Example of dynamics are altruism, scarcity, identity, status, etc.
- *Components* element defines those elements involved in the creation of dynamics and feedback that will create game mechanics. For example, points, badges, levels, missions, avatars, etc.
- *Mechanics* are the various actions, behaviours and control mechanisms afforded to the player within a game context. It describes the rules of the game with components for creating game dynamics.
- *Platforms* element defines the environment physical or virtual, on which to implement game mechanics.
- *Costs* element describes the investment needed to develop the game.

In the following section, we present the proposed extensions to GMC framework.

4   Proposal

4.1   GMC New Element - End Game

Each iteration in GMC helps to further define and validate the hypothesis associated to those elements of the model defined in previous steps. Specifically, the *mechanics* element, which is core in the gamification process, is the section that requires more iterations and refinements. This is the case even if all the components of the rest of the elements are well-designed, since the complexity of designing game mechanics is intrinsically high. In fact, some initiatives plan to provide tools to aid gamification designers with the transformation of selected components in the GMC workflow into specific mechanics that turn out to be suitable for the gamification process at hand.

---

[5] Gamification World Congress 2015, https://gamification.world/congress/gwc-2015.

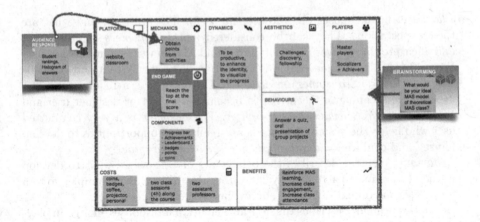

Fig. 1. Design of the gamification experience applying the Extended GMC.

Moreover, Mora et al. [17] point out that specific hypothesis referred to the logics of the game, such as game on-boarding or end game rules, do not appear explicitly in any element of the GMC framework. Certainly, although one may argue that some of these rules could be defined during the subsequent refinement steps of the *mechanics* element, its design becomes unavoidably complex when combining all actions, behaviours and components to define all the rules of the gamified activity. Therefore, to isolate the specific rules of the end of the game, would help in the modularity of the overall design process.

Thus, we propose to extend the GMC framework with a new element named *end game* (see Fig. 1). This element integrates different actions and behaviours to create specific game dynamics that will reach the end of the game. These dynamics will lead to a final state of victory or goal accomplishment which, most often, will stretch players to the limits of their abilities in their pursuing of this final (desirable) state. In the case of a learning serious activity, our claim is that students will make further progress in their skills and knowledge acquisition. To become a top user - with the highest score in a competitive environment - or to become the most popular player - with greater peer recognition in a collaborative context - are some examples of end-game rules.

4.2 GMC Extensions

As we consider *revenues*, *players*, *aesthetics* and *mechanics* rough elements in the GMC framework, we propose to extend it with two external systems that may help designers in these elements. Figure 1 depicts this extended GMC framework.

On the one hand, we suggest the use of tools that involve users to: corroborate *revenues* (we also refer to them as *benefits*); refine user profiles (*players*); and let them provide suitable and creative solutions (*aesthetics* and *mechanics*). The LSP is one representative example of these tools.

On the other hand, *mechanics* can be deployed by using ARS. For example, ARS quizzes create a competitive atmosphere, including timed responses, real-time feedback, and points. Additionally, ARS Surveys, which lack of any competitive aspect, can be used for getting feedback from learners, being more suitable for group discussions.

5   Case Study

In order to explore the application of our extended GMC framework, we performed a case study of teaching Multi-Agent Systems, an optional subject in the fourth-year of a Computer Engineering degree. It has 6 ECTS (European Credit Transfer System), students attend two 2-hour-long in-class activities per week.

As for class attendance, a total number of 26 students were enrolled in the course. Nevertheless, just a few of them (less than 20 %) attended all theory classes. In fact, none of the theory classes did surpass fifty percent attendance. Additionally, when attending, the majority of students did not actively participate in class discussions. Therefore, our gamification goals (i.e., *benefits*) are to increase both class engagement and attendance, as well as to reinforce MAS learning, considering that concepts introduced in MAS theory classes are often abstract and difficult to grasp.

5.1   Design

The design of the gamification was conducted by a team formed by a game designer coach, the teacher of the MAS subject, and two collaborator teachers who also actuated as assistants during sessions.

In the starting point of the design process, we involved a group of students in a brainstorming session to corroborate our diagnosis of the problem and our definition of the solution (i.e. gamification goals). We also aimed at obtaining students' feedback as well as collecting their opinions and ideas. To do so, we scheduled an LSP activity (see the blue box in the rightmost part of Fig. 1) with eight voluntary students distributed in two groups of four students each.

Upon coach's requests, students built a model about an MAS application in the real world, built a model of a novel MAS model that could improve the world, and built a model of their ideal class to learn MAS topics. Finally, students answered a survey that gathered their opinions about the LSP activity and current dynamics of (non-gamified) MAS theory classes.

All students agreed that the activity of modelling an MAS application with Lego bricks had helped them conceptualise and reinforce concepts of the subject. They also claimed that they had learned from the MAS application proposals made by their fellows. They imagined their ideal class as an engaging and collaborative activity with the teacher giving support to groups of students, who interact among themselves and apply theoretical concepts to real applications. It is noteworthy that during the LSP activity they had fun and felt committed and motivated.

These results helped us to confirm the suitability of the gamification project. Moreover, some students suggestions about their ideal class inspired our class gamification design, which is depicted in Fig. 1 and detailed in the following.

The *revenues* (benefits) to achieve with the gamified class are: reinforce MAS learning, increase class engagement and increase class attendance.

Related to *players*, students could be considered *master players* in GMC framework because they are familiar with the basic concepts of MAS. Furthermore, the design team agreed that user types were socializers and achievers.

As students usually have difficulties with the first contact with MAS concepts, and also to be continuously engaged during the class, our proposal of *behaviours* to develop in the players is increase attendance and participation in MAS classroom sessions by means of several quizzes with real-time feedback along the class and oral presentations of group projects.

The *aesthetics* –desirable emotional responses evoked in students– we considered are: to overcome a challenge, explore MAS concepts, and fellowship.

As for *dynamics*, we chose to: be productive or contribute to reinforcing concepts for all class students, enhance the group identity and progression within the classroom, and visualize the progress of each student inside the gamified MAS session.

Components we used are leaderboards, progress bars, achievements, badges, coins, and points.

The *mechanics* we defined revolve around point rankings. First, students answer an interactive quiz –performed by means of an ARS– and obtain individual points. The student at the top of the ranking earns a badge, and each student adds his points to a paper scoreboard. Afterwards, students design an MAS project consisting of several activities that include the build-share-reflect sequence from LSP. Along this sequence, students share proposals and get rewards: physical coins that correspond to a number of points on the scoreboard. Badges are also awarded for most valued (voted) projects. Additionally, a shared coffee break was included to promote group identity.

The *end game* consists in, firstly, choosing (and rewarding) the three students with the higher scores (that is, the number of points accumulated along the performed activities) and, secondly, declaring the absolute winner.

Regarding *platforms* where to apply gamification, we required using both the physical classroom (and resources) environment as well as an ARS website.

Finally, some *costs* are identified to be necessary to get some of the resources required to develop the gamification project. These are coins, badges, class projector, and personnel.

Next section explains the actual execution of these *mechanics* and *end game* as well as the usage of *platforms* and incurred *costs*.

5.2 Gamified Class

We conducted a two-hour-long theory class with 24 students which were familiar with the subject, and thus, they could be considered as *master players*. The session was first introduced by recalling our gamification goal (i.e., expected *benefit*) and describing its outline: reviewing theoretical concepts and designing a Multi-Agent System.

Fig. 2. Top-left: Question projected. Top-right: Mobile student interface. Bottom-left: Histogram of answers. Bottom-right: Quiz scoreboard.

Thus, the class started by reviewing theoretical concepts for half an hour. This activity was designed to consolidate MAS concepts by means of an ARS that induced the 'answer a quiz' *behaviour* with 'individual challenge' *aesthetics*.

Specifically, students participated in an interactive quiz we created at Kahoot![6] web *platform*. It consisted of 5 consecutive theory questions posted on the class projection screen. The top left image in Fig. 2 shows the first question. Students answered (and received feedback) by means of their mobile phones. Figure 2 also depicts the colour-and-shape-code user-friendly interface that students are provided to select their individual answer (See top right image in Fig. 2) where the left-most image shows possible answers to choose from whereas the rest provides student feedback. The cross-marked red screen stands for the time-out or incorrect answers (no points awarded in any case), for both cases, the correct answer is provided. The tick-marked green screen indicates the answer is correct as well as the number of awarded points. They were awarded up to 1000 *points*[7] if they answered each question correctly and within a 30 second timeout period, so that the quicker they answered, the most points they got. For each question/answer cycle, the class projection screen showed a histogram of aggregated answers indicating how many students had chosen each option. When figures showed that some concepts were not clear enough, the teacher opened a discussion about most common errors (see the bottom left image in Fig. 2).

The *mechanics* of this ARS incorporated different ways of providing immediate feedback to students. On the one hand, as the top right image in Fig. 2 shows, each mobile phone showed individual achievements: if the answer was correct or wrong, the awarded points, and current position in the class ranking. On the other hand, the class projection screen showed student rankings after each question (see the bottom right image in Fig. 2). Afterwards, at the end of the quiz,

---

[6] https://getkahoot.com.

[7] For the sake of readability, we also use italics to highlight previously designed components from Fig. 1.

the winner got a badge and students were asked to write their total awarded points in a paper *scoreboard*. We had provided beforehand this scoreboard for including subsequent activity scores, and thus, it also acted as a *progress bar*.

Afterwards, we devoted most of the session to experience with the design of an MAS. Here the teacher first presented subsequent parts a Multi-Agent Based Simulation research project, and then we encouraged the students to collaboratively design related examples of MAS –so we induced an MAS design *behaviour*.

Simweb is a former European research project that aimed at defining and studying alternative market models for the distribution of electronic contents – such as music or pieces of news. It involved the definition of a market as an MAS including both market stakeholders as well as those products being traded. Thus, it required characterising: (i) buyer and provider agent roles and associated behaviours, and (ii) product ontologies. Different actions and strategies were defined for each role: "imitation", "innovation", or "reputation leadership" constituted alternative provider strategies; whereas "buy cheapest offers", "satisfy requests exactly", or "be loyal to provider" were some buyer strategies. Additionally, products were defined in terms of its attributes and associated value domains. These definitions were key to define provider product offers as well as buyer preferences.

Students were asked to design an MAS market collaboratively. Initially, student pairs had assigned 3 different products (a party organizing service, a drone, and an electronic book), and the various provider and buyer strategies mentioned before. Each pair had a specific product, buyer and provider strategies assigned such that there were 12 different pair assignments but 4 pairs traded the same product —so that they could form 3 bigger groups afterwards. When working collaboratively, MAS principles were somehow mapped into an experiential and immersive design, where each student had autonomy to design and play one agent (i.e., its behaviour) but student interaction was key to agree on the overall system orchestration (i.e., common product definition and interaction).

MAS market design was partitioned in two phases, each following a (i) design -(ii) share -(iii) reward sequence similar to the one from LSP. The first phase required students to define the product, provider offers, and buyer preferences. Whereas in the second, students specified the agent interaction protocol and executed the system so that agent decision making –based on computing buyer requirement satisfaction from considering providers' offers– become apparent. For each phase: (i) design was done in pairs; then (ii) each pair shared their definition with those 3 other pairs trading the same product and finally, (iii) students awarded each others' work by awarding physical *coins* that were initially equally distributed. Specifically, each pair agreed on the design they liked the most and awarded this other pair by giving 2 of their coins (one coin from and for each student). Moreover, it is worth mentioning that these tree stages had a 3-to-5-minute time limitation that kept students focused on their tasks.

This activity was quite demanding. Therefore, a shared coffee break was introduced to relax students a bit. Students had an opportunity to socialize in a more relaxed atmosphere and to *enhance the group identity*.

Considering the overall activity from a gamification point of view, our final goal was to increase the mastery (i.e., knowledge) of 'master' players, but students were also considered as both 'socializers' and 'achievers' players since they worked collaboratively to achieve their design task. Furthermore, the *aesthetics* were that of 'discovery' and 'fellowship' and main *dynamics* pursued students to be productive while learning to design an MAS market.

Students obtained points from different activities so that the *End game* was defined by accounting for the students that reached the top at the final *score*. Thus, the *mechanics* consisted in:

1. Sharing: The pair having most coins within each group explained their market design to the rest of the class. As a result, 3 pairs explained market examples that traded different products.
2. Reward: Classmates voted for the preferred one. Each member of the winner pair won a badge.
3. Teacher's feedback: The teacher provided final remarks on MAS design such as model visualization or MAS execution indicators.
4. Ranking: Students updated their paper *scoreboards* by computing their total number of points and by considering that both *coins* and *badges* accounted for 1000 *points* each.
5. Winner and price assignment: top-three-scored students raised their subject grades proportionally. The overall winner was also acclaimed by classmates.

6 Results

Based on data gathered from surveys filled by students after the gamified class, we present the following results:

- 96 % of students considered that their knowledge or skills in MAS concepts had increased after hands-on activities during the gamified MAS class.
- 96 % of students indicated that tools used in class (interactive game, participatory activities, group work, awards, etc.) had helped them to be engaged, motivated, and also to reinforce and further learn MAS concepts.
- 92 % of students had fun during the gamified theory session.
- 88 % of students believed that classes could include gamified dynamics.
- 83 % of students would attend more classes, if they were gamified.
- 96 % of students would recommend their fellows to attend gamified sessions.

Analyzing these results, we can conclude that the majority of students perceived knowledge acquisition during the session. We can also observe that students were a bit more engaged and motivated than took pleasure. It could be due to the fact that they probably did not follow well the activities due to an overloaded agenda, as they themselves said. Then, as a lesson learned, we could say that gamified activities must be carefully designed to facilitate participation and engagement of students in class (Fig. 3).

Related to students' opinions about the use of gamification in theory classes and if they would attend classes more frequently, the reason of the decrease of

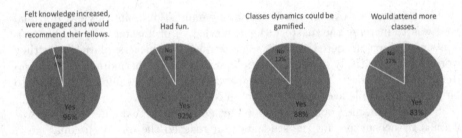

Fig. 3. Results of gamified MAS class about students.

values until 88 and 83 percent respectively may result from (i) the preferences of some students of "learning by example", which demands from them a less cognitive effort (they play a passive rol) in contrast to their active rol during gamified classes, (ii) and the coincidence of studies and work timetables. Recall that this is a subject of last year of studies, so that many students work and study at the same time. Additionally, it should be noted that the majority students had fun with ARS quiz and found it interesting. Nevertheless, some others did not liked the competitive aspect of gamification.

7   Conclusions and Future Work

This paper presents a methodology to improve traditional classroom dynamics and knowledge acquisition. Specifically, it aims at promoting student's perfor-mance, in-class participation, and attendance. This methodology is based on the Gamification Model Canvas framework but extends it to include MAS principles, as well as those of Lego Serious Play and Audience Response System, so that its application in current academic contexts become most suitable.

We have developed a use case consisting of the design and implementation of a gamified class in the subject of MAS in a university level course. 96 % of students believed that activities and tools used in the gamified class had helped them to consolidate and deepen their knowledge, besides got them engaged and motivated during class. As future work, we expect to be able to further evaluate the proposal extending this experience to next year MAS course as well as to other subjects.

Acknowledgments. We thank projects TIN2012-38876-C02-02, 2014SGR623, TIN2015-66863-C2-1-R (MINECO/FEDER), Carolina Foundation, and Pontificia Uni-versidad Católica del Perú for supporting the development of this research.

References

1. Barreteau, O., Bousquet, F., Attonaty, J.M.: Role-playing games for opening the black box of multi-agent systems: method and lessons of its application to senegal river valley irrigated systems. J. Artif. Soc. Soc. Simul. 4(2), 5 (2001)

2. Bartle, R.: Hearts, clubs, diamonds, spades: players who suit MUDs. J. MUD Res. **1**(1), 19 (1996)
3. Beer, M.: Multi-agent Systems for Education and Interactive Entertainment: Design, Use and Experience: Design, Use and Experience. IGI Global, Hershey (2010)
4. Bellanca, J.A.: 21st Century Skills: Rethinking how Students Learn. Solution Tree Press, Bloomington (2011)
5. Casasola, E., De, V., Cliffe, O., Padget, J.: Teaching MAS in the UK and in latin America. Innov. Teach. Learn. Inf. Comput. Sci. (2005)
6. Deterding, S., Dixon, D., Khaled, R., Nacke, L.: From game design elements to gamefulness: defining gamification. In: International Academic MindTrek Conference: Envisioning Future Media Environments, pp. 9–15. ACM (2011)
7. Domínguez, A., Saenz-de Navarrete, J., De-Marcos, L., Fernández-Sanz, L., Pagés, C., Martínez-Herráiz, J.J.: Gamifying learning experiences: practical implications and outcomes. Comput. Educ. **63**, 380–392 (2013)
8. Gauntlett, D.: Creative Explorations: New Approaches to Identities and Audiences. Routledge, London (2007)
9. Hunicke, R., LeBlanc, M., Zubek, R.: MDA: a formal approach to game design and game research. In: AAAI Workshop on Challenges in Game AI, vol. 4 (2004)
10. Ibanez, M.B., Di-Serio, A., Delgado-Kloos, C.: Gamification for engaging computer science students in learning activities: a case study. IEEE Trans. Learn. Technol. **7**(3), 291–301 (2014)
11. Iosup, A., Epema, D.: An experience report on using gamification in technical higher education. In: Proceedings of 45th ACM Technical Symposium on Computer Science Education, pp. 27–32. ACM (2014)
12. Kapp, K.M.: The Gamification of Learning and Instruction: Game-Based Methods and Strategies for Training and Education. Wiley, New York (2012)
13. Kay, R.H., LeSage, A.: Examining the benefits and challenges of using ARS: a review of the literature. Comput. Educ. **53**(3), 819–827 (2009)
14. Kurkovsky, S.: Teaching software engineering with Lego Serious Play: conference workshop. J. Comput. Sci. Coll. **30**(6), 13–15 (2015)
15. Li, C., Dong, Z., Untch, R.H., Chasteen, M.: Engaging computer science students through gamification in an online social network based collaborative learning environment. J. Inf. Educ. Technol. **3**(1), 72–77 (2013)
16. Marczewski, A.C.: Even Ninja Monkeys Like to Play. CreateSpace Independent Publishing Platform (2015)
17. Mora, A., Riera, D., González, C., Arnedo-Moreno, J.: A literature review of gamification design frameworks. In: 2015 7th International Conference on Games and Virtual Worlds for Serious Applications (VS-Games), pp. 1–8. IEEE (2015)
18. Nicholson, S.: A user-centered theoretical framework for meaningful gamification. In: Proceedings of GLS 8.0 Games+Learning+Society Conference, pp. 223–229 (2012)
19. Richter, G., Raban, D.R., Rafaeli, S.: Studying gamification: the effect of rewards and incentives on motivation. In: Reiners, T., Wood, L.C. (eds.) Gamification in Education and Business, pp. 21–46. Springer, Switzerland (2015)
20. Sakellariou, I., Kefalas, P., Stamatopoulou, I.: Teaching intelligent agents using NetLogo. In: ACM-IFIP IEEIII (2008)

Analysis of Market Trend Regimes for March 2011 USDJPY Exchange Rate Tick Data

Lukáš Pichl[✉] and Taisei Kaizoji

International Christian University, Osawa 3-10-2, Mitaka, Tokyo 181-8585, Japan
lukas@icu.ac.jp
http://www.icu.ac.jp/

Abstract. This paper reports the analysis of the foreign exchange market for the USD and JPY currency pair in March 2011 for the period of 23 trading days comprising 3,774,982 transactions. On March 11, 2011 the disaster of the Great Tohoku Earthquake disaster accompanied by tsunami took place; the event was followed by a highly turbulent market with JPY appreciating without limits in the panic that ensued; major central banks of the world intervened since after to weaken the yen. We analyze the tick data set using the criteria of aggregate volatility, extreme-event distribution, and singular spectrum analysis to discover the market microstructure during the central bank interventions. In addition, a multi-layer neural network algorithm is designed to extract the causality regime on the microscale for each trading day. At the beginning of the month, the success ratios in the trend prediction hit levels as high as the order of 70 %, followed by about a 10-point decrease for the rest of the data set. Distribution of intra-trade times shows clear signs of algorithmic trading with the transaction clock ticking at the time intervals of 0.1, 0.25 and 10.0 s. The extracted trend prediction rates represent lower bounds with respect to other methods. The present work offers a useful insight into algorithmic trading and market microstructure during extreme events.

1 Introduction

On March 11, 2011, at 14:46 JST the Great Tohoku Earthquake of magnitude 9.0 stroke, followed by a massive tsunami, leaving 15,894 dead, 6,152 injured, and 2,562 people missing, according to the National Police Agency (data of February 10th, 2016) [1]. The overall property damage reached hundreds of billions of dollars. The Japanese yen rapidly strengthened once the scale of the damage became known. This has happened in contrary to increased concerns about the future exports of Japan or the increased expectation of government default due to the forthcoming revitalization cost burden. The two major reasons for the sudden speculative appreciation were according to Neely [2] (i) expectations that Japanese insurance companies would need to liquidate and repatriate reserves from overseas, and (ii) the closing of carry-trade positions in which investors borrowed yen to lend abroad. The appreciation was rapid and

© Springer International Publishing AG 2016
N. Osman and C. Sierra (Eds.): AAMAS 2016 WS, Visionary Papers, LNAI 10003, pp. 184–196, 2016.
DOI: 10.1007/978-3-319-46840-2_12

significant: whereas on March 10, at 9 PM JST, one USD traded at 82.936 JPY, one week after, on March 17, at the same time, the trading level was 78.899 JPY. The finance ministers of the group of G-7 announced on March 17 late evening a coordinated intervention to weaken the yen [3]. Although the exact amounts are not known, the Fed announced, for instance, that it sold yen from the U.S. reserves worth the equivalent of 1 billion dollars. The Bank of Japan sold between 1–2 trillion yen on the same day, too [4]. In this paper, we embark on an empirical study of the USD/JPY exchange rate using a data set of market tick transactions in March 2011 (bid and ask price range is available, but transaction volumes are not). In Sect. 2, we describe the structure of the data set and its empirical characteristics, such as the distribution of log returns, intra-trade time intervals, or the evidence of algorithmic trading on the real time scale. Section 3 presents our attempt at discovering high volatility regimes characteristic of sudden market speculations or central bank interventions. We focus on the distribution of extreme events and visualization of their density in the form of barcode diagram. Singular Spectrum Analysis (Principal Component Analysis on the lagged time series) is used to find the events of dimensional collapse when the eigenvalue of the first principal components represents all the standard deviation in the time series - this criterion appears to correlate with the high volatility regimes of market interventions. In Sect. 4, motivation for trend prediction by multi-layer neural network algorithm is described, and the results presented for each trading day of March 2011. We conclude with final remarks in Sect. 5.

2   Data Set

The data set consists of trade records that include the currency pair indicator, USD/JPY, date in the form of YYYYMMDD, and the price pair of bid and ask values, in the format of NN.NNN (units of JPY). The source is True FX company (http://www.truefx.com/). The exchange rate time series are depicted in Fig. 1 (time scale in seconds is used from the reference point of March 1st, 2011, 0:00 JST), which shows the sudden speculative appreciation of yen after the earthquake and tsunami disaster (2011 3 11 14:46, t(sec)= 1,003,593 and t(tick)=1,303,200). The peak effect of this speculative bubble took place on 2011 3 16 21:15 (t(sec)=1,459,100, t(tick)=1,993,900). The intervention of the G-7 group lead by Bank of Japan started on 2011 3 18 00:02 (t(sec)=1,555,300, t(tick)=2,350,600). An aggregated volatility criterion depicts one more significant event on 2011 3 21 13:40 (t(sec)=1,863,600, t(tick)=2,728,200), during which the market was largely unstable, perhaps due to the ongoing battle of the speculative trend of yen appreciation and the central bank intervention to depreciate the currency. Although none of these events appears significantly in the Singular Spectrum Analysis of the FX time series shown in Fig. 2, the SSA will be proven useful on the lagged copies of logarithmic returns, defined as

$$R_t = \log\left(\frac{F_{t+1}}{F_t}\right),\tag{1}$$

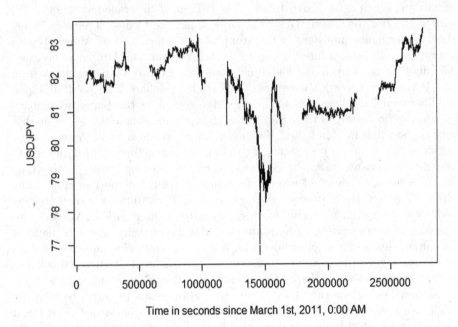

Fig. 1. The exchange rate of USD/JPY in March 2011 for the period of 23 working days. The breaks in the line correspond to weekends.

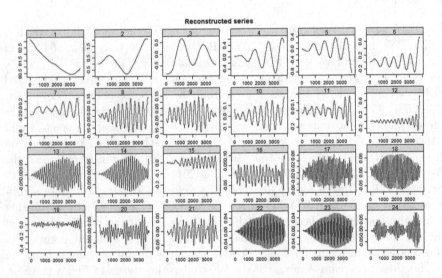

Fig. 2. Reconstruction of the price time series from Fig. 1 using Singular Spectrum Analysis.

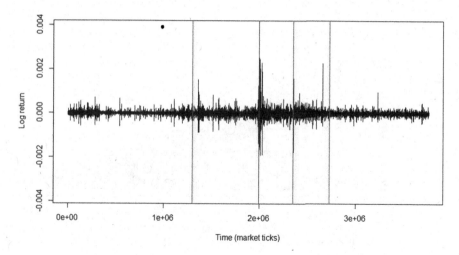

Fig. 3. Tick-to-tick log returns for USDJPY exchange rate.

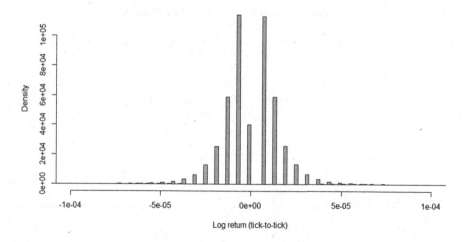

Fig. 4. Histogram of log returns.

where the F_t is the price at (tick) time t defined by the average of the bid and ask exchange rate values. In Fig. 3, the time series of Fig. 1 transformed to logarithmic returns are shown. The vertical lines correspond to the events of the earthquake, speculative bubble, and the 1st and 2nd interventions against this trend. Figure 4 provides the discrete version of the log return histogram, on which the quoting step is visible (order of $10^{-3}/\text{FX}$). The histogram has a power-law tail, as can be seen from the straight-line region of the histogram in a log-log plot shown in Fig. 5.

Next, we proceed to the analysis of intra-trade times. In the inset of the histogram in Fig. 6 for the first 0.6 s, it can be seen that every 0.1 s, there is a peak

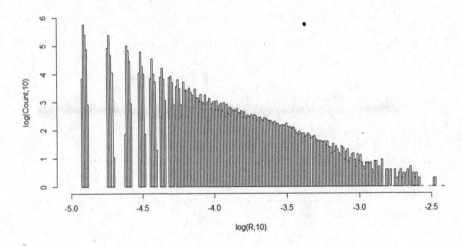

Fig. 5. Histogram of log returns (log-log plot).

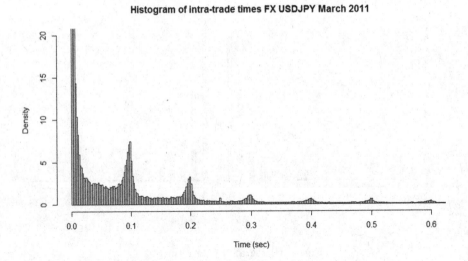

Fig. 6. Histogram of intra-trade times.

of increased trading activity, indicating the physical clock at the market being used for transaction clearing and algorithmic trading. In addition to the 0.1 s stepping, there is also a small peak distinguishable at a quarter of a second. The effect is more pronounced on a longer time grid in Fig. 7 using the logarithmic scale. Notice the higher-than-regular effect at 10 s interval, too.

In order to asses the volatility of the market, focusing especially on the central bank interventions, one useful criterion is the distribution of extreme events. Using the n-gram analysis with n=10, we define an extreme events as a

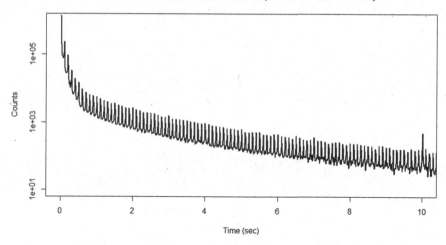

Fig. 7. Clock ticks at intra-trade times (log scale).

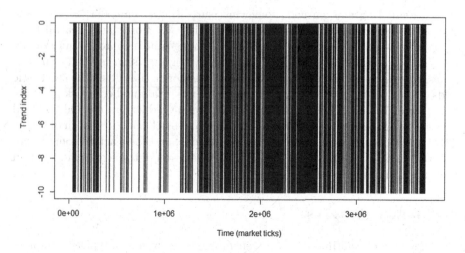

Fig. 8. Barcode of extreme-event occurrence in tick data.

sequence of 10 adjacent log returns of negative sign. Since the probability distribution of log returns is symmetric, the odds for this event to occur are 1 in 1024. Next, we define an indicator, which is equal to 0, when the extreme event was not recorded in the moving window, and −10, in case the extreme event was detected. A line plot of this indicator results in a barplot, from which clustering of volatility and the distribution of extreme 10-grams may easily be seen.

The result for March 2011 is given in Fig. 8. It can be seen from Fig. 8 that until the earthquake, the extreme events were rare (and clustered). This has changed profoundly since-after March 11, and two continuous blocks of

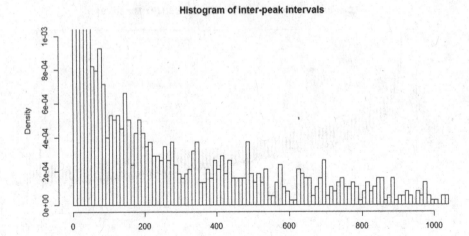

Fig. 9. Distribution of time intervals between extreme events.

the extreme 10-grams ensued, somewhat surprisingly, immediately with the start of the speculative bubble, and then at the G-7 coordinated central bank intervention. The barplot thus indicates the changes in the market microstructure, namely, the departure from clustering of 10-grams seen in the usual time series, to a more equidistant distribution. Let us notice that given the stochastic odds of 10^{-3} for the extreme 10-gram to occur, the total number of tick points in the order of 10^6, and the line thickness, the referential barplot of equally spaced n-grams would be represented by the entire area in black. For the month of March 2011, the statistical estimate of extreme 10-grams, and their actual count, coincide to 3 digits precision. An inset from the histogram of these extreme 10-gram inter-event times is given in Fig. 9.

3   Market Patterns

The modeling of volatility effects of central bank interventions typically employs an extra variable representing whether the intervention is taking place or not [5]. We do not have this kind of information for March 2011; also not all of the interventions are publicized, even though the public announcement beforehand often adds to the scale of the resulting effect [6]. We thus select a simple criterion for volatility detection using the tick-to-tick time scale, on which we add up the absolute values of the realized log returns (rather than their squares, in order to allow for a more robust behavior with regard to outliers). When the indicator exceeds the threshold value of 0.1, we detect an extreme event. As can be seen in Fig. 10, this criterion clearly detects the speculative bubble and the two interventions events on March 18 and March 21, without fail.

When a market panic occurs, or a massive intervention takes place, an overall trend emerges that reduces the number of degrees in the time series of log returns.

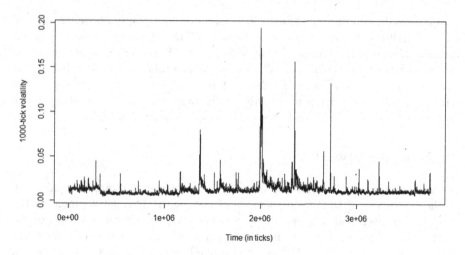

Fig. 10. Volatility detection using $\sum_{1}^{1000} R_t$.

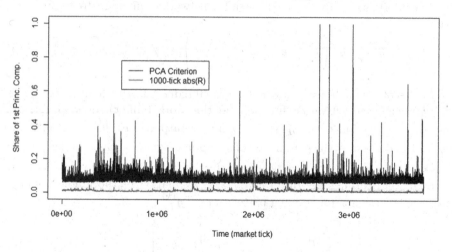

Fig. 11. Trend collapse detection using Singular Spectrum Analysis. (Color figure online)

We have attempted to test this hypothesis using the Singular Spectrum Analysis, i.e., the Principal Component Analysis applied to k-lagged copies of the time series [7]. The particular setting is a 100-tick long subset of the time series, each lagged with $k = 0, 1, \ldots, 19$ steps. From these, the symmetric 20 by 20 covariance matrix is formed, and its eigenvalues are computed. To account for the sudden dimensionality collapse, we take the ratio of the standard deviation of the first principal component to the standard deviations of all principal components. We remark that this criterion is again more robust that it would be in case of taking the ratio of variance explained. The time series of the resulting criterion values are shown in Fig. 11. The red line indicates the log return time series for comparison. If we select the threshold of the order of 0.9 and above, then three dimensionality collapse events are detected, falling within the time of the unannounced second intervention event of March 21. This completes our empirical analysis of market patterns, volatility and extreme event criteria that distinguish the different market regimes. In the next section, we will apply the standard backpropagation algorithm to investigate the degree to which causality can be extracted for the case of trend prediction on the market tick scale.

4   Neural Network

Artificial feed-forward neural networks are currently undergoing a renaissance in the prediction of time series because of the algorithmic development in the discipline of deep learning [8–10]. Although recent research focuses mostly on the relation of information and market returns, using, e.g., deep belief networks [10], this computational model has been applied successfully to trend-extraction in a number of studies [11–15].

The information propagates through the network from inputs to outputs [16], where

$$h_i^{(k)} = g_k \left(\sum_{j=1}^{n^{(k-1)}} w_{i,j}^{(k)} h_j^{(k-1)} + b_i^{(k)} \right) \quad i \in \langle 1, \ldots, n^{(k)} \rangle, \tag{2}$$

with k denoting the hidden layer index ($k = 0$ reduces to the input layer, $h_i^{(0)} \equiv x_i$), g_k being the activation function (in this work $\tanh(x)$ for $k = 1, \ldots H$, and the identity function, $g_{H+1}(x) = x$ in the output layer; $h_i^{(H+1)} \equiv y_i$). The network is defined by the parameters of synaptic weights $w_{i,j}^{(k)}$ and hidden neuron biases $b_i^{(k)}$ in each layer k. The parameters of the network are initialized at random; the learning algorithm consists in evaluation of the gradient of the objective function J for training pattern $\{x^{(n)}, y_d^{(n)}\}$,

$$J^{(n)} = \frac{1}{2} \sum_{k=1}^{d_o} \left[y_k(x^{(n)}) - y_{dk}^{(n)} \right]^2, \tag{3}$$

by means of error backpropagation [17]. The optimization method of choice is typically of the conjugate gradient class combined with stochastic sampling of initial conditions. Upon training of the neural network, i.e. having optimized its parameters, Eq. (2) can be used to predict the out-of-the-sample values. In the present work, the dimension of input vector x is $d_i = 5$ and dimension of output is $d_0 = 1$. The number of hidden layers is $H = 4$. An actual example of a neural network of this type showing the topology used in this work is given in Fig. 14. The bias values for hidden and output neurons are in blue with constant input value 1; weights are shown in black for each synaptic connection. All the calculations are performed using the open source free software R [18,19]. Artificial neural networks as described above have already been used extensively in the prediction of market returns [20].

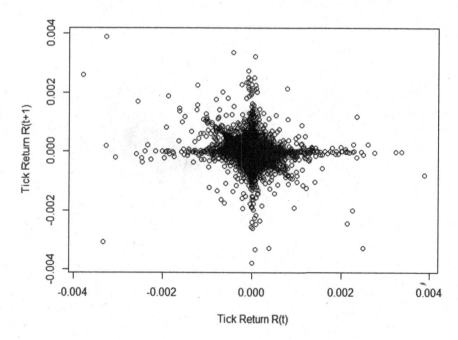

Fig. 12. Correlation of subsequent log returns.

In order to extract the causality degree from the time series data set, we select as predictors the variables R_{t-5}, R_{t-4}, R_{t-3}, R_{t-2} and R_{t-1} in a 5-step back moving window. Normally, the one-step legged time series are negatively correlated with the original ones; the feature of the mutual log return distribution in the data set can be seen from the scatter plot in Fig. 12. The diagonal line pattern corresponds to the negative correlation of R_t and R_{t-1}. To represent the correlation of R_t with the recent trend, we compute the moving window return $R_{t-5} + R_{t-4} + R_{t-3} + R_{t-2} + R_{t-1}$, which is positively correlated with R_t as can be seen in Fig. 13. Both plots indicate the existence of partial patterns that are subjected to the neural network learning algorithm. Figure 14 then shows the multi-layer architecture of the artificial neural network. There are 5 inputs, plotted as full blue circles on the left part of the picture, and a single output neuron, depicted in red. The neurons of the four hidden layers are shown as empty circles. Weight parameters are shown as numbers for each synaptic connection. Bias parameters are represented as constant inputs of value 1, and the respective weight for each extra synaptic connection to the constant input. The parameters of the nework were learnt on the March 31st, 2011, data set. The one-month data set is divided into 23 subsets of one day trading data.

Table 1 shows the neural network predicted result for the trend, i.e. the sign of the log return, or the so called hit ratios (66.6 % of the tick data is used for training, 33.4 % of the data for prediction testing). The minimum value is 53.98 %, the median 60.9 %, the mean 61.27 %, and the maximum 72.92 %.

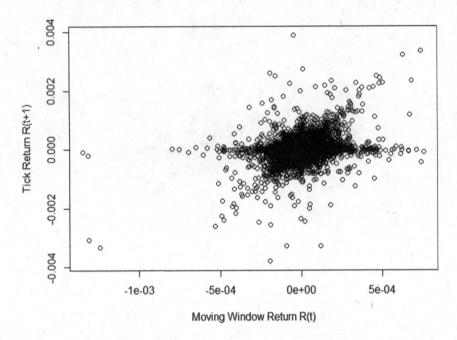

Fig. 13. Trend correlation of log returns.

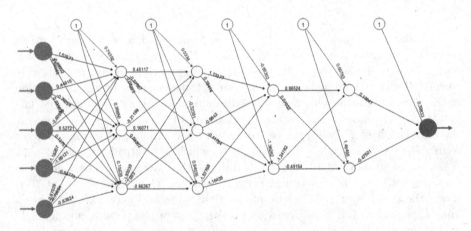

Fig. 14. Neural network in multi-layer configuration. (Color figure online)

It can be seen from the data that on the Great Tohoku Earthquake day the rates
dropped from around 70 % of the preceding week by 10 points, and remained
at the lower levels throughout the central bank interventions. These values were
obtained by repeatedly re-initializing the neural network parameters, to avoid
the trapping in a local minimum problem. They can be considered as the lower
bounds for estimates obtained by more sophisticated methods.

Table 1. Trend prediction success rates (hit ratios) for trading days of March 2011.

Mon	Tue	Wed	Thu	Fri
	01	02	03	04
	54.40	57.67	54.35	53.99
07	08	09	10	11
72.92	72.43	72.05	71.40	63.69
14	15	16	17	18
56.04	57.33	53.98	56.07	57.09
21	22	23	24	25
58.55	61.62	61.65	60.23	62.65
28	29	30	31	
65.73	61.19	63.35	60.90	

5   Conclusions

We have analyzed the statistical properties and the trend regimes in the tick data set of USD/JPY foreign exchange trades. A simple volatility criterion that uses the sum of the log returns over a moving window interval correctly extracts the periods of the speculative bubble and the central bank market interventions. Singular spectrum analysis applied to the lagged log return series indicated a dimensionality reduction events in the market microstructure during the market interventions on March 21st. Starting with the earthquake event, the distribution of extreme events using 10-grams of negative log returns changed substantially - covering the speculative bubble formation and the subsequent central bank intervention. Trend prediction success rates computed with the neural network also drop by about 10 points from the pre-disaster level, indicating market turbulence and chaotic behavior of market participants. The present work is believed to provide a useful insight to the turbulent foreign exchange market episodes, for which networked agent simulations are appropriate [21].

References

1. National Police Agency of Japan. http://www.npa.go.jp/archive/keibi/biki/higaijokyo_e.pdf. Accessed 16 Feb 2016
2. Neely, C.J.: A Foreign exchange intervention in an era of restraint. Fed. Reserve Bank St. Louis Rev. **93**(5), 303–324 (2011)
3. Reuters Markets. G7 Cenbanks in rare currency action after yen surge. http://www.reuters.com/article/us-global-economy-idUSL3E7EH14Q20110318. Accessed 16 Feb 2016
4. Bloomberg Business. http://www.bloomberg.com/news/articles/2011-05-13/fed-bought-1-billion-of-u-s-currency-during-march-g-7-yen-intervention. Accessed 16 Feb 2016

5. Dominguez, K.M.: Central bank intervention and exchange rate volatility. J. Int. Money Finance **17**, 161–190 (1998)
6. Tsen, W.H.: Exchange rate and central bank intervention. J. Glob. Econ. **2**(e104), 1–4 (2014)
7. Hsieh, W.W.: Machine Learning Methods in the Environmental Sciences. Cambridge University Press, Cambridge (2009)
8. Bengio, Y.: Learning deep architectures for artificial intelligence. Found. Trends Mach. Learn. **2**(1), 1–127 (2009)
9. Haykin, S.: Neural Networks and Learning Machines, 3rd edn. Pearson International Edition, New Jersey (2009)
10. Kuremoto, T., Kimura, S., Kobayashi, K., Obayashi, M.: Time series forecasting using a deep belief network with restricted Boltzmann machines. Neurocomputing **137**, 47–56 (2014)
11. Mizuno, H., Kosaka, M., Yajima, H., Komoda, N.: Application of neural network to technical analysis of stock market prediction. Stud. Inform. Control **7**(3), 111–120 (1998)
12. Chen, A.-S., Leung, M.T., Daouk, H.: Application of neural networks to an emerging financial market: forecasting and trading the Taiwan Stock Index. Comput. Oper. Res. **30**, 901–923 (2003)
13. Sitte, R., Sitte, J.: Analysis of the predictive ability of time delay neural networks applied to the S&P 500 time series. IEEE Trans. Syst. Man Cybern. **30**, 568–572 (2000)
14. Zhang, G.P., Kline, D.: Quarterly time-series forecasting with neural networks. IEEE. Trans. Neural. Netw. **18**, 1800–1814 (2007)
15. Clements, M.P., Franses, P.H., Swanson, N.R.: Forecasting economic and financial time-series with non-linear models. Int. J. Forecast. **20**, 169–183 (2004)
16. McCulloch, W., Pitts, W.: A logical calculus of the ideas immanent in nervous activity. Bull. Math. Biophys. **7**, 115–133 (1943)
17. Rumelhart, D.E., Hinton, G.E., Williams, R.J.: Learning representations by back-propagating errors. Nature **323**, 533–536 (1986)
18. Core, R., Team, R.: A language and environment for statistical computing. R Foundation for Statistical Computing, Vienna, Austria (2016). https://www.R-project.org/
19. Fritsch, S., Guenther, F., Suling, M.: neuralnet: Training of neural networks. R package version 1.32 (2012). http://CRAN.R-project.org/package=neuralnet
20. Castiglione, F.: Forecasting price increments using an artificial neural network. Adv. Complex Syst. **4**(1), 45–56 (2001)
21. Sun, X.-Q., Shen, H.-W., Cheng, X.-Q.: Trading network predicts stock price. Sci. Rep. **4**(3711), 1–6 (2014)

Author Index

Printed in the United States
By Bookmasters